# BUSINESS MANAGEMENT IN IRELAND

## Competitive Strategy for the 21st Century

John J. Lynch

Frank W. Roche

Oak Tree Press

Dublin

Oak Tree Press
Merrion Building
Lower Merrion Street
Dublin 2, Ireland

A catalogue record of this book is
available from the British Library.

ISBN 1-872853-68-4

Printed in Ireland by Colour Books Ltd.

# CONTENTS

**CHAPTER THREE:**
**The State and Industrial Development**          **63**

# LIST OF TABLES

CHAPTER THREE: The State and Industrial Development

CHAPTER FOUR: Traditional Industry

CHAPTER FIVE: Resource-Based Industry

CHAPTER SIX: Modern Industry

CHAPTER SEVEN: Services Industries in Ireland

CHAPTER EIGHT: Strategy

CHAPTER ELEVEN: Financial Management

CHAPTER TWELVE: Human Resource Management

# LIST OF FIGURES

CHAPTER ELEVEN: Financial Management

CHAPTER TWELVE: Human Resource Management

# INTRODUCTION

*T*he objective of this book is to describe the critical role played by strategy formulation and implementation in Irish business on the threshold of the twenty-first century. The business community worldwide is experiencing a period of fundamental change. This could be considered the fourth revolution (the first three being the early industrial, manufacturing and services revolutions). Business people are becoming aware of the need to manage and exploit the dramatic changes that are occurring in markets and industries. Some of the key changes taking place in the overall business environment, the business structure and in business processes utilised are listed below.

## Business Environment

- The shift in the manufacturing base towards Asia, Eastern Europe and South America.

- The increasing role of the European Union in Irish economic affairs.

- The use of improved technology in all its forms.

## Business Structure

- The movement in employment away from traditional and resource-based industries towards modern manufacturing and services.

- The rise in importance, in terms of job creation, of small and medium-sized enterprises (SMEs).

## Business Processes

- The increase in attention being given to high standards of product and service quality and its management via World Class Business (WCB), Business Process Re-engineering (BPR) and Total Quality Management (TQM).

These changes are creating both opportunities and threats for Irish firms. Some have the necessary competencies, skills, resources and competitive advantages to exploit the opportunities. These firms most likely utilise a strategic planning process that couples their key strengths and capabilities with market requirements. Others do not possess these skills and probably will not survive in the twenty-first century.

Managers and business students in Ireland must appreciate the phenomenon of change and accept that an understanding of business strategy will be crucial for survival in the business arena of the next century.

Business strategy can be divided into two distinct areas: strategy formulation and strategy implementation. In essence, formulation and implementation occur at three distinct levels within the firm:

• The *Strategic* level, where decisions specify *what* to do

• The *Tactical* level, where decisions specify *how* and *where* to do it

• The *Operational* level, where decisions are *converted* into action.

Figure 1 on the following page describes this process graphically.

Firms exist to create and deliver goods and services to their customers. Therefore, firms should be designed to support the processes required to meet this primary objective. In general, it is the linking of overall business strategy with the functional strategies of marketing, operations, human resources and finance at these three levels which allows the business transformation process to occur effectively and efficiently. This is one reason why so many firms are "re-engineering" their business activities in the 1990s.

**Figure 1: The Three Levels of Business Strategy**

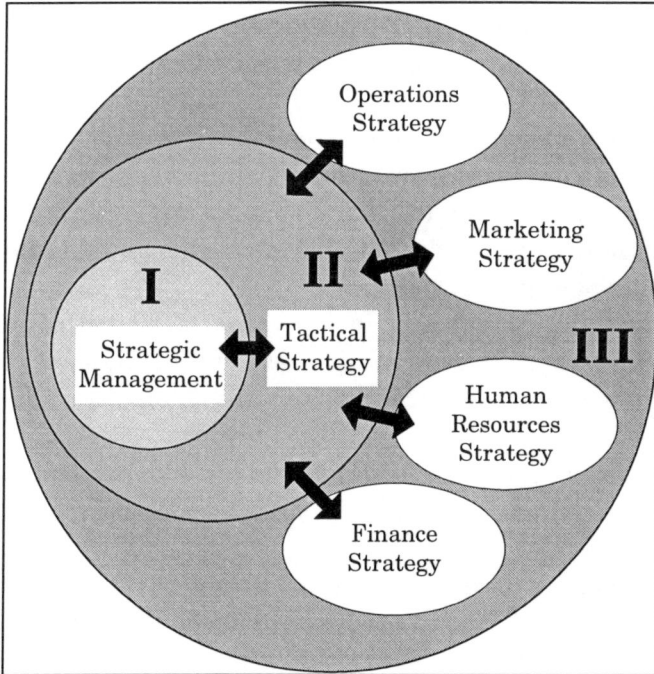

## The Objectives and Structure of the Book

The objectives of this book are threefold. First, it attempts to describe the overall business environment in Ireland in terms of the business structure, the business environment and the role of the state in industrial development. Second, it looks at the four primary industry sectors, namely Traditional, Resource-based, Modern and Services. Third, the book attempts to describe the nature of business strategy in the Irish context in terms of strategy formulation and implementation.

Following this introduction, the book progresses as follows:

In Chapter One the overall structure of Irish business is analysed. The chapter profiles the Irish economy in terms of size, sectoral breakdown and historical development. It also analyses the importance of foreign firms, large firms, SMEs and state-sponsored enterprises in the context of future growth in the economy.

Chapter Two looks at the business environment in which Irish firms compete. It describes the global, European and national drivers of change that effect Irish firms.

The important and evolving role that the state plays in Irish industrial development is analysed in Chapter Three, in terms of both commercial and non-commercial involvement.

Chapter Four moves away from the macroeconomic level and begins the sectoral review. This chapter deals with traditional industry and, in particular, the drivers of change that affect Irish-owned companies in this sector.

Resource-based industry in Ireland is dealt with in Chapter Five, which concentrates on agri-food and drink-based industry. Other sub-sectors reviewed include mining, forestry, fishing, turf and gas.

Chapter Six examines modern industry with particular emphasis on computers, chemicals, pharmaceuticals and electrical engineering.

Service-based industries are investigated in Chapter Seven, including domestic and internationally-traded sectors.

The final section of the book looks at the role of business strategy and how it relates to the core functions of marketing, operations, finance and human resource management.

Chapter Eight reviews the key concepts involved in strategy and strategic management.

The functional strategy review begins in Chapter Nine with an analysis of marketing strategy and its evolving role in overall business strategy in the 1990s.

Chapter Ten addresses the increasingly important area of operations management, with a focus on the key concepts of World Class Manufacturing (WCM), Business Process Re-engineering (BPR), and World Class Business (WCB).

Chapter Eleven looks at the critical role that financial strategy plays in allowing business strategy to be implemented.

The section ends with an analysis of human resource management in Chapter Twelve, with a focus on the increasing importance of employee involvement in both formulating and implementing strategy.

The relationship between, and interdependence of, the twelve chapters in the book are depicted in Figure 2.

**Figure 2: *Structure of the Book***

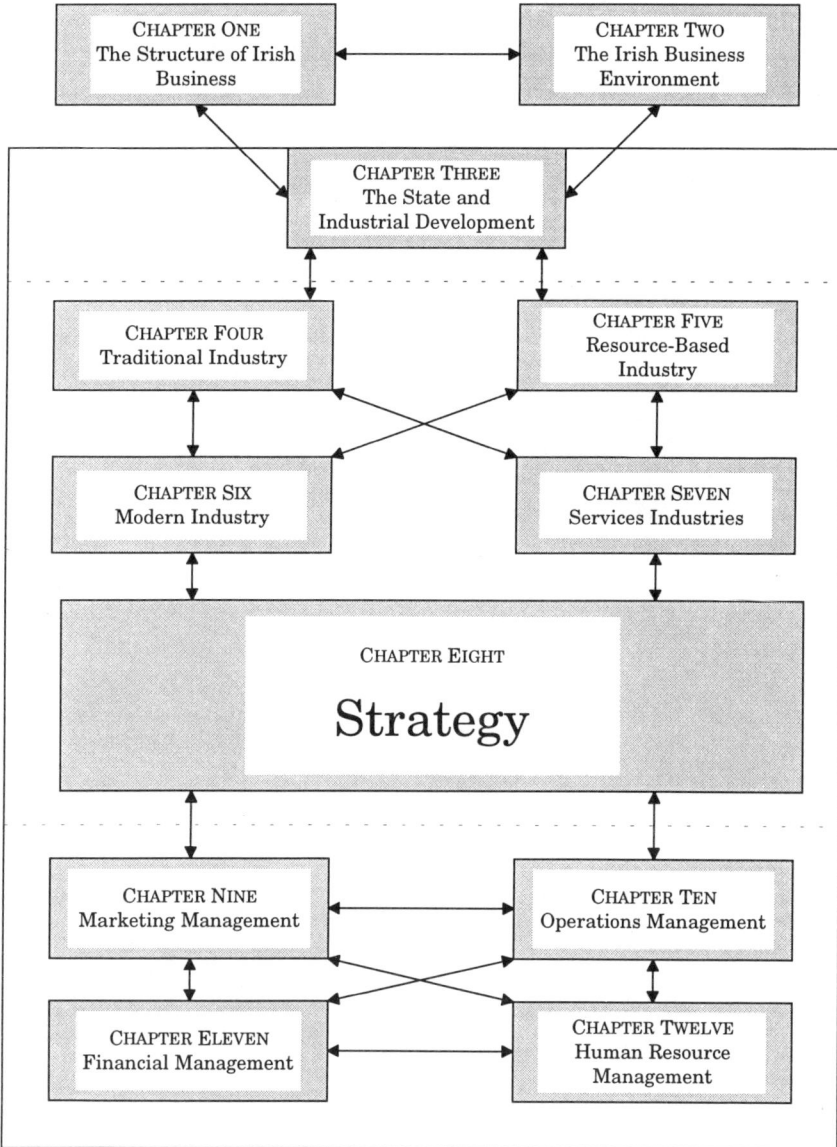

CHAPTER ONE

# THE STRUCTURE OF IRISH BUSINESS

*T*his chapter provides a broad outline of how Irish business is currently structured and looks at the forces which have shaped this structure. Such an overview is a necessary prelude to assisting the development of a coherent and workable strategy. Businesses are, in the long run, dependent on the societies which support them and it is therefore an essential part of strategic management to understand the nature of the social forces shaping demand and supply and the general operating environment.

## 1.1 HISTORICAL BACKGROUND

This section provides a brief overview of the development of the Irish economy from the 1920s to the 1990s. Ireland has been trying to achieve economic development since the Industrial Revolution. But, up until independence in 1922, economic progress was hampered by discriminatory trading and economic conditions imposed by Britain. In common with many other newly liberated countries, Ireland went through a phase of "economic nationalism", where policy tended to focus on the promotion of infant industries through the use of protective barriers. Although of questionable efficiency, manufacturing employment reached one of its highest levels ever in the mid-1930s. From then until the late 1950s, government policies attempted to achieve self-sufficiency in food and manufactured goods. By the end of this period, however, the strains caused by the self-sufficiency philosophy were beginning to show. As detailed below, strong forces were coming into operation, which caused Ireland to have a very high propensity to trade. Recognition of these forces led successive governments to adopt policies designed to achieve trade growth and to develop manufacturing industry.

In roughly a decade and a half — from the initial negotiations to join the European Economic Community (EEC) in 1962 until the late 1970s when oil shocks and world recession began to bite deeply — Ireland experienced a period of very high growth. Agricultural output (and prices), manufacturing output, population, size of the labour force, standards of living and expectations all grew at a rate faster than Ireland had ever experienced (with the exception of population growth in the 50 years leading up to the Famine), and at a faster rate also than most other developed economies. These growth processes were fuelled by the Anglo-Irish Free Trade Agreement in 1966, membership of the European Free Trade Association (EFTA), and by EEC membership when it finally occurred in 1973.

The high growth, which was latterly accompanied by high inflation rates, disguised the fact that infrastructure and social development were being funded by borrowings increasingly denominated in foreign currencies. During the period of general growth there was only a slight increase in total employment. This apparent stability in employment in fact marked a large-scale structural change: public sector employment had grown by one-third; foreign industry now accounted for one-third of manufacturing employment; indigenous industry, faced with intense competition, had dwindled by 40 per cent; and agricultural employment had declined, by 1981, to 45 per cent of what it had been in 1961. Table 1.1 analyses the change in sectoral employment between 1926 and 1966. Agriculture declined in importance during this time from 53 per cent to 17 per cent of total employment.

The second oil shock and the subsequent world recession were a great blow to Ireland's development aspirations. Nevertheless, the people and respective governments chose not to reduce their standards of social public expenditure, and borrowing, especially foreign borrowing, took place on an increasing scale. The labour force grew by an average of 22,000 per annum from 1977 to 1982, but there was no increase in employment during the same period. These events resulted in a lowering of ability to continue the

funding of borrowings from domestic income increases, and led to
still higher foreign borrowings as old debts were rolled over.

*Table 1.1: Historical Employment in Ireland, 1926–81*

|  | % in Agriculture | % in Industry | % in Services | Total at Work 000 |
|---|---|---|---|---|
| 1926 | 53 | 13 | 34 | 1,222 |
| 1936 | 50 | 16 | 34 | 1,234 |
| 1946 | 47 | 17 | 36 | 1,227 |
| 1951 | 41 | 23 | 36 | 1,217 |
| 1961 | 36 | 25 | 39 | 1,053 |
| 1966 | 31 | 28 | 41 | 1,067 |
| 1971 | 26 | 31 | 43 | 1,055 |
| 1981 | 17 | 32 | 51 | 1,138 |

*Source*: "Report of the Task Force on Jobs in Services", Department of the
Taoiseach, December 1993.

The economy continued to stagnate in the 1980s and Ireland did
not benefit from the world upturn of 1983/84, except in the foreign
industry sector, which enjoyed an upsurge in export demand; but
this was met more by increases in productivity than by increases
in employment. Meanwhile, foreign debt continued to grow, as did
unemployment.

Drastic fiscal contraction in the mid-1980s by means of tax
increases and, more importantly, spending reductions, turned the
economy around from a position of near bankruptcy. The cost was
a significant shake-out of traditional manufacturing and service
employment, a surge in unemployment and high emigration,
which reached record levels at this time. A long-term benefit was
that Ireland experienced a boom between 1987 and 1990 in line
with worldwide trends. The rate of growth since then has been
among the highest in the industrial world. The average growth in
GNP between 1987 and 1992 was 4.6 per cent — despite a worldwide recession following the Gulf War of 1990. This growth is

broadly in line with the average Irish experience of the 1960s and 1970s.

## 1.2 THE OVERALL STRUCTURE OF IRISH BUSINESS

In 1993, the Government Task Force on Small Business analysed the structure of Irish business with a view to creating a focus on the importance of small business to the Irish economy. The analysis of this Task Force is reviewed in this section.

### 1.2.1 The Number of Establishments in Ireland

The Task Force on Small Business estimated that there were approximately 160,000 non-farm businesses in Ireland in 1993. However, nearly half of these were one-person operations. The Central Statistics Office (CSO) restricts its analysis to enterprises with more than three employees. The Task Force went further and analysed the structure for enterprises with more than one employee.

### 1.2.2 Size Profile of Irish Firms

According to the Task Force, most businesses in Ireland are small, and most small businesses are very small. Around 98 per cent of enterprises employ fewer than 50 persons and around 90 per cent employ fewer than 10 persons. Less than 1 per cent (0.3 per cent) of establishments employ over 500 people. Table 1.2 describes the very marked difference in Irish businesses by establishment and by employment.

However, the 0.3 per cent of firms with over 500 employees account for 40 per cent of total employment, while firms with over 50 employees account for 68 per cent of the total. This biased share of employment among large firms is heavily influenced by the inclusion of large public sector enterprises such as the ESB, Aer Lingus, Telecom Éireann, An Post, the Health Boards and Government bodies. If these establishments are omitted, over 30 per cent of the total private sector labour force is composed of people who work in enterprises employing less than 10 people, and over 50 per cent in enterprises with less than 50 employees. Job generation in recent years has been disproportionately concentrated among small businesses, while the share of employment among large firms has fallen.

*Table 1.2: Number of Establishments and Employment, 1993*

| No. of Employees | Establishments | | Employment |
|---|---|---|---|
| | Number | % | % |
| 1–4 | 62,953 | 71 | 9 |
| 5–9 | 12,413 | 14 | 6 |
| 10–49 | 10,640 | 12 | 17 |
| 50–99 | 1,153 | 1.3 | 10 |
| 100–499 | 1,153 | 1.3 | 18 |
| 500+ | 266 | 0.3 | 40 |
| Total | 88,578* | 100 | 100 |

* Employers employing more than one person.
*Source*: Government Task Force on Small Business (1994).

### 1.2.3 Sectoral Breakdown and Global Comparison

Table 1.3 provides a breakdown of employment by sector. It shows that manufacturing industry's share of the total number of enterprises is relatively modest compared with its contribution to wealth creation, export earnings and employment. It must be noted that 80 per cent of small businesses are in services.

A study carried out for the European Commission by the European Network for SME Research found that Ireland is below the European average in terms of the number of enterprises per 1,000 population. However, as the proportion of the population that is economically active is lower than in most industrialised countries, Ireland ranks quite well in terms of enterprises per 1,000 working population.

**Table 1.3: Sectoral Breakdown of Employment, 1992**

| Description of Category | No. of Establishments | % of Total |
|---|---|---|
| Hotels, Guest Houses | 1,168 | 0.9 |
| Catering | 2,948 | 2.3 |
| Entertainment | 448 | 0.4 |
| Builders | 16,240 | 12.8 |
| Hire Purchase | 139 | 0.1 |
| Services | 38,929 | 30.7 |
| Grocers | 4,451 | 3.5 |
| Groceries with Public House | 860 | 0.7 |
| Public Houses | 6,615 | 5.2 |
| Unprocessed Goods | 5,197 | 4.1 |
| General Stores | 1,206 | 1.0 |
| Cake, Tobacco, Paper Shops | 2,152 | 1.7 |
| Shoe Shops | 452 | 0.4 |
| Drapers | 3,212 | 2.5 |
| Garages, etc. | 5,818 | 4.6 |
| Chemists | 1,187 | 0.9 |
| Builders' Providers | 1,538 | 1.2 |
| Electrical Dealers | 1,403 | 1.1 |
| Jewellers | 484 | 0.4 |
| Booksellers | 731 | 0.6 |
| Furniture | 967 | 0.8 |
| Department Stores | 73 | 0.1 |
| Variety Chain Stores | 77 | 0.1 |
| Fuel Merchants | 552 | 0.4 |
| Other Distributors | 9,107 | 7.2 |
| Manufacturers | 8,457 | 6.7 |
| Other | 12,343 | 9.7 |
| Total | 126,754 | 100 |

*Note*:    Percentage figures may be rounded.
*Source*:  Government Task Force on Small Business (1994).

Table 1.4 compares Ireland with the major developed countries.

### Table 1.4: Comparison with Other Countries

| Country | No. of Enterprises (000) | No. of Enterprises per 1,000 inhabitants | No. of Enterprises per 1,000 of working age | No. of Enterprises per 1,000 in labour force |
|---|---|---|---|---|
| Belgium | 530 | 53 | 79 | 128 |
| Denmark | 180 | 35 | 52 | 62 |
| France | 2,040 | 36 | 55 | 84 |
| Germany | 2,160 | 35 | 50 | 73 |
| Greece | 670 | 67 | 101 | 169 |
| Italy | 3,170 | 55 | 80 | 131 |
| Luxembourg | 20 | 43 | 77 | 112 |
| Netherlands | 420 | 28 | 41 | 63 |
| Portugal | 640 | 62 | 99 | 139 |
| Spain | 2,020 | 52 | 79 | 135 |
| UK | 2,630 | 46 | 70 | 93 |
| Ireland | (a) 130<br>(b)* 160 | (a) 37<br>(b) 45 | (a) 60<br>(b) 74 | (a) 99<br>(b) 122 |
| Total EU | 14,600 | 45 | 67 | 101 |
| Japan** | 6,622 | 54 | 77 | 107 |
| US | 18,979 | 77 | 117 | 154 |

\*        1992
\*\*       1993
*Note*:    The figures for Ireland include both (a) the original European Commission survey estimates of 130,000 and (b) the Task Force estimate of 160,000 enterprises in Ireland.
*Source*:  Government Task Force on Small Business (1994).

At this point it would be beneficial to look at the importance of both large companies and small/medium sized-companies in the overall economy.

### 1.2.4 An Analysis of Large Companies

An analysis of the top 1,000 Irish companies from the *Business and Finance* listing undertaken in 1995 shows how few companies there are in the whole Irish economy (see Table 1.5).

**Table 1.5: Analysis of the Top 1,000 Companies, 1995**

| No. | Turnover £ m | Employment | Industry |
|---|---|---|---|
| 1 | 1,427 | 11,751 | Building Material Supplier |
| 2 | 1,317 | 18,267 | Print and Packaging |
| 3 | 1,280 | 8,000 | Supermarkets |
| 4 | 1,214 | 2,300 | Export of Dairy Products |
| 5 | 1,129 | 6,219 | Dairy and Pigmeat Processing |
| 10 | 871 | 13,069 | Telecommunications |
| 20 | 498 | 970 | Wholesale Grocery |
| 40 | 245 | 2,305 | Industrial Holding |
| 60 | 170 | 437 | Cash and Carry |
| 80 | 130 | 97 | Vehicle Import Distribution |
| 101 | 104 | 863 | Builders Merchants |
| 150 | 68 | 510 | Airline |
| 250 | 37 | 493 | Computer Manuals |
| 400 | 21 | 259 | Crane Manufacturer |
| 550 | 14 | 50 | Freight Forwarding |
| 700 | 9.5 | 45 | Provender Miller |
| 850 | 6.5 | 53 | Adhesive Manufacturer |
| 1,000 | 4 | 115 | Electronic Components |

*Source*: *Business and Finance*, "Top 1000 Irish Companies", January 1995.

The thousandth company had a turnover of £4 million. The largest 100 firms account for about the same turnover as the next 850. Foreign ownership among large companies was high — 24 of the 70 largest industrial enterprises were foreign-owned — and the top 10 foreign-owned businesses reported sales in excess of £6.3 billion, with massive sales growth being experienced by the foreign-owned computer companies such as Microsoft, Intel, Apple and Dell.

In terms of business activities, the 100 largest firms provide Ireland's basic infrastructural services, dispose of the bulk of agricultural produce, obtain and distribute our major imports, and account for most of our manufactured exports (see Table 1.6).

*Table 1.6: Industry Sectors of the Top 100 v. Top 1,000, 1995*

| Sector | Top 100 % | Top 1,000 % |
|---|---|---|
| Agriculture, Agri-food and Drink | 19 | 32 |
| Manufacturing Industry | 37 | 25 |
| Distribution | 23 | 27 |
| Transport/Utilities | 10 | 10 |
| Other Services | 11 | 6 |
| Total | 100 | 100 |

*Source*: *Business and Finance*, January 1995 and authors' estimates.

As in other developed economies, manufacturing employment losses in the 1980s occurred mainly in large indigenous firms. Manufacturing employment gains in the 1990s have been primarily among smaller firms. Foreign firms suffered in the early 1980s but this trend was reversed in the late 1980s and has continued into the 1990s.

### 1.2.5 An Overview of SMEs

In common with all western economies, Ireland's small firm sector accounts for the bulk of all enterprises. Ninety per cent of firms in Ireland employ 10 people or fewer. The amount of employment accounted for by this sector is about average for developed economies, with 30 per cent of manufacturing firms and over 95 per cent of all enterprises. However, there is evidence to suggest that this proportion is low for the size of the economy — although the small firm sector accounts for over one-third of indigenously-controlled employment, which might be more in line with its potential.

The small firm manufacturing sector comprises about 4,500 firms with a total employment of 57,000 people. Output per employee is lower than in other size sectors, which reflects lower capital intensity and greater dependence on the home market. Small firms exhibit a marked tendency to operate in certain industries, as illustrated in Table 1.7. below.

**Table 1.7. Small Industry Share of Total Manufacturing Employment**

| Sector | % |
|---|---|
| Wood and Furniture | 63 |
| Paper and Printing | 27 |
| Metals | 25 |
| Clothing and Footwear | 25 |
| Miscellaneous | 25 |
| Minerals | 22 |
| Food | 19 |
| Chemicals | 15 |
| Textiles | 12 |
| Drink and Tobacco | 10 |
| All Sectors | 30 |

*Source*: Forfás and estimates.

The size of a manufacturing establishment is largely determined by the economies underlying the production process and by the character of the market for the goods. Some of the major economic and structural factors which apply to small firms are outlined by Kieran Kennedy (*IBAR,* Vol. 7, No. 1, pp. 17–8) below:

There are three classes of reasons for the existence of small firms. First, the minimum economic scale of plant remains small. Broadly speaking the activities most favourable to small firms are those involving low capital intensity, low fixed costs, batch production techniques, non-repetitive tasks, and personalised skills.

Moreover, unit cost may be minimised at different scales for different dimensions of cost, and the weights of these costs may differ at different stages of the production process — leading to the parcelling out of some activities on subcontract to small firms.

Second, market factors may enable firms to survive below the minimum economic scale of production. This is more probable where markets are localised by reason of transport costs, where advertising is unimportant, and where there is a high degree of service in delivery. Small firms may be used by large firms to meet unanticipated increases in demand or seasonal peaks. Where there are major economies of scale in marketing or other significant entry barriers in penetrating markets, small firms can still survive if pooled marketing arrangements are available.

Third, there are dynamic factors at work all the time. The industrial structure is constantly changing, and at any given time the small firm sector will include formerly large firms in decline and new firms on the way up. Moreover, as already noted, the minimum economic scale itself changes with technological change, the life cycle stage of products, and relative cost of transport, communications, fuel etc. It had commonly been thought that these changes made for ever-larger scale of operations, but developments in the seventies have caused some revision of that review.

In general, the economic and structural factors that permit and encourage the existence of small firms also militate against their growth beyond a certain stage. Growth beyond a particular product/market niche usually requires very large cost increments and management capabilities that are difficult to develop within the business. In Ireland, state funding is available to small companies, and this can help the development of the firm beyond the small stage.

Irish small businesses seem to have evolved on a stand-alone basis, which makes growth difficult. In countries that develop many large firms, such as Japan, small firms have more opportunities as suppliers.

## 1.3 AN OVERVIEW OF THE MANUFACTURING SECTOR OF IRISH INDUSTRY

Because of its importance in overall economic development, it is appropriate at this stage to analyse the manufacturing sector in more detail. The Irish manufacturing industry can be divided into three sectors: traditional, resource-based, and modern industries. These sectors are analysed in more detail in Chapters Four, Five and Six. The three sectors may be defined as follows:

- **Traditional** industries produce "mature" product types where low-skilled labour is an important input. Classic examples of traditional industries include textiles, clothing, footwear, furniture and printing and publishing. In general, these industries have been shifting steadily to low-wage countries, which then export the goods to the industrially developed nations.

- **Resource-based** industries may be "traditional" or "modern" in many respects, but because they reflect individual national resource endowments, different cost and market structures prevail. The key resource-based industries in Ireland are agribusiness, drinks, forestry, fishing and mining.

- **Modern** industries in general produce products that embody a high level of knowledge and technical infrastructure and thereby add a great deal of value to the raw materials and labour used in production. The most important modern Irish industries include electronics, chemicals, pharmaceuticals, health care and precision engineering.

The three industry types by sector are classified in Table 1.8.

Overall employment in manufacturing industries has remained quite stable in the 1990s, in contrast to the 1980–85 period when total employment fell by almost 40,000. Traditional industries are beginning to stabilise after a disastrous period in the 1980s. Strong growth continues to be experienced in the modern sector.

Output in traditional manufacturing industry is driven by domestic demand, international demand and the ability of Irish firms to be competitive *vis-à-vis* foreign counterparts in terms of technology, labour and capital costs. Output in resource-based Irish industry is constrained by quota restrictions on agricultural production as a result of the Common Agricultural Policy (CAP) and its reform. Output in the modern or high-technology sector is driven by world demand, world supply by competitor countries and the ability of Ireland to attract mobile foreign investment. A key factor in Irish.competitiveness is the low corporate tax rate afforded to foreign direct investors.

## Table 1.8: Classification of Industry Sub-Sectors

| Modern | Resource-based | Traditional |
|---|---|---|
| Preliminary Processing of Metals | Slaughtering and Meat | Cement, Concrete Products |
| Chemicals, Oil and Tar | Dairy Products | Glass and Glassware |
| Paint and Varnish | Seafood Products | Ceramic Goods |
| Pharmaceuticals | Grain Milling | Textiles |
| Toiletry Preparations | Bread and Flour | Knitted Goods |
| House and Office Chemicals | Fruit and Vegetable Products | Carpets and Floor Coverings |
| Man-made Articles | Confectionery | Leather and Tanning |
| Mechanical Engineering | Other Foodstuffs | Clothing |
| Precision Toolmaking | Soft Drinks | Household Textiles |
| Computer and Office Software | Tobacco Products | Paper |
| Electrical Engineering | Alcoholic Beverages | Printing and Publishing |
| Health-Care Products | Timber Products | Rubber Products |
| Instrument Engineering | Wooden Furniture | Plastic Products |
| Motor Vehicles and Parts | | Toys, Sports and Musical Instruments |
| Other Transport | | |

*Source*: Irish Productivity Centre, 1994.

Table 1.9 analyses output, employment and productivity among the three manufacturing sectors through the 1980s and into 1992.

**Table 1.9: Performance Indicators in Manufacturing, 1989–92 (1986–89 in brackets)**

|  | Output<br>% p.a. | Employment<br>% p.a. | Productivity<br>% p.a. |
|---|---|---|---|
| **Modern** | | | |
| Computers and High Tech Engineering | 6.7 (24.4) | 2.8 (4.6) | 3.8 (19.0) |
| Chemicals | 13.7 (13.2) | 5.9 (2.4) | 7.4 (10.5) |
| Total Manufacturing Industries | 6.0 (11.5) | 1.0 (0.8) | 4. 9 (10.6) |
| **Resource-based** | | | |
| Food | 5.7 (6.7) | 1.1 (-1.3) | 4.6 (8.1) |
| Drink and Tobacco | 1.6 (4.7) | -2.7 (-5.1) | 4.4 (10.4) |
| Miscellaneous | 3.3 (4.4) | 2.1 (4.8) | 1.2 (-0.4) |
| **Traditional** | | | |
| Textiles | 4.1 (3.9) | -0.6 (0.0) | 4.8 (3.9) |
| Clothing and Footwear | -5.4 (-3.7) | -3.1 (-4.8) | -2.4 (1.2) |
| Traditional Metals and Engineering | 0.8 (4.2) | -2.7 (-2.8) | 3.6 (7.2) |
| Timber and Furniture | 2.7 (5.1) | -0.9 (1.3) | 3.6 (3.7) |
| Paper and Printing | 6.3 (8.8) | 0.5 (2.7) | 5.8 (5.9) |
| Clay Products | 0.8 (4.2) | -2.7 (-2.8) | 3.6 (7.2) |

*Source*: Department of Enterprise and Employment, Operational Programme (1994–97), 1994.

As can be seen, clear differences in performance exist between the three sectors, the main trends being summarised as follows:

- There was a very significant drop in the growth rate of output and productivity in the modern or high-technology group of sectors in 1989–92, compared to the previous period, although growth rates remain relatively high compared to the other two sectors. Employment growth was not affected as much because of the decrease in productivity.

- The growth rate of the traditional group of sectors in output and productivity fell sharply in 1989–92 from the very strong

1986–89 (post-recession) growth rates, with little change in the aggregate employment level. Clothing and footwear showed particularly poor performance.

- There was growth in output in food, drink and tobacco sectors, although this did not translate into employment growth because of growth in productivity.

Exports for 1992 are analysed in Table 1.10. It is clear that only one-third of indigenous firms are exporting, compared with over 85 per cent of non-indigenous firms.

**Table 1.10: Export Propensity of Foreign-owned and Indigenous Firms (IR£ million)**

|  | Foreign-owned | Indigenous |
|---|---|---|
| Gross Output | 10,918 | 9,050 |
| Gross Output of Exporters | 10,558 | 6,398 |
| Exports | 9,363 | 3,023 |
| Export Propensity (%) | 88.7 (85.8) | 47.3 (33.4) |

*Note*:   Propensity shares in brackets represent all manufacturing industry rather than exporters.
*Source*:   Census of Industrial Production, 1990.

## 1.4 THE IMPORTANCE OF FOREIGN-OWNED INDUSTRY

This section analyses foreign-owned industry and the important role it plays. Ireland's business structure — in particular, the structure of manufacturing industry — has been enormously affected by a very high level of direct foreign investment. The sustained growth in overall manufacturing output has primarily occurred in foreign firms, which account for nearly 55 per cent of gross manufacturing output and approximately 45 per cent of manufacturing employment. These percentages are by far the highest among European countries. In addition, the few large Irish-owned manufacturing concerns have undergone increased internationalisation in the form of increased foreign investment. Tables 1.11 and 1.12 analyse the total sales and expenditure in

Ireland of foreign-owned (organised by IDA Ireland) and indigenous industry (organised by Forbairt).

As these tables show, sales in the foreign-owned sector at £9.5 billion in 1993 were growing at a faster rate than those in the indigenous sector (£11.4 billion). Irish economy expenditure is much higher in the indigenous sector at 68.9 per cent of sales as opposed to 32.5 per cent in foreign-owned businesses. However, expenditure is growing at a much faster rate in the foreign-owned sector (61.9 per cent against 31.6 per cent between 1987 and 1993).

**Table 1.11: Total Sales and Expenditure in Ireland of Foreign-owned Manufacturing Industry, 1987–93 (IR£ million, constant 1993 prices)**

|  | 1987 | 1990 | 1993 | % Change 87–93 | % Change 92–93 |
|---|---|---|---|---|---|
| Sales | 5,829 | 7,670 | 9,464 | 62.4 | 8.9 |
| Irish Economy Expenditure of which: | 1,903 | 2,537 | 3,080 | 61.9 | 6.9 |
| Labour Costs | 868 | 1,107 | 1,226 | 41.2 | -1.4 |
| Irish Raw Materials | 357 | 566 | 791 | 121.6 | 13.8 |
| Irish Services | 672 | 852 | 1,057 | 57.3 | 12.8 |
| Employment | 56,949 | 64,587 | 66,738 | 17.2 | 0.6 |

Source: Forfás Survey of Manufacturing Expenditure, 1994.

For almost 30 years Ireland's industrial policy has been focused on attracting foreign manufacturing concerns to locate here. This policy has been very successful and foreign firms have brought with them existing markets, developed technologies and modern management practices. However, it is sometimes difficult to integrate some of these foreign firms into the remainder of the economy in terms of sub-supply, technology transfer and other economic linkages.

*Table 1.12: Total Sales and Expenditure in Ireland of Indigenous-owned Manufacturing Industry, 1987–93 (IR£ million, constant 1993 prices)*

|  | 1987 | 1990 | 1993 | % Change 87–93 | % Change 92–93 |
|---|---|---|---|---|---|
| Sales | 8,132 | 9,810 | 11,398 | 40.2 | -2.4 |
| Irish Economy Expenditure | 5,975 | 6,507 | 7,864 | 31.6 | 3.6 |
| of which: | | | | | |
| Labour Costs | 1,352 | 1,400 | 1,596 | 18.0 | -1.1 |
| Irish Raw Materials | 3,303 | 3,445 | 4,295 | 30.0 | 5.1 |
| Irish Services | 1,106 | 1,380 | 1,596 | 44.3 | 7.1 |
| Employment | 82,160 | 83,431 | 91,492 | 11.4 | -0.7 |

*Source*: Forfás Survey of Manufacturing Expenditure, 1994.

In terms of employment and output, and most especially in terms of exports, the foreign sector of manufacturing industry has become essential, almost compensating for the job losses in the traditional sectors, which followed the introduction of free trade. The overseas companies operate mainly, but not exclusively, in the modern industry sectors, and output growth is higher than in indigenous firms. Recent industrial growth has taken place in just a handful of sectors where the share of wages in net output is barely 10 per cent, according to the ESRI. These sectors include:

• Pharmaceuticals

• Data Processing Equipment

• Software Production

• Miscellaneous Foods.

By 1990, these four sectors accounted for 27 per cent of manufacturing value added (up from 11 per cent a decade before) but they accounted for only 10 per cent of manufacturing employment. The arrival and expansion of firms with a wage share as low as 10 per cent inevitably contributes to expansion of measured output disproportionate to employment growth, thereby contributing to the impression of "jobless growth".

Table 1.13 shows some principal employment and output characteristics of both Irish and foreign manufacturing concerns. Some of the more important features are listed below.

**Table 1.13: *Manufacturing Industry by Nationality of Ownership, 1993***

| | Employment | | Gross Output | | Net Output | | | |
|---|---|---|---|---|---|---|---|---|
| | No. | % | £ m | % | £ m | % | Wages & Salaries | Per Person |
| Irish | 92,103 | 57.2 | 11,130 | 54.9 | 3,537 | 38.4 | 55.6 | 38,403 |
| Foreign | 66,353 | 41.2 | 8,708 | 42.9 | 5,253 | 57.1 | 42.9 | 79,167 |
| Unclassified | 2,458 | 1.5 | 438 | 2.2 | 411 | 4.5 | 1.5 | N/A |
| TOTAL | 160,914 | 100 | 20,276 | 100 | 9,201 | 100 | 100 | 58,785 |

*Source:* Adapted from Forfás Survey of Manufacturing Expenditure, 1994.

- One in seven manufacturing enterprises in Ireland is foreign-owned.

- Foreign firms are larger than indigenous firms, employing on average more than three times as many people per establishment. Together they account for nearly four out of every ten employees engaged in manufacturing industry.

- Foreign firms produce just over 40 per cent of gross output, but nearly 60 per cent of total net output.

- Foreign firms have a higher output per person than Irish firms, both in gross and in net terms. Net output per person is more than twice as high (£79,167 compared to £38,403).

- Total Irish economy expenditures are lower for foreign than for indigenous firms, both in absolute terms and also relatively.

Foreign firms, as a group, have a very different cost structure from Irish-owned firms. Significant differences include lower labour costs, lower materials costs, a higher propensity to import raw materials and, most importantly, much higher profit levels. The higher profit levels are partly a result of transfer pricing practised by these companies on an international basis.

## 1.5 ANALYSIS OF STATE-SPONSORED ENTERPRISES

In this section we look briefly at how direct state involvement in industry fits into the overall business system. Beginning with the Electricity Supply Board (ESB), which was set up in 1925, the state has founded about 100 commercial enterprises for pragmatic strategic reasons (in marked contrast to the UK, where ideology informed the growth of state enterprises). Many state-sponsored bodies are natural or legal monopolies and this market power has often been reflected in their pricing policies. Originally, these bodies were set up to provide essential services which were beyond the scope of private enterprise — Córas Iompair Éireann (CIE, now Iarnród Éireann, Bus Éireann and Dublin Bus), Aer Lingus and the ESB are examples. Others were created to exploit natural resources (Bord na Móna, Bord Gáis) or because their industries were of strategic supply importance (Comhlucht Siúcra Éireann (CSE), Nitrigin Éireann Teoranta (NET), Irish Steel, Irish Life). The types of state-sponsored enterprises, the industry sectors in which they operate, and the sectors' relative importance in the economy are broadly in line with other European countries. About 30 of these firms have more than 100 employees, and the largest 10 rank among the top 60 companies. It was expected that the state-sponsored commercial enterprises would be self-financing and would generate an adequate return on government investment. In practice, performance has been very uneven and, although important social and strategic functions are served, the net financial benefit to the state from its commercial activities is questioned by some commentators. Nevertheless, the importance of these bodies in the total economy is considerable. Public enterprises account for about:

- 7 per cent of national income
- 7.5 per cent of all employees
- 15 per cent of national investment
- 40 per cent of public sector investment.

As in the UK, the trend has been towards increased privatisation of state enterprises. This has been driven by the belief that the private sector can achieve higher levels of efficiency and competitiveness and the fact that many semi-state enterprises are competing in global industries against more efficient private sector multinational corporations (MNCs). Privatisation or semi-privatisation has changed the status of the following companies in recent years:

- Comhlucht Siúcra Éireann (Irish Sugar)
- Irish Life
- Kilkenny Design
- B and I.

The role of the state in Irish business is analysed in more detail in Chapter Three.

## 1.6 SECTORAL EMPLOYMENT

The work that people do falls into three categories of economic importance:

- Services
- Agriculture
- Manufacturing.

This is a broad classification, and there are many examples of firms which do not fit clearly into one of these categories. However, most economic activity can be usefully classified in this way; the cost structures and markets are more similar within the sectors than between them. Table 1.14 gives a breakdown of sectoral employment as it has developed since 1985. Agriculture has continued its decline in overall employment, with a move towards service employment. Manufacturing industry employment is similar to many European countries.

*Table 1.14: Sectoral Employment in Ireland, 1985–93*

|        | Agriculture % | Services % | Industry % | Total at Work 000 |
|--------|---------------|------------|------------|-------------------|
| 1985   | 16            | 56         | 28         | 1,079             |
| 1986   | 16            | 56         | 28         | 1,081             |
| 1987   | 15            | 57         | 28         | 1,080             |
| 1988   | 15            | 57         | 28         | 1,092             |
| 1989   | 15            | 57         | 28         | 1,090             |
| 1990   | 15            | 57         | 28         | 1,126             |
| 1991   | 14            | 58         | 28         | 1,125             |
| 1992   | 13            | 59         | 28         | 1,125             |
| 1993*  | 12.5          | 60         | 28         | 1,144*            |

\*          Estimate — ESRI Medium Term Review 1994.
*Source*:   CSO Labour Force Survey.

### 1.6.1 Employment in Services
In line with other countries, the services sector has become the major area of employment (Figure 1.1). This is generally explained by rising consumer demand for services, combined with increased labour productivity in industry and agriculture as total capital investment increases.

Between 1980 and 1993 employment in services grew by 113,000. This growth has been primarily in the market service sector rather than in non-market services (i.e. health, education, public administration). This is a worldwide phenomenon.

The reasons for the worldwide growth in services employment include increased specialisation and outsourcing of business services, which means that much of the growth in services employment represents merely redefinition and reclassification of industrial work. The growth of information technology and the labour-saving nature of technology suggest that in the past few years it is the relative shortfall in the growth in service jobs (compared to other countries) which is a major factor in Ireland's disappointing employment performance.

### Figure 1.1: Employment in Services, 1990–94

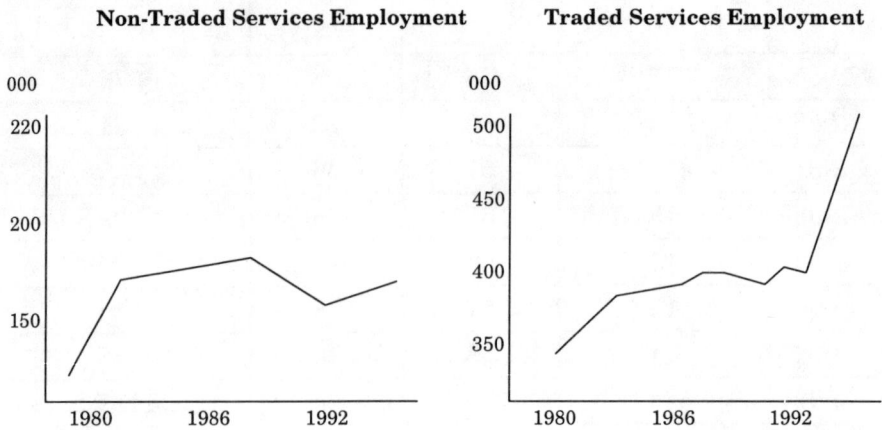

Source: *Medium Term Review*, ESRI, 1994.

The high levels of employment in services, and particularly public services, must be seen in the light of Ireland's relatively low per capita GNP; yet there are important results, as the IPC notes:

> Supplying the traded sector of the economy is not the primary economic function of the services sector (or even of market services) and economic policy towards the services sector should not be formulated as if it were. The two most important economic functions of the services sector are (a) its output goes mostly directly to consumers and that output determines to a major extent Irish living standards, and (b) it is by far the most important provider of employment.

At the same time, the cost of achieving employment objectives is a major component in the national debt, and measures taken to reduce the debt, and may result in increased unemployment and decreased consumer services. Every government must attempt to balance the needs of reducing levels of unemployment against reducing national debt, and this has proved extremely difficult in Ireland in recent times given its demographic structure.

### 1.6.2 Employment in Agriculture

Although agricultural employment has decreased steadily to its present 13 per cent of total employment, productivity gains since accession to the EC in 1973 have resulted in large output increases. Agriculture accounts for about 35 per cent of total manufacturing output and 27 per cent of exports, much of it directed at the EC surplus markets. The industry structure has changed radically, mainly as a result of the Common Agricultural Policy (CAP) and its reform, with production now concentrated in a few very large companies. Of Ireland's top 100 firms, about one-third are agriculture-based. They include beef and dairy processors, and companies which further process or distribute agricultural products. The absorption of smaller producers is likely to continue as CAP support diminishes and as economies of scale become more important. At the same time, a number of smaller producers have growth prospects because they have succeeded in addressing specialised product/market niches.

### 1.6.3 Employment in Manufacturing

Manufacturing employment has declined since 1980 and in particular in the 1980s, both in absolute terms and as a proportion of total employment, itself declining. Despite the decline in employment, net output increased somewhat, driven primarily by export demand from European economies recovering from recession. Ireland's overall economy did not share the general recovery after 1984.

However, since 1986, Ireland has been one of the few European countries to have avoided a significant decline in industrial employment. When the statistics underlying output growth and productivity are examined more closely, it can be seen that the Irish economy has a dual industrial structure. Modern industries account for most of the productivity improvements and non-food exports, while traditional industries focus mainly on supplying the domestic market. Traditional manufacturing industry is still trying to adjust to the competitiveness of an open economy. The modern sector is dominated by foreign companies attracted to Ireland as a manufacturing base for their world markets; and while intensive efforts are being made to develop indigenous modern industry, the total contribution may be slight for some time to come.

## SUMMARY

An understanding of the environment in which a firm operates is a necessary prerequisite to developing a coherent strategy. This chapter provides a broad outline of the structure of Irish business in the 1990s and tracks the economic development that has helped to form this structure. The major points of this chapter may be summarised as follows:

- The Irish economy has achieved average growth rates of 4 per cent per annum since the 1960s, apart from the recessionary period of the early 1980s. This growth rate is one of the highest in the industrialised world.

- There are at least 160,000 non-farm enterprises in this country. Most of these businesses are very small; around 90 per cent employ less than 10 people. However, less than 1 per cent of establishments employ 40 per cent of the total workforce.

- The services industry now accounts for 60 per cent of employment in Ireland, while agriculture now accounts for only 13 per cent (compared with 53 per cent in 1926). Industrial employment at around 28 per cent is reasonably stable and similar to other European countries.

- Most output growth has occurred in the modern or high-technology sector, which is dominated by foreign-owned companies.

- Job creation has been concentrated among the small business sector and services sector. Small and medium-sized industry and services enterprises are strategically important for long-term growth in the Irish economy.

- State-sponsored enterprises account for 7 per cent of national income, 7.5 per cent of employees, 15 per cent of national investment and 40 per cent of public sector investment. In common with international trends, some state companies are being privatised, primarily because of the competitive pressures from multinational corporations (MNCs).

- There are some 990 foreign-owned firms operating in Ireland at present, employing around 90,000 people, equivalent to 40 per cent of the industrial workforce. They represent approximately 50 per cent of manufactured output and three-quarters of industrial exports.

---

## FURTHER READING

*Business and Finance*, "Top 1,000 Irish Companies", January 1995.

Central Statistics Office, "Labour Force Survey", Government Publications Office, 1992.

Central Statistics Office, "Census of Industrial Production", Government Publications Office, 1990.

Department of Enterprise and Employment, "Operational Programme 1994–1997", Government Publications Office, 1994.

Department of Industry and Commerce, "Review of Industrial Performance", Government Publications Office, (PL. 7423) 1990.

Department of the Taoiseach, "Report of the Task Force on Jobs in Services", Government Publications Office, 1993.

Economic and Social Research Institute (ESRI), "Medium-Term Review — 1994–2000", Government Publications, 1994.

Forfás, various reports and surveys, Government Publications Office.

IDA Ireland and Forfás Annual Reports.

Kennedy, Kieran A. , "The Relevance of Small-Scale Manufacturing in Industrial Development", *IBAR*, Vol. 7, No. 1, pp. 10–32.

Quarterly Review Economic Trends, September 1994, IBEC.

"Report of the Government Task Force on Small Business", Government Publications, 1994.

CHAPTER TWO

# THE IRISH BUSINESS ENVIRONMENT

*I*t is often very difficult for the practising manager to assess the impact of the environment on the enterprise's operations. Part of the reason for this problem is that day-to-day operations are so demanding of attention, and also that the relevant "environment" is inherently difficult to define and analyse. Nevertheless, every firm is deeply embedded in an environment that is much wider than the activities of customers, suppliers and competitors. As with industrial structure, the broad societal background is dynamic and can deliver threats and opportunities to the firm. For this reason, strategic management must make an attempt at assessing the broad patterns of environmental trends.

Managers working in Ireland face an environment that is considerably different in important respects from that facing their peers in other countries. Some of the more obvious differences include a low level of industrialisation compared to trade partners, a very open economy, low per capita income (compared to trade partners), geographical isolation from markets, and a very small domestic market. In addition to these static descriptions, there are dynamic forces operating. This chapter outlines the broad shape of the drivers of change as they affect the general business environment in Ireland, and how they may impact on Irish firms.

The following areas are discussed here to examine the business environment:

- The global business environment and trends in major economic power blocs

- The European business environment and its effect on separate member nation states, and the political/legal environment

- The current economic situation within Ireland in terms of

output, income and employment

- The technological environment and the importance of Science and Technology to economic development

- The political-legal environment in terms of regulations and legislation in the area of business

- The physical environment and the effects of environmental concern on business behaviour.

The chapter concludes with an analysis of some of the unique features of the Irish economy that result from the business environment. Figure 2.1 graphically portrays the business environment as it affects Ireland in the 1990s.

## 2.1 THE GLOBAL ECONOMIC ENVIRONMENT

Three main drivers of economic activity in a global sense are:

- The traditional power blocs

- The emerging power blocs

- WTO and its effects on world trade.

As already mentioned, the Irish economy is small and open and it is greatly affected by economic activity in the rest of the world — in particular, the UK and Europe. This section looks briefly at the state of the world economy in the 1990s and the influence it is having on the Irish economy.

### 2.1.1 Global Economic Activity in the 1990s

All the major trading blocs simultaneously suffered from stagnation in economic performance in the early 1990s after the Gulf War, which caused a recession. The recession was not too severe relative to previous recessions, but it was reasonably long and protracted, particularly in Europe.

A major reason for continued European recession were the knock-on effects of German unification, which led to expansionary fiscal policy and tight industry policy by the German Bundesbank. The reluctance of other countries within the European Monetary System (EMS) to devalue their currencies added to upward pressure on interest rates at a time when a more expansionary monetary policy might have been more appropriate. Large fiscal deficits worked against many European countries in their attempts to manoeuvre themselves out of recession, and despite cutbacks in spending, budget deficits in many countries rose in the early 1990s.

**Figure 2.1: The Business Environment and Forces**

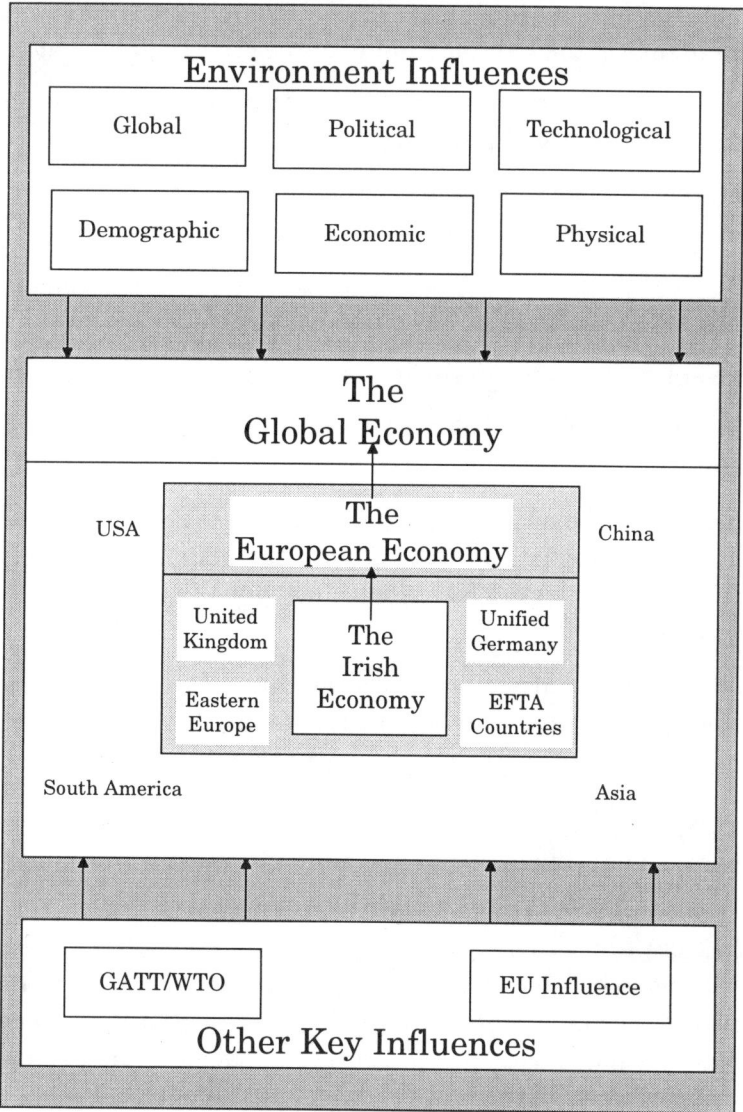

The mid-1990s sees economic activity and output in a growth phase of approximately 5 to 6 per cent per annum, and this is expected to continue at a more conservative level until the year 2000. As we near the twenty-first century, world economic activity is in a state of dynamic change. Fundamental developments are occurring in the levels of competitiveness between trading blocs. The following are some of the main influences on world economic activity in the mid to late 1990s:

- The creation of the World Trade Organisation (WTO), and acceptance of the Uruguay round of the GATT agreement

- The decline in importance of the nation-state and the emergence of new as well as the traditional power blocs

- The rise of corporate power as the larger MNCs become global companies with outputs greater than some nation-states

- The emergence of the "Four Dragons" (South Korea, Singapore, Taiwan, Hong Kong) as key economic powers

- The emergence of China as another emerging economic power

- The growth of some South American countries as low-cost manufacturers on the world stage

- The emergence of the "Visegrad" countries (Poland, the Czech Republic, Hungary, and the Slovak Republic), particularly in the areas of agri-food processing and traditional manufacturing

- A shift in the centre of gravity of the European Union, with the acceptance of most European Free Trade Association (EFTA) countries in 1996 and East European countries after 2000.

All of these influences will have a great effect on the way in which business is undertaken in Europe, and in particular in Ireland.

### 2.1.2 Europe
The European economy was relatively stagnant in the early 1990s because of focused attention on EU integration and tight German monetary policy pushing up interest rates. Modest growth is being experienced in the mid-1990s as a result of a continued lack

of consumer and business confidence, the need for fiscal rectitude among many countries and continued high interest rates.

## Germany
The health of the German economy is crucial to European growth. After a period of increased public expenditure and growth in inflation after reunification, the German economy is expected to experience modest growth of 2.5 per cent per annum to 1996, rising to 3.5 per cent thereafter.

## United Kingdom
The state of the UK economy has always had a major influence on Irish economic activity, although this has diminished somewhat. In relative terms, the UK came out of recession quickly in the period 1992–94; unemployment dropped significantly and this is expected to continue. GDP growth was between 2 and 3 per cent between 1992 and 1995, and further growth is dependent on the rate of economic growth in other European economies.

## Eastern Europe — The "Visegrad" Countries
Developments in the Visegrad countries of Poland, the Czech Republic, Hungary and the Slovak Republic have been remarkable since the demise of Communism. Both the manufacturing and agricultural sectors are driving growth under a high level of political stability. This growth is expected to continue throughout the 1990s, primarily as a result of an upturn in the German economy, although necessary industrial reform may push up unemployment and budget deficits. Table 2.1 describes the key economic indicators up to 1995.

**Table 2.1: Economic Activity in the "Visegrad" Countries 1990–95**

|  | GDP (% change per annum) | | | Inflation (%) | Current Deficit ($ million) |
|---|---|---|---|---|---|
|  | 1990 | 1993 | 1995 | 1995 | 1995 |
| Poland | -8 | 3.5 | 3.5 | 25 | -2,500 |
| Czech Republic | -1.5 | -15 | 3 | 10 | -500 |
| Hungary | -3.5 | -12 | 1 | 20 | -2,500 |
| Slovak Republic | -2.5 | -15 | 1 | 10 | -300 |

*Source:* EIU, "The World in 1995", Economist Publications, 1995.

### 2.1.3 Asia
*Japan*

The early 1990s recession in Japan was deeper and more fundamental than that in Europe or the USA. Japan's recession was
caused by the weak international environment, a sharp appreciation in the yen which reduced competitiveness, an overheating
of the domestic economy in the late 1980s and adverse demographic shifts affecting consumption and savings. Japan is currently trying to stimulate growth through public-expenditure
programmes. Weak growth was experienced in 1994 (0.4 per cent)
and it is expected to remain low in the mid-1990s but to improve
thereafter as Japan benefits from growth in world trade.

### *The Dragon Economies in South Asia*

The so-called Dragon economies of South Korea, Singapore,
Taiwan and Hong Kong avoided the world recession of the early
1990s and enjoyed strong growth, together with the other "dynamic" Asian economies of Malaysia and Thailand. Co-operation
with China will affect each Dragon economy between 1995 and
2005 as trade increases between the nations. Table 2.2 describes
the main economic indicators for the countries in 1995.

**Table 2.2: Economic Forecasts for "Four Dragons", 1995**

|  | 1995 Forecasts | |
| --- | --- | --- |
|  | **GNP Growth (%)** | **GNP per Capita ($)** |
| South Korea | 7.4 | 9,600 |
| Singapore | 7.6 | 24,900 |
| Taiwan | 6.6 | 12,620 |
| Hong Kong | 3.6 | 22,840 |

*Source:* EIU, "The World in 1995", Economist Publications, 1995.

### 2.1.4 South America

After many years of debt-mismanagement and hyper-inflation,
economic growth based on more sound fiscal policies and open
markets is being experienced in most major Latin American
countries, with the possible exception of Mexico. The economic
rebirth of Latin America is predicted to be as profound as that

begun by East Asia 20 years ago and by Europe 40 years ago, depending on continued political and military reform. Latin America as a region is expected to become a major low-cost producer on the world market. Table 2.3 gives the main economic indicators for the key economies.

**Table 2.3: Economic Forecasts for Latin America, 1995**

|  | Inflation (%) | Economic Growth (%) | Current Account ($ billion) |
|---|---|---|---|
| Mexico | 7.5 | 4.8 | -28 |
| Argentina | 4.3 | 3.5 | -11 |
| Brazil | 205 | 2.5 | -8.3 |
| Chile | 12 | 5.7 | -1.3 |

*Source:* EIU, "The World in 1995", Economist Publications, 1995.

## 2.2 THE EUROPEAN BUSINESS AND ECONOMIC ENVIRONMENT

The main influences of the European business environment on the Irish Economy are in the areas of:

- The Single European Market

- Fiscal and Currency Policy

- Common Agricultural Policy (CAP)

- EU Competition Policy

- The Social Charter

- Taxation and VAT

- Environmental Legislation.

### 2.2.1 The Single European Market

Membership of the EU has had a profound influence on the course of development of the Irish economy. The cumulative effect, which has not yet been realised, will be to integrate the Irish economy into the largest macroeconomic entity in the world. This substantially exists already, in the core economies of Germany, the Netherlands, Belgium, France, Italy and the United Kingdom. The fundamental stability of the system is a result of the strength and continued growth of the unified German economy. There are six EU policy areas of particular economic importance to Ireland, because of the Single European Market (SEM). They are: Fiscal and Monetary Policy, the Common Agricultural Policy (CAP) and Reform; Competition Policy; the Social Charter and Labour law; Taxation Reform; and, finally, Environmental Policy.

The basis for the Single Market is the unhampered movement between member states of persons, goods, services and capital. In order for this market to function effectively, great changes in member states' regulatory systems had to occur, and many of these structural changes are now in place or are well advanced. In 1987, a major step towards European integration took place when Ireland's ratification of the Single European Act (SEA) enabled all member states to formalise and give national statutory effect to the complex set of mechanisms which had evolved to create a true Common Market. The SEA went further, providing a public statement of intent to continue the process of integration, and it provided for many new mechanisms to allow this to take place. In 1992 the Maastricht Agreement paved the way for clearer political and economic union among the member states.

The key to effective European economic union is the elimination of economic and non-economic internal frontiers; to create a common external frontier; to provide strengthened powers to act against distortions of trade caused by monopolies and restricted practices; and to institute more effective mechanisms for the harmonisation of laws and economic and commercial policies between member states. The following legal changes will continue to have a major impact on European business:

- The removal of all trade barriers raises the threat of increased competition, and at the same time provides opportunities for expansion.

- The removal of barriers to free movement of goods and the harmonisation of VAT rates lead to greater alignment of prices throughout the Community, with both gains and losses in Irish terms.

- Community attempts to eliminate market distortions provide for tests for competition, which may have to be taken into account in developing marketing strategies.

- For some items, there are hidden costs resulting from harmonisation measures: paperwork, testing, composition, certification, and quality.

- Bidding for public contracts is on a Community-wide basis which is having implications for Irish construction and engineering firms and printing firms.

## 2.2.2 Fiscal and Currency Policy

The first EU-derived economic force lies in the area of European fiscal and currency policies, mentioned above. The main effect of these as far as Ireland is concerned has been to stabilise exchange rates with its main trading partners (except the largest, the UK, since sterling left the EMS system). Membership of the EMS has also led to a further opening of the Irish economy to external influences. While integration of the domestic economy into the EU macroeconomy is not yet fully complete, the forces behind integration are strong. With the advent of the Maastricht Treaty, the focus of financial integration has been on the establishment of monetary union and the creation of a European Central Bank.

## 2.2.3 CAP, ERDF and ESF

The second and most overtly beneficial area of policy in the past has been the Common Agricultural Policy (CAP). The CAP began in the early post-war years with the twin intentions of achieving agricultural self-sufficiency and maintaining farm incomes. CAP has consistently absorbed about two-thirds of the entire Community budget. The mechanisms used mainly involve guaranteeing prices and markets, subsidising certain farm inputs, and subsidising exports to countries outside the Community. While satisfying the original aims of CAP, implementing these policies has led to intractable food surpluses, higher-than-world prices for foodstuffs, and an unacceptable drain on Community funds. Ireland's agricultural industry had benefited enormously from CAP intervention, but the reform of CAP, begun by Commissioner

MacSharry in 1991, is likely to be the most serious challenge for the Irish agricultural industry up to the turn of the century. This issue is dealt with in more detail in Chapter 4 on Resource-based Industries.

The areas of regional and social policy within the EU are addressed by the European Regional Development Fund (ERDF) and the European Social Fund (ESF). These funds are intended to help bring certain disadvantaged regions within the Community up to the general level of social and economic development. Ireland as a whole has been designated as a disadvantaged region, and the economy has received considerable EU grant-aid for infrastructural development, manpower training, and research support services. In the Community Support framework agreed with the EU for the period 1994–99 Ireland will receive £6.5 billion from the EU to support economic and social development. It is unlikely that this level of support will continue beyond 1999, as by that time Ireland will have closed the gap in living standards with other EU member states, and new member states such as Poland and Hungary will then attract higher levels of support.

### 2.2.4 Competition Policy
The Treaty of Rome (1957) lays down the basis for creating a common market and free trade between member states, and competition policy was spelt out in Articles 85 and 86 of the Treaty. European competition policy is crucial to the development of the European Union in that it helps to maintain or establish a genuine competitive structure. The thrust of Article 85 is to prohibit agreements or concerted practices between enterprises that prevent, restrict or distort competition. Article 86 is aimed at curbing the abusive behaviour of monopolies. Regulation 17 of the Article deals with the registration of mergers and acquisitions. Competition policy has had a major effect on many areas of European and Irish industry — in particular the airline industry, telecommunications and energy.

### *Airline Industry*
The restrictive practices undertaken by many state-owned airlines up until the 1970s were broken by the EU "open skies" policy, which allowed private and non-domestic airlines to

compete on all European routes (e.g. Ryanair and Virgin CityJet). This policy has dramatically changed the structure and competitiveness of the European airline industry, very much to the benefit of travellers.

### Telecommunications
Following the "open skies" policy and in an attempt to improve the overall competitiveness and efficiency of telecommunications in Europe, this industry is now being deregulated. This will allow non-state-owned enterprises to compete for domestic and international business, and it will result in a search for strategic alliances between global telecommunications companies and less competitive state-owned enterprises.

### Energy
As in the case of telecommunications, state-owned monopolies in energy are being forced to compete against private operators. Electricity generation in Ireland is subject to the same pressures. The structures are now being examined by the Government to determine the most appropriate future structure for Ireland.

### 2.2.5 The Social Charter and Labour Law
The relationship between labour and its social partners, employers and government is undergoing considerable change in Ireland. The reasons for this change are EU membership; economic forces acting on traditional workforce practices; and the increased emphasis at a regional and national level on equality and safety in the workplace.

Some of the more obvious of these transitional effects are:

- Increased worker participation in the workplace
- EU trends towards increased worker participation at board level
- The potential adoption of minimum wage rates because of harmonisation of labour policies
- More contractual relationships between unions and employers
- A movement away from National Wage Agreements to more localised solutions.

## 2.2.6 Taxation Mechanisms

The tax system in Ireland is likely to undergo a change in the near future. There are two main areas of impact. The first derives from the need to restructure the tax collection mechanisms — archaic and ineffective in many respects. Legislative steps are likely to be taken to improve them. As an example of ineffective collection, in 1986 there was a backlog of over £600 million in uncollected taxes, mainly VAT and payroll taxes due from companies.

The tax amnesties of 1987 and 1993 were one approach to rectifying under-collection, and the amount collected surpassed estimates almost by an order of magnitude, indicating significant under-collection in the past.

The second area of impact derives from SEM regulations making illegal certain forms of taxation and costs now applying in Ireland. Some examples of these are:

• Important and forced paperwork costs

• Restrictions on import quantities, especially consumer purchases from Northern Ireland

• Conditions of payment, such as VAT at point of entry

• Reduction of VAT rates to European levels

• Charges and limitations on the movement of capital.

Corporate tax rates may be affected in the longer run — Ireland has already been forced by the EU to extend the low (10 per cent) rate of tax on export profits to all manufacturing industry, in order to remove what was in effect an export subsidy.

The harmonisation of taxes to be brought about by the SEM mechanisms will cause a net loss to the Irish Exchequer, estimated at £500 million to £600 million annually. Some other form of tax revenue will have to be obtained to replace this if the public sector deficit is not to be expanded. Otherwise, public spending will have to decrease.

## 2.3 THE ECONOMIC ENVIRONMENT IN IRELAND

The economic environment consists of factors affecting purchasing power and spending patterns. This section looks at Irish indicators in areas such as income, spending, savings and labour-cost competitiveness.

### 2.3.1 Standards of Living and Disposable Income

The usual indicator of standard of living is GDP per capita, which in Ireland has shown one of the strongest growth rates in Europe in the 1990s. However, this has come to be known as "soufflé" growth, as disposable income has not grown at a similar rate. The reasons for this are the amount of leakage from the economy in the form of profit repatriation by foreign companies and debt interest payments abroad. Two other major influences on the Irish standard of living are changes in terms of trade and EU funding.

The Economic and Social Research Institute (ESRI) uses an indicator which accounts for these variables called "National Resources" (Gross National Disposable Income plus Capital Transfers), which acts as a true indicator of standard of living. Figure 2.2 shows historical and economic growth rates in Ireland.

**Figure 2.2: "National Resources" Growth Rate, 1984–2000**

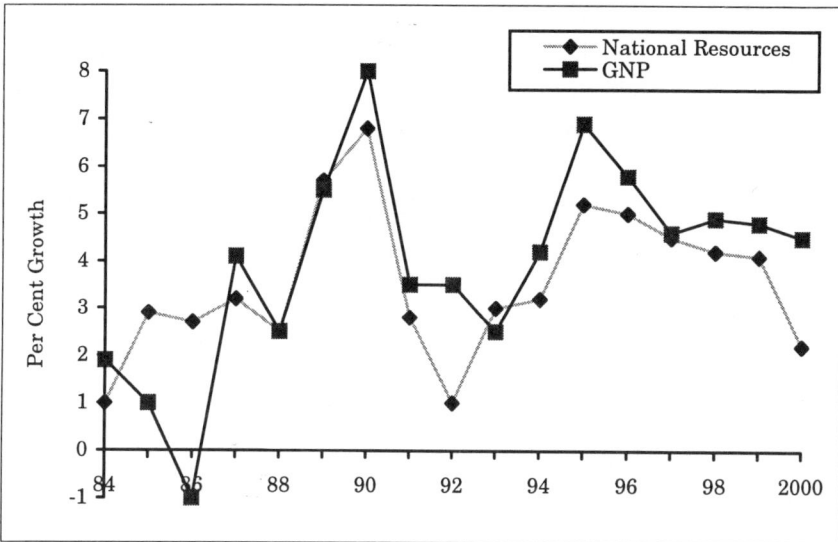

*Source*: ESRI, Medium Term Review, 1994.

## 2.3.2 Consumption, Savings and Debt

The amount of consumption and savings in Ireland is intrinsically linked not only to current disposable income, but also to future expectations of economic growth, unemployment and interest rates. For example, savings rose to a very high level of 15 per cent of disposable income in the early 1980s because of fears of the economic crisis.

The mini-boom of 1988–90 saw savings fall to a low of 8 per cent and economic slowdown pushed savings to 12.4 per cent in 1993, probably because of volatility in the EMS and possible rises in interest rates. The improvements in expectations since 1993 should push savings to below 10 per cent in 1995, averaging 11.5 per cent beyond 2000.

The anticipated fall in savings combined with a rise in real after-tax income should push consumption up to high growth levels by 1995, levelling off to 4 per cent by 2000.

## 2.3.3 Investments and Balance of Payments

We now look at the resources available to the economy and how they have been used (national production, EU transfers etc.). Throughout the 1970s and early 1980s, domestic spending through consumption and investment exceeded available resources. Therefore, balance of payments deficits were experienced with foreign indebtedness and acquisitions of domestic assets by non-residents.

These deficits occurred until 1988 when balance of payments surpluses began, and GNP was up to 6 per cent in 1993 accompanied by virtually no net borrowings by Government from non-residents and no accumulations of foreign assets by financial institutions or the domestic private sector. Five interrelated factors were working in the 1990s, namely:

- Tighter fiscal policy

- Favourable external environment for demand, exchange-rate development and international interest rates

- Increased transfers from the EU

- Reduction in the propensity of businesses to invest domestically out of earnings

- Wage restraint in the private sector.

**Figure 2.3: Ireland's Balance of Payments Surplus, 1960–93**

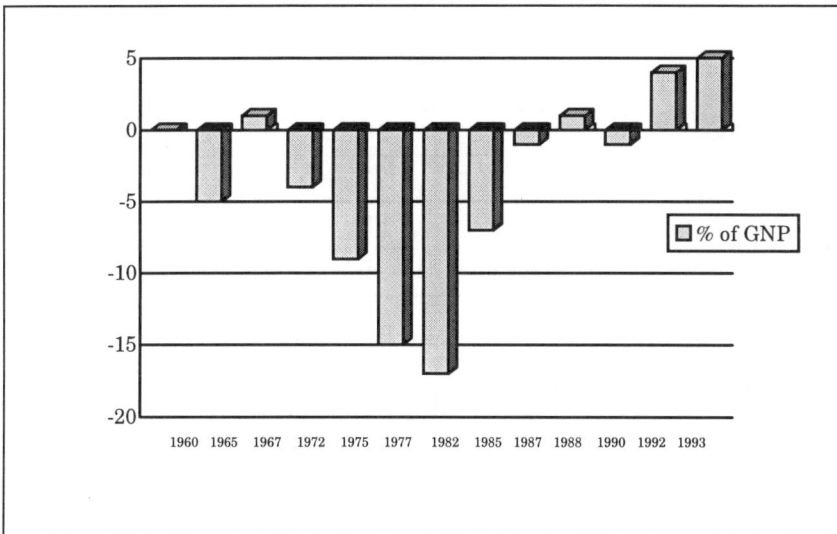

*Source:* ESRI, Medium Term Review, 1994.

### 2.3.4 Labour Cost Competitiveness

The labour cost competitiveness of Irish firms *vis-à-vis* UK counterparts has changed considerably over the past 30 years. In 1960 Irish wage levels were 70 per cent of those in the UK, compared to parity in 1980. This represents a considerable loss of competitiveness in 20 years. Without Government protection, many traditional firms were uncompetitive and very dependent on domestic markets. Only the consumer boom of the 1970s allowed them to stay in business; the domestic spending squeeze resulting from fiscal contraction from 1981 devastated much traditional industry.

The competitiveness of Irish firms improved significantly between 1986 and 1989 and has remained stable since, enabling employment in traditional industries to stabilise. In terms of agri-business development, growth has been high in the past few years as this industry is beginning to be dominated by a handful of large firms with sophisticated product-development marketing and labour-saving technology change. This has not meant increases in employment, however.

### Table 2.4: Relative Wage Rates in Manufacturing — Ireland Compared to the UK

| Year | % |
|------|-----|
| 1963 | 70 |
| 1967 | 77 |
| 1971 | 85 |
| 1975 | 98 |
| 1979 | 103 |
| 1983 | 95 |
| 1987 | 105 |
| 1991 | 90 |
| 1993 | 96 |

*Source*: ESRI, Medium Term Review, 1994.

## 2.4 DEMOGRAPHIC/SOCIOCULTURAL FACTORS

Demographic and sociocultural factors determine the background market conditions and influence the growth processes in an economy. This section looks at population and employment trends in Ireland and examines how they differ from other markets.

### 2.4.1 Population Trends

According to the ESRI, Irish society is likely to undergo a radical change between 1995 and 2005, as a result of major demographic changes in the population — the pattern of births, deaths and migration over the past 10 years. The key features being experienced are:

- A reduction in the number of children being born

- A rapid fall from 2000 onwards in the net entry into the labour force

- A major increase in the proportion of the population in working age groups

- A substantial reduction in the dependency ratio regardless of unemployment levels.

Although Ireland has always had a high birth rate in relation to its European neighbours, the total population declined slowly from the foundation of the state until 1961, when it reached its nadir of 2.818 million. In the 1970s it began to increase rapidly. Until then, natural population increases had always been exceeded by emigration. In the decade of the 1970s net immigration of just over 100,000 took place, almost one-third of the natural increase. This may have been a one-off response to employment conditions in Ireland approaching comparability with those obtaining in the UK, thus attracting emigrants back. The 1986 census shows that net emigration resumed in the early 1980s. Between 1981 and 1986, 75,000 people left the country, 31,000 in 1986 alone. Despite this, the Irish population reached its levels over 3.5 million, primarily because of the baby boom and return migration of the 1970s. Emigration pushed total population down until 1990, albeit at a slower rate. The ESRI estimate that the population of Ireland in 1994 was 3.57 million.

*Table 2.5: Population Trends in Ireland, 1971–2000*

| Year | 000 |
|------|-----|
| 1971 | 2,978 |
| 1981 | 3,443 |
| 1986 | 3,540 |
| 1991 | 3,526 |
| 1994 | 3,573 |
| 2000** | 3,568 |

**       Forecast.
*Source:* CSO and ESRI.

The Irish population make-up is different from that of its neighbours in several important respects. In the late 1980s the proportion of population under 25 was about 48 per cent, compared with a European average of about 38 per cent. This high ratio was part of the explanation for an exceptionally high dependency ratio, and it also resulted in some 70,000 young people leaving school each year. However, this level has dropped to about 40 per cent and is expected to drop lower in the years to 2000 (see Table 2.6).

*Table 2.6: Age Distribution of the Population of Ireland, 1971–2000 (%)*

|              | 1971  | 1981  | 1986  | 1991  | 1994  | 2000** |
|--------------|-------|-------|-------|-------|-------|--------|
| 0–14         | 31.3  | 30.1  | 29.5  | 26.7  | 24.7  | 20.1   |
| 15–24        | 16.2  | 17.7  | 17.4  | 17.1  | 18.3  | 17.6   |
| 25–64        | 41.4  | 41.5  | 42.4  | 44.8  | 45.6  | 49.6   |
| 65+          | 11.1  | 10.7  | 10.7  | 11.4  | 11.5  | 11.8   |
| TOTAL (000)  | 2,978 | 3,443 | 3,540 | 3,526 | 2,573 | 2,568  |

** Forecast.
*Source:* CSO and ESRI.

A major reason for the change in the demographic structure is the declining birth rate. The number of children under the age of 15 will fall dramatically between 1995 and 2005, dropping from 22 births per 1,000 to 15. According to the ESRI, by 2005 there will be 25 per cent less children under the age of 15, which will be closer to the EU average. Because of its existing demographic structure and levels of emigration, Ireland has and will continue to have a small proportion of its population over 65. The high dependency rates experienced in the 1980s are forecast to decline dramatically to the EU norm. Between 1995 and 2005, the ESRI forecasts that the numbers in the working age group 15–65 will rise from 60 per cent to almost 70 per cent (see Table 2.7).

In terms of female employment, Ireland has always had a higher non-participation rate than other European countries. As Table 2.8. shows, women made up only 34 per cent of the workforce in 1991, compared to a European average of 40 per cent.

## Table 2.7: Labour Force Trends, 1961–2000

|        | Labour Force (000) | At Work (000) | Unemployed | % * | Dependency Ratio |
|--------|------|------|------|------|------|
| 1961   | 1,060 | 1,018 | 43  | 4.1  | 2.77 |
| 1971   | 1,080 | 1,030 | 49  | 4.5  | 2.89 |
| 1981   | 1,264 | 1,151 | 113 | 8.9  | 2.99 |
| 1986   | 1,308 | 1,081 | 227 | 17.4 | 3.27 |
| 1993   | 1,379 | 1,144 | 235 | 17.0 |      |
| 2000** | 1,484 | 1,285 | 200 | 13.5 |      |

*       Inclusive of net migration.
**      Forecast.
*Source*:  CSO, Labour Force Surveys, and ESRI.

## Table 2.8: Female Employment-Global Comparisons — Women as Percentage of Total Workforce

|      | IRL  | UK   | EUR  | USA  | JAP  |
|------|------|------|------|------|------|
| 1988 | 32.5 | 43.6 | 39.2 | 45.0 | 40.1 |
| 1989 | 32.7 | 44.0 | 39.5 | 45.2 | 40.4 |
| 1990 | 33.3 | 44.2 | 39.9 | 45.4 | 40.6 |
| 1991 | 33.9 | 44.8 | 40.0 | 45.6 | 40.7 |

*Source:*  European Commission/Eurostat, 1994.

### 2.4.2 Unemployment

The absolute number of unemployed has already become a social force with economic effects. During the 1980s and early 1990s the number of unemployed in Ireland was very nearly the same as the total numbers engaged in manufacturing industry — about 250,000 each, representing some 20 per cent of the total workforce and 7 per cent of the total population. These figures probably understate the size of the potential workforce, and hence the real number of the unemployed. School-leavers are excluded for a period, women are probably under-represented, and there are large numbers of people undergoing training (much of it paid for by the European Social Fund whose criteria focus on the young unemployed) who are not classified as unemployed, although in receipt of equivalent benefits.

There are a few main areas where the scale of unemployment has a major impact. Perhaps the most important of them is emigration. Aside from the social disquiet that follows realisation of the likelihood of widespread emigration (perhaps equivalent to one in three school-leavers), and the sense of loss resulting from leaving itself, the exodus represents a very large outflow of educational capital. There is an irony in this — a portion of Ireland's national debt is re-exported free of charge to the creditor countries in the form of skilled labour.

A second effect of widespread unemployment has been the enlargement of the "black" sector of the economy, as the unemployed seek both to augment and to maintain their state-provided benefits. For the unemployed, the marginal benefits of obtaining legitimate employment — especially low-paid employment — are often small, and can be negative, insofar as actual work must be performed. For the small business purchasing black-economy labour, services and even goods, there is usually a flexibility and cost advantage that cannot be ignored. There are severe inadequacies in the tax collection mechanisms that favour the growth of the black economy. These illegal activities, which may be of the order of 8 to 10 per cent of total economic activity, increase the tax burden of the "white" sector, and can distort certain labour markets (such as clothing manufacture) to the point where it is necessary to be "black" in order to continue in existence. Whether or not to participate in the black economy poses a very real dilemma for many small businesses.

One response of the state to the unemployment problem has been to increase post-school training of all sorts. There have been two main thrusts to this development: an increase in the quality and diversity of technical education at third level; and at the same time, large numbers undergoing short-term vocational training. FÁS, for example, completed the training of nearly

40,000 people in 1994. Government policies have led to a generally well-educated workforce, whose desire to realise the financial benefits of their education has provided a strong motive to
emigrate.

The interaction of these aspects of unemployment — that is,
education, the development of the black economy, and manpower
policy — has fostered changing attitudes of people to the economic
system and their roles in it. In the absence of more quantitative
sociological research in this area, an impressionistic view of atti-
tude changes might encompass the following:

- Increased disrespect for government institutions

- Increased public support for black activities

- Low expectations of finding employment coupled with high
  awareness of emigration possibilities among youth

- Perception of "permanent" training and make-work activities
  by state

- Awareness of individual poverty and hardship.

In summary, the sociocultural factors operating in Irish society
could have a destabilising influence on the Irish economic structure. The natural growth in population cannot be absorbed by
employment growth, and this leads to increased state spending on
unemployment benefits, on training, and on direct and indirect
aid to small and start-up businesses for providing employment. At
the same time, and for the same reasons, emigration is increasing, personal taxes are high, and the tax base is narrowing.
Action to reduce the budget deficit, the biggest component of
which is current state expenditure, is being undertaken at a time
when demand for state-supplied services is increasing. There is a
danger of an increase in the already high poverty level of the Irish
people.

## 2.5 THE TECHNOLOGICAL ENVIRONMENT

A country's technological infrastructure is a major influence on its
economic growth and productivity. As mentioned in the previous
chapter, the Irish economy is heavily influenced by the integrated

global economy, an economy which is being driven more and more by the commercialisation of technology. New growth theories suggest that "knowledge subsumed as human capital is now the key factor in economic growth and in National competitive advantage" (Kinsella and MacBrierty, 1994). The rate of innovation is largely shaped by technology, which is an output of scientific endeavour. Technology subsumes:

- The products made within an economy

- The processes employed to make such products

- The organisational structure used to co-ordinate activity

- The institutions that constitute the basic structure within which the economy functions (Lipsey, 1993).

Research and Technological Development (R & TD) helps to create wealth and jobs directly and also adds to the national knowledge base, thereby increasing the economy's potential for generating future growth. It is a key aspect of the Culliton Report.

This section analyses the technological environment as it affects the business environment by first looking at current spending on Research and Development (R & D) in Ireland. EU policy on Science and Technology (S & T) is then analysed followed by a description of the Irish organisational structure for S & T development.

### 2.5.1 R & D Expenditure in Ireland

Expenditure on R & D was approximately £183 million from all sources (in-house and external) in 1991. This has grown from a very low level of £42.5 million in 1982. However, R & D expenditure in Ireland remains very low by international standards. Table 2.9 shows an international comparison of R & D spending in 1991. Despite major growth in Ireland, spending only represents 1.1 per cent of sales. In comparison, Japan spent 6 per cent of sales and Germany nearly 7 per cent. Ireland ranks eighth in Europe in R & D outlay, ahead of Spain, Greece and Portugal, and spends roughly half the European average.

**Table 2.9: Total R & D Expenditure in Various Countries**

| Country | R & D Exp. (Stg£ bn.) | % Change Previous Year | R & D as % of | | |
|---|---|---|---|---|---|
| | | | Sales | Profit | Dividends |
| US | 41.2 | +3 | 4.4 | 72 | 185 |
| Japan | 26.6 | -1 | 5.9 | 176 | 856 |
| Germany | 12.0 | -3 | 6.8 | 481 | 922 |
| UK | 4.7 | +9 | 2.3 | 29 | 74 |
| Sweden | 1.7 | +13 | 7.3 | 212 | 621 |
| Holland | 1.6 | -6 | 5.7 | — | — |
| Ireland | 0.174 | +20 | 1.1 | — | — |

*Source*: Kinsella, R.P. and V.J. MacBrierty, *Economic Rationale for an Enhanced National Science and Technology Capability*, 1994.

Not only does Ireland rank low on the European R & D spend league, but when compared to the USA and Japan, Ireland and Europe in general perform badly (see Table 2.10).

**Table 2.10: Comparison of Expenditure on R & D in Europe, USA and Japan, 1991**

| | Total Spending (ECU bn.) | Spending per Capita | GNP % | Business Contrib. | No. of Researchers & Engineers |
|---|---|---|---|---|---|
| EU | 104 | 302 | 2.0 | 52 | 630,000 (0.4%) |
| USA | 124 | 493 | 2.8 | N/A | 950,000 (0.8%) |
| Japan | 77 | 627 | 3.0 | 78 | 450,000 (0.9%) |

*Source*: European Commission/Eurostat, 1994.

In-house expenditure amounted to £175.9 million in 1991. Seventy-five per cent of this is spent on experimental development, with less than 5 per cent being spent on basic research.

**Table 2.11: Varieties of R & D Expenditure by Type of Research (In-house Expenditure)**

|                            | IR£ m | %    |
|----------------------------|-------|------|
| Basic Research             | 6.9   | 3.9  |
| Applied Research           | 37.0  | 21.1 |
| Experimental Development   | 132.0 | 75.0 |
| TOTAL                      | 175.9 | 100  |

*Source*: Forfás Statistics, 1992

The figures can be further analysed by comparing expenditure among foreign-owned and indigenous-owned companies (see Table 2.12). It is noted that Irish firms, which account for 44 per cent of total employment, spend only 37 per cent of the total R & D expenditure. This represents only 0.6 per cent of sales, whereas foreign firms in contrast spend 1.9 per cent of sales in Ireland, despite the fact that so few foreign companies actually base R & D facilities in Ireland in the first place.

**Table 2.12: R & D Dimensions of Irish Business (indigenous v. foreign-owned), 1991**

|                                                   | Irish            | Foreign          | Total            |
|---------------------------------------------------|------------------|------------------|------------------|
| Personnel                                         | 1,729.5          | 2,241.9          | 3,971.4          |
| Total Spend (£ m)                                 | 64.4             | 111.3            | 175.9            |
| Spend as % of Sales                               | 0.6              | 1.9              | 1.1              |
| Spend on R & D in H.E. Sector                     | 0.3 (16.3%)      | 0.7 (48.7%)      |                  |
| Spend on Technical Consultancy in Irish H.E. Sector | 0.24 (12.1%)   | 0.25 (15.7%)     | 0.485            |
| No. Involved in R & D Consortia with Irish H.E. Sector | 82 (17.1%)   | 45 (23.4%)       | 127              |
| No. of Formal R & D Depts.                        | 232 (62.7%)      | 138 (37.3%)      | 370 (100%)       |

*Source:* Forfás Statistics, 1992

One reason for this dearth of investment in S & T in Irish firms is the small size structure of the economy. As mentioned in Chapter One, 85 per cent of Irish enterprises employ fewer than 10 people. For a small firm, the costs of generating and/or acquiring and exploiting knowledge are often prohibitive. Small scale limits the capacity of small firms to absorb costs and capture the benefits of R & D. Therefore, a national S & T policy is critical in offsetting these weaknesses.

### 2.5.2 EU Policy on Science and Technology

According to the European Commission's White Paper on growth, competitiveness and employment, "Europe's competitive edge has been eroded, and it is not in a strong position with regard to future technology". Specifically, this paper concluded that:

- The EU's R & TD effort was inadequate relative to the US and Japan (see Table 2.11. for comparison).

- Europe is relatively strong in basic research but the R & TD needs of industry are less developed. Relative technical advantage in basic research does not always translate into absolute commercial advantage in products or services.

- Japan's leading position in world trade exports is a measure of its ability to diffuse technology into the marketplace.

The central motivation behind the single market is European competitiveness *vis-à-vis* the US and Japan. The Maastricht Treaty embodied a desire to strengthen and extend the scope of its industrial dimensions by strengthening the S & T base, exploiting Europe's R & TD and unifying the EU's R & TD through multinational budgets and financial programmes. Another key objective of EU policy is to integrate R & D policy into cohesion policy — reducing differences within countries.

The thrust of this policy is outlined in the White Paper. According to the paper, the new knowledge-based industries and community research must strive to address technology-driven problems and socially relevant programmes. While not ignoring the importance of basic research, there is a clear leaning towards industrially relevant research. The White Paper calls for:

- An adequate level of funding for research
- An appropriate range of research activities
- Effective technology transfer.

The Office of Science and Technology (OST) based in the Department of Enterprise and Employment has been directing science policy since 1987. In 1988, the Government formed a new institutional structure, Eolas, which took over from the former National Board for Science and Technology (NBST) and the Institute for Industrial Research and Standards (IIRS). It was given responsibility for implementing S & T policy. This corresponded with a significant rise in funds for Irish research from the EU framework programme.

The agency S & T structure was altered following the Culliton and Moriarty Reports. The IDA was restructured into three entities, Forfás, Forbairt and IDA Ireland. Forfás now encompasses the policy wing of the former Eolas.

## 2.6 THE PHYSICAL ENVIRONMENT

The growing awareness of the need to protect the natural and physical environment worldwide and the awareness of the long-term effects of man-made ecological problems have many implications for Irish economic and industrial policy at national industry and firm level. This section examines the importance of the physical environment, by looking at the trends driving increased environmental awareness, and then by discussing the response to the environmental challenge.

### 2.6.1 Environmental Trends

In global terms, there are three environmental trends affecting the business environment:

### *Increased Levels of Pollution*

Pollution, created either by industrial activity or by ecological disasters such as Exxon Valdez or Chernobyl, is damaging the quality of the natural environment. Examples of this pollution are:

- Improper disposal of chemicals and radioactive waste

- Overuse of chemicals in agricultural production

- Use of non-biodegradable products in primary and secondary packaging

- Improper control of industrial and agricultural effluent

- Deterioration of the atmosphere environment because of industrial and automotive emissions

- Deterioration of the ozone layer because of overuse of chloro-flourocarbons (CFCs).

### Shortage of Raw Materials

Sustained industrial development for the past 200 years has depleted the world's raw materials. Two forms of raw materials exist:

- Infinite resources, such as air and water — despite being infinite they are being affected by ozone-layer depletion, "smog" and "oil spills"

- Finite resources, consisting of renewable resources such as forests, arable land; and non-renewable resources such as oil, coal precious metals.

The increasing cost to the consumer and increasing pressure from environmentalist lobby groups and political groups are forcing developments in synthetic materials and alternative sources of raw materials.

### Cost of Energy

Over-reliance on finite non-renewable energy sources, such as oil, and the "owners" of the resource, such as OPEC, greatly effects the world economy. For example, the oil crisis of the early 1970s "fuelled" hyper-inflation and created a recession, whereas the Gulf crisis in 1990 has been one of the main forces driving the economic recession for four years. This over-reliance is driving research and development in alternative energy sources such as solar, nuclear, wind and natural gas, as well as more efficient use of scarce energy by industry and consumers.

### 2.6.2 European Response to the Environmental Challenge

The environmental trends mentioned above have had serious influences on government and consumer attitudes. Two key areas of influence are increased environmental regulation and legislation, and increased consumer pressure.

### Environmental Regulation/Legislation

The principles of EU environment policy are sustainable development, precautionary action and integration of environmental considerations in all aspects of project-funding decisions. This policy is being implemented through increased regulation and legislation on waste disposal in agri-food processing, environmentally friendly packaging and recycling and licensing of industrial activities.

### Increased Consumer Pressure

Consideration must be taken for the response of many European consumers to environmental concerns through altering consumption or purchasing decisions or by taking a more active role through political parties or lobby groups. See Chapter Nine on marketing strategy for a more detailed discussion on this issue.

### 2.6.3 EU Environmental Funding Sources

### ENVIRREG

This is an ERDF regional fund to assist regions where environmental problems hold back socioeconomic development. Support is available for the treatment and disposal of household waste and sewage in urban areas, port facilities for the disposal of effluent etc. ENVIRREG applies to all coastal areas in the most disadvantaged regions and on the Mediterranean coast. The ENVIRREG budget was ECU 500 million between 1989 and 1993. Ireland received ECU 24 million in this period.

### R & D Funding

A total of ECU 5,100 million was set aside in the Third Framework Programme 1990–94 to fund research and technology development programmes in new areas, alternative technologies, etc.

**Thermie Programme**
This is the main instrument of the EU in promoting the uptake of efficient and clean energy technologies and meeting its environmental objectives.

### 2.6.4 Response to the Environmental Challenge in Ireland
Ireland has a competitive advantage in the environmental area. The eco-industry in the areas of environmentally friendly technologies, products and services shows much potential. Ireland in general has a high-quality physical environment in comparison to other industrialised countries. In addition, consumers and industrialists in Ireland and worldwide hold strong perceptions of Ireland as having an attractive environment and being a producer of "green" products. An example would be the high regard for Irish beef in Germany among retailers and consumers. However, this perception needs to be managed and reinforced where necessary.

According to the National Development Plan 1994–97, the maintenance of Ireland's high-quality environment is a key ingredient in allowing the economy to develop and generate employment. Therefore, the industry operational programme for 1994–97 will be built on principles of natural and environmental policy, and development will entail:

- Using cleaner technologies and production techniques

- Preventing or reducing waste production and, where possible, increasing re-use of recycling activities

- Pursuing a policy of conservation of energy and other raw materials.

To this end, the Environmental Protection Agency (EPA) was set up under the EPA Act, 1992 with the purpose of protecting Ireland's natural environment. The powers and functions of the EPA include licence control, monitoring general environmental quality, co-ordinating environmental research programmes, advising on environmental quality standards and supervising environmental monitoring.

A draft operational programme for environmental services was submitted for approval to the EU in 1994 and forms the basis for drawing down EU funding.

Although the current focus on environmental activity could be regarded as a cost burden on Irish businesses and Irish society, as already mentioned, the environment has become such an important issue on global markets that an environmentally-concerned image — more than just being "green" — could become a source of competitive advantage for some Irish firms, depending on their product market positioning.

### Recycling

A five-year national recycling plan was established in 1994. In 1993, 1.7 million tonnes of municipal waste were generated in Ireland, which included 0.4 tonnes of packaging waste. The strategy sets a target of 20 per cent for recycling of municipal waste compared to the current rate of 7.4 per cent. This will be achieved by increasing the recycling of packaging waste from 42,000 tonnes (10.3 per cent) to 133,000 tonnes (33 per cent) (see Table 2.13 for details). The proposed EU directive on packaging and packaging waste requires a minimum 25 per cent recovery rate in any event. The principle of producer responsibility is adapted as a basic element in the approach to recycling.

## 2.7 EFFECTS OF THE BUSINESS ENVIRONMENT ON THE IRISH ECONOMIC STRUCTURE

The chief structural features of the Irish economy stem from the country's geography and history. It is a small island, lying beside a much larger island, and it is thinly populated in comparison to its European neighbours. The fact that Ireland is an island leads to natural trade barriers arising from logistics costs and cultural differences. Ireland's history and small size have left a legacy of relative underdevelopment in terms of capital infrastructure and also in terms of international trade. There are very few large, strong indigenous firms. Ireland's long domination by the United Kingdom had led, among other things, to the inherently small economy of the island being further split into two smaller and increasingly divergent economies.

*Table 2.13: Recycling Rates in the Packaging Waste Stream*

| Packaging Material | Recycling Rates % | |
|---|---|---|
| | 1993 | 1999 |
| Paper | 14.0 | 25 |
| Glass | 21.0 | 55 |
| Plastics | 0.1 | 25 |
| Metals | 1.5 | 25 |
| Ferrous Metal | 0.3 | 25 |
| Aluminium | 4.1 | 25 |
| TOTAL % | 10.3 | 33 |

*Source*: Department of the Environment, 1994.

The size of the economy of the Republic of Ireland is about twice that of Northern Ireland. However, Northern Ireland's economy is tightly integrated with that of the UK and it is difficult to disentangle the two sufficiently to allow much detailed comparison with the economy of the Republic. The small absolute size of the economy, combined with a small dispersed population, results in natural cost disadvantages in the distribution of goods and services. The absolute size of the domestic market with 3.6 million consumers is not large enough to allow certain kinds of industry to develop or to achieve economies of scale. Many infrastructural services are expensive since they are supplied to only a small number of dispersed consumers.

### 2.7.1 The Drive to Export
Ireland has some mineral resources of importance. There are fairly extensive deposits of tin, lead and zinc, and traces of copper and gold. Non-metallic minerals include turf, natural gas, barytes, gypsum, dolomite and quartz. However, the country is dependent on the outside world for most manufacturing raw materials.

Ireland's main natural capital asset is a soil/climate combination that particularly favours grass-growing, and hence there is a large agricultural sector dominated by dairy and beef production.

The operation of EC agriculture policies (Common Agricultural Policy — CAP) has led to an output of these products considerably in excess of the needs of the domestic market. Curtailing the production of such surpluses, while at the same time maintaining agricultural incomes, is probably one of the most difficult challenges faced at the moment by the EU. Irish agriculture is at present almost completely dependent on the operation of the CAP, and regardless of what level of permanent support emerges from the political process, the agricultural sector must continue exporting to survive.

There is a similarly strong logic behind the strategic need to increase manufactured exports. The domestic market cannot grow as fast as manufacturing output, and so output growth is largely determined by export demand. The companies that respond to this demand are largely in modern industries and are usually large and foreign-owned. Most of these companies could never have been founded to service the Irish market alone, and their establishment is a result of the industrial policy followed since the late 1950s. The traditional industries dealing in traded goods also have a strong need to export in order to employ the benefits of scale which modern processes allow — and to combat erosion of domestic markets by imports which are the fruit of more recent technology.

Services too may be exported, and increasing attention and resources are being devoted to this area. Apart from the invisible exports of tourism and logistic services, some interesting export services are being explored — financial services, scientific and medical research, agricultural consultancy, aircraft leasing and maintenance, computer software, product and process development, are all in advanced stages of establishment. Many of these new service exports have their origins in state enterprises — PARC, ESB and Aer Lingus, for example. Although these services could generally be produced in Ireland at no cost disadvantage, the primary drive to export comes from the large, often vast markets that can be reached, which either spread initial costs among more consumers, or have low marginal unit relative to sales price.

A final reason why Ireland must continue to be export-oriented is in order to avoid balance of payments constraints on economic growth. Export earnings are needed to fund the high dependence on imports of industrial raw materials, energy products, heavy industrial goods and consumer and industrial products.

There are policies and programmes in place, especially in the area of industrial sub-supply, to encourage import substitution, but for many classes of goods it will never be possible to obtain indigenous supplies. In the period 1991–94, Ireland has experienced positive and growing trade balances (see Table 2.14).

*Table 2.14: Exports to Imports — Volume (1985 = 100)*

| Year | Exports | Imports | Balance of Trade |
|------|---------|---------|------------------|
| 1991 | 161.2 | 142.7 | 18.5 |
| 1992 | 182.0 | 150.4 | 31.6 |
| 1993 | 189.0 | 155.7 | 33.3 |
| 1994 | 197.7 | 162.7 | 35 |

*Source*: European Commission/Eurostat, 1994.

### 2.7.2 The Openness of the Irish Economy

The high propensity to trade, in combination with a small absolute value of trade relative to the size of trading partners, places Ireland in a vulnerable position. By international standards, the Irish economy is very open. The degree of openness is defined by the ratio of exports plus imports to GNP. In recent years, the total value of trade has been around 130 per cent of GNP. Being so open and so small, the Irish economy is particularly vulnerable to trends in the economies of its trading partners. This vulnerability manifests itself in two particular ways:

• Trends in world demand dictate the demand for Irish exports. Since exports constitute such a large proportion of GNP, world trade conditions play a dominant part in dictating the economy's overall growth rate.

• In the financial sector, trends in the interest and inflation rates of those trading partners with which we maintain quasi-

fixed exchange rates, the members of the European Monetary
System (EMS), are imposed on the Irish economy through the
exchange rate mechanisms.

The business environment sets basic conditions for the Irish
economy. Where Irish costs start to rise above costs in competitor
countries, Irish products are displaced by foreign products both in
markets at home and abroad. The results are a deterioration in
the trade balance, and lower growth. Where Irish costs are below
those of the country's trading partners, Irish goods improve their
market share both at home and abroad. This leads to a strengthened trade position, higher output and exports. It is for this
reason that competitiveness is given such emphasis: it determines
the market share that will be commanded by the Irish industrial
sector.

## SUMMARY

This chapter outlines the broad shape of the forces driving change
as they affect the business environment in Ireland. It is crucial
for effective strategic management to analyse the broad patterns
of societal and economic change and to assess the impact at
national, industry and business level. The major "uncontrollable"
factors affecting the Irish business environment are global business trends, economic and demographic factors, technological and
political factors and the physical environment. The main trends
are:

- **The Global Economy:** The worldwide recession of the early
  1990s has been replaced by sustained growth, which is
  expected to continue to the turn of the century. Traditional
  economic powers will be threatened by the "Dragon Economies"
  of Asia, the "Visegrad" nations of Eastern Europe and, in the
  longer term, the key economic powers of South America.

- **Euro-Influence:** The European Union affects the Irish environment in terms of fiscal and currency policy, competition
  policy, labour legislation and the social charter, taxation policy
  and environmental legislation. Naturally, membership of the

Union has both positive and negative effects. On the positive side, the SEM gives Ireland greater access to the European market of 300 million consumers. As part of the Greater Europe, Ireland receives high levels of social and regional funding, although this will change after the year 2000. On the negative side, membership increases access to the Irish market for multinational companies (MNCs) and reduces the control Ireland has over its economy.

- **Irish Economic Indicators:** Very high GNP growth rates in Ireland have not resulted in high growth in employment or disposable income, partly because of the openness of the economy. Consumption is expected to grow substantially as a result of increased consumer confidence and a drop in personal savings. After a loss of labour competitiveness in the 1970s and 1980s, Irish firms have now returned to a strong position in this area.

- **Demographics:** Irish society is undergoing a radical demographic change in the 1990s because of major changes in the population structure. The main effect of this change will be a substantial reduction in the dependency ratio, regardless of the levels of unemployment that prevail.

- **Technology:** Spending on R & D in Ireland is very low in European terms and extremely low compared to America and Japan. It is particularly weak in indigenous Irish industry, partly because of the small size of Irish firms and the need for scale to gain returns on R & D expenditure. To help overcome these problems, the state has played an important role in providing funds to enhance the R & D capability of firms.

- **The Environment:** Concern for the natural environment is increasing. A greater responsibility is being placed on the firm by the EU and national governments, to ensure that EU environmental policy is properly implemented.

All these environmental factors combine to make Ireland more open, more dependent on world economic activity, more dependent on exports and more vulnerable to countries with higher levels of competitiveness. Membership of the EU and the EMS places constraints on Ireland's freedom to pursue independent monetary, fiscal and trade policies.

---

**FURTHER READING**

CSO statistical bulletin, Government Publications, 1995.

Department of the Environment,"Developments in the Area of Environmental Protection", in *Environment Bulletin*, Issue 23, August 1994.

Economic and Social Research Institute (ESRI), "Medium-Term Review — 1994–2000", Government Publications, 1994.

Economist Intelligence Unit (EIU) *The World in 1995*, Economist Publications, January 1995.

EPA annual report and various literature, 1995

European Commission/Eurostat, *Eurostatistics: Data for Short-Term Economic Analysis*, 8–9, 1994.

Kinsella, R.P. and V.J. MacBrierty, *Economic Rationale for an Enhanced National Science and Technology Capability*, 1994.

Lynch, John, *Legal Aspects of Marketing*, Marketing Institute of Ireland, 1987.

# CHAPTER THREE

# THE STATE AND INDUSTRIAL DEVELOPMENT

*T*his chapter looks at the important role that the state has played in overall economic and industrial development since independence, and the continued and developing role it plays in an era of transition for the country. Following this introduction the objectives of state involvement and the policy rationale for state intervention are addressed. The history of industrial policy development is then analysed as is the changing role of the state *vis-à-vis* privatisation. Commercial semi-state bodies are next examined, followed by an analysis of the non-commercial state sector.

## 3.1 OVERVIEW OF STATE INVOLVEMENT IN IRISH BUSINESS

The state intervenes in many areas of Irish business and the broader Irish society for a variety of pragmatic as well as ideological reasons. From a business point of view, the state intervenes in the business environment for two reasons:

1. To maintain a competitive business infrastructure it is vital that strategically important services or raw materials are developed, maintained and offered at competitive rates. This is necessary in order to enhance Ireland as a business location for both foreign firms and domestic firms. In general, commercial semi-state bodies were created to satisfy these objectives, in particular, in the three key areas of energy, transport and communications, but also in other areas including finance and industry.

2. To assist and support the development of the various sectors of

Irish industry. It is important that Irish industry develops on a balanced sectoral level and that the players receive guidance, assistance and funding where appropriate to accomplish this development. In general, two forms of state agency exist:

- *Business Development Agencies.* These agencies deal with overall policy development in Irish industry. The main agencies include Forfás, Forbairt, IDA Ireland, Shannon Development and Údarás na Gaeltachta.

- *Functional Development Agencies.* These agencies offer guidance, assistance and funding in functional areas such as marketing, training, finance and technological support. The main agencies include FÁS, The Irish Trade Board/An Bord Tráchtála (ABT) and an Bord Bia.

In total, there are 103 state-sponsored enterprises (not all dealing with the business sector), 17 of which are commercial semi-state enterprises. It must be noted that direct state involvement is effected by policy and funding levels laid down by the various government departments and, increasingly, by EU policy, legislation and funding. Figure 3.1 shows the general structure of state involvement in Ireland.

### 3.2 POLICY RATIONALE FOR STATE INTERVENTION

In general, government intervention worldwide has been justified for four distinct reasons, namely:

- To protect or foster infant industry
- To benefit from economies of scale in individual businesses
- To correct market failure
- To control "externalities".

In the first case, government intervention may take place to foster infant industries behind protective trade barriers, where the country is underdeveloped. Government may also intervene to protect strategic industries which face sharp foreign competition, as the Irish Government did in the case of companies like Irish Steel, TEAM Aer Lingus and Irish Sugar Co. (now Greencore plc).

## Figure 3.1: State-Sponsored Network in Ireland

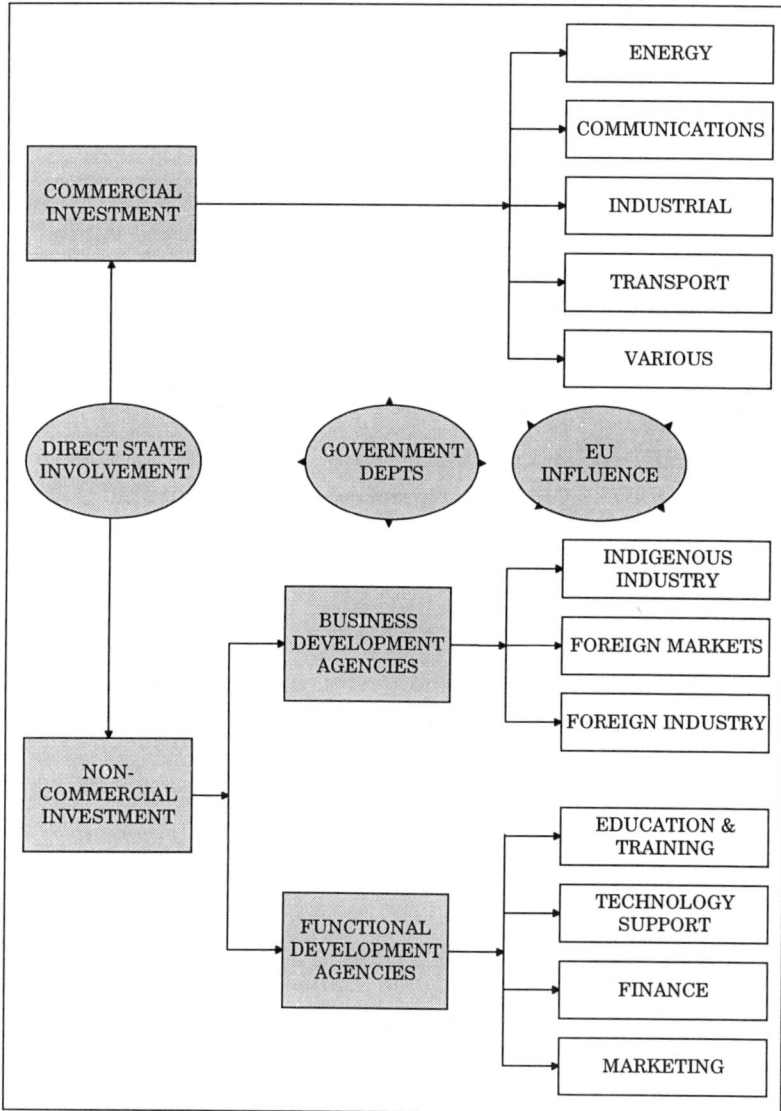

In the second case, government intervention may arise where the economies of scale created by a large monopoly will help to ensure supply at an optimal or acceptable price to consumers, whereas small firms would be unable to supply at the same prices. This has been the rationale in the case of telecommunications, post and energy. This situation is not unique to Ireland. At present, governments in all countries in Europe are examining their strategic position in this area *vis-à-vis* private industry. Governments should be continuously examining whether protected industries remain strategic and would not benefit from competition.

In the third case, government intervention steps in to correct market failure where the market may fail to deliver the socially necessary goods and services. Such failures can arise from natural monopolies — as with electricity, where the state established the ESB to supply electricity to all parts of Ireland. Similarly, it was the unavailability of finance for industry that led to the creation of the Industrial Credit Corporation (ICC) in 1932.

Finally, government intervention arises where a firm or industry is affected by "externalities", such as costs or benefits which are not captured in individual firms' profit and loss accounts. Hence, the state may enact legislation aimed at curbing pollution (where the cost to society is not a charge on the firm) or at ensuring certain health and safety standards for workers, as in the mining or asbestos industries.

There is a considerable ongoing debate about the validity of government intervention in the business sector. It is argued that protectionism fosters inefficiency and complacency, leaving firms ill-prepared to face the rigours of free trade. This has certainly been the case in Ireland — when tariff protection was removed, many traditional industries collapsed.

The end of the protectionist era witnessed the substitution of indirect industrial supports in the form of grants and tax benefits for direct restraints on foreign competition. However, the present level of government spending on industry is continually being questioned both by the taxpayers of Ireland and by the free competition rules of the EU.

The National Development Plan (1994–99) has made a number of changes in the area of state involvement. One major change is the attempt to reform the economic environment directly, rather than provide supports which enable selected firms to avoid the impact of adverse environmental conditions. This involves tackling the national debt, tax reform, improving transport and communications, more extensive and appropriate education, raising confidence levels and readjusting labour-force attitudes.

Industrial policy itself is trying to develop a closer focus on selected industrial growth sectors — mainly in technology- or knowledge-driven industries — and this has been accompanied by a shift from hard to soft supports — that is, from grant-aiding fixed assets to grant-aiding the employment of high-quality labour and advice. These changes have been accompanied by structural changes in the support system as agencies with over-lapping functions have been merged.

How these policy shifts affect the Irish economy and the business system, and how world economic events will interact to foster or destabilise the system further, will be revealed in the future. As mentioned in Chapter Two, the immediate and medium-term outlook is for sustained growth in all world markets. Conditions of growth and change pose threats and provide opportunities to all participants, and this highlights the necessity for each business to analyse and monitor the broad environment within which it operates.

## 3.3 THE DEVELOPMENT OF INDUSTRIAL POLICY

This section traces the development of industrial policy in Ireland from the early years to its present position, and examines the issue of privatisation. The small size of the Irish economy, its underdeveloped status, and its consequent vulnerability have, from the foundation of the state, led to extensive government intervention in the development of the business system. This is a common stage in the development of newly-independent countries, and in Ireland appears to be fundamentally grounded in pragmatism rather than ideology.

The Industrial Development Authority (IDA) was set up originally in 1954. The primary focus of government intervention before 1960 was the protection and fostering of indigenous, traditional and resource-based industries. As useful as this policy was in developing infant industry, it failed in principle in developing the competitiveness of the Irish economy in an increasingly open and competitive world market. As a consequence, from the early 1960s onward, the primary thrust of government policy was to attract foreign manufacturing companies into Ireland, principally by means of grant-aids for capital equipment, and full tax-exemption for export profits. The government also invested in ensuring a competitive infrastructure of vital services and raw materials.

In 1968, the IDA's regional industrial policy reflected the changing role of many provincial cities, notably Cork and Galway. The relative success in ensuring the new industrial areas meant that escaped the ravages of the first oil crisis. But the detrimental impact of the combination of two oil shocks had a serious impact on the success of attracting overseas investment into Ireland.

In 1982, a major review of industrial policy was carried out by the Telesis group of consultants, and many of its recommendations were later embodied in official government policy, with the publication of a White Paper on industrial policy in 1984. The main finding of the Telesis Report was that although the policy of attracting foreign firms had been a major factor in maintaining employment levels during a period when employment was being eroded by job losses in traditional industries, the structural adjustment of indigenous Irish industry — the part controlled by Irish owners — was inadequate. The major problem was that only a handful of Irish firms had managed to achieve strong, internationally competitive positions in traded goods or services. Many firms in traditional industries — even companies which were large by Irish standards — did not survive the transition to free trade conditions. To develop products and implement strategies for export markets typically requires resources that are not available to most firms, and even state aid on a considerable scale could not overcome this.

The Telesis recommendations were: (a) to continue the policy of attracting foreign firms (with some modifications); (b) to improve the support systems; and, above all (c) to adopt a more selective and interventionist approach to helping indigenous firms to develop. Telesis suggested that the goals of industrial policy should be:

• To exploit natural resources where competitive advantage can be gained

• To restructure industry in order to phase out those areas competing with low-wage countries

- To gain competitive advantage through productivity gains in selected areas of manufacturing business

- To substitute for imports of non-traded goods.

The government's White Paper response was broadly in line with the Telesis proposals, although with some shifts of emphasis. Thus, policies were adopted to shift incentives selectively towards firms producing traded goods, to shift resources away from fixed assets and towards technology acquisition and marketing, and to select foreign firms for their capacity to integrate into the Irish economy. There was also to have been a greater integration of state-agency activities.

A Government White Paper in 1984 introduced a triennial industrial policy review, published in 1986 and 1989. In 1991, nearly a decade after the Telesis report, and in response to deteriorating economic conditions and rising unemployment, a new and more fundamental examination of industrial policy was undertaken. The report of the Industrial Policy Review Group (the Culliton Report) was published in 1991. This report concluded that:

- The formation of policy needed a broader outlook to take account of all major relevant factors, including taxation, infrastructure, education and training.

- There was a need for a more market-led and production-oriented enterprise sector.

- Irish industrial performance needed to be built on national sources of competitive advantage.

- Industrial policy interventions needed to be delivered in a more integrated and cost-effective manner.

The main recommendations of the Industrial Policy Review Group (IPRG) were as follows:

- A new agency should be established for the development of indigenous, Irish-managed industry, to bring together, in a more integrated way, the developmental and support services formerly provided by IDA, ABT and Eolas in particular.

- A separate agency should be established to maximise the levels of internationally mobile investment in Ireland.

- State assistance should be focused on types of projects which would, because of their risk pattern, have difficulty in obtaining finance from existing financial institutions.

- Greater use should be made of equity, including preference shares, in the provision of support to industry.

- Agencies should become more selective, with the selectivity directed towards the establishment of industrial clusters around industrial segments and niches of national competitive advantage.

The Group stressed that there were no simple policy solutions to unemployment. It emphasised the need for a systematic integrated and sustained effort to improve the competitiveness of the economy and to promote active involvement and enterprise throughout it. The Moriarty Task Force was created to advise the Government on how the Review Group's recommendations should be implemented — a step which was missing with Telesis.

Following the report of the Moriarty Task Force, the government's response, entitled "Employment through Enterprise", generally endorsed the Moriarty Task Force and the Review Group's recommendations, and a more comprehensive and integrated approach to industrial policy emerged. As a result, the industrial policy objectives for the period 1994–99 focus on the promotion of a strong, internationally competitive enterprise sector comprising both Irish-owned and foreign-owned companies making the maximum contribution to sustainable employment growth. The main objectives are:

- The generation of sustainable employment in the industrial and services sectors

- A greater integration of industrial activity with other sectors of the economy, with the effect of increasing the Irish value-added share of industrial output

- The development of our natural resources as a foundation for increased industrial development, with particular emphasis on the development of the food-processing and timber industries

- The growth of indigenous firms utilising best-practice modern technology and having the ability to compete successfully in technology-based sectors and on home and overseas markets

- Higher living standards in Ireland

- The achievement of a satisfactory regional balance in economic development.

### 3.3.1 Direct State Involvement in Business

Throughout the 1990s, there has been a continuing debate as to whether the state should be involved in commercial activities or whether it should be limited to general policy development and technical assistance to the commercial business sector. Privatisation and semi-privatisation are key trends in most countries in the 1990s, and the following are the drivers of change making this happen:

- EU deregulation of state-owned incumbent monopolies

- Increased competitive threats from the private sector

- Reductions in subsidies to state-sponsored enterprises and the need for rationalisation.

This trend toward privatisation is influenced mainly by EU competition policy as it endeavours to create an open and freely competitive single market, and by the increased openness of the Irish economy which has little by way of protectionism. While many non-commercial bodies have been merged, a few of the commercial semi-state companies are being privatised or semi-privatised in line with European trends. This occurs when the assets that belong to the public sector are sold or transferred to the private sector. In certain cases, the government retains a "golden share" or a veto to prevent those who buy a semi-state body from selling it without government approval. Examples of semi-state bodies that have been privatised include:

- The Irish Sugar Co. — now Greencore plc

- B and I Shipping Line — sold to Irish Continental Group (ICG) plc

- Irish Life Assurance — which became Irish Life Assurance plc.

Naturally, there are many arguments for and against privatisation, and it has become a highly emotive and politically sensitive issue. If one looks at the UK experience, privatisation and increased competition have improved the competitiveness of many enterprises, particularly in the areas of telecommunications and automotive industries. However, in other sectors privatisation has resulted in much downsizing and redundancy without increased efficiency. In some cases this occurred as the consumer price increased— British Gas and the regional electric companies, for example. Elsewhere — France and the Nordic countries, for example — the government has retained state monopolies to a greater extent, while focusing on increasing efficiency and productivity and co-operating with the private sector. There are no set or definitive criteria for deciding on the level of direct involvement. They vary according to government and political policy, specific industry requirements and the competitive situation which prevails. A judgment has to be made by the government in power, taking these criteria into account.

The key to the effective role of the state in direct involvement in business in the modern global business environment would seem to be an optimal level of privatisation. This increases technology transfer between the public and private sectors and benefits from effective private-sector management expertise, while ensuring moderate price levels and scale economies — hence the importance of strategic partnerships or alliances between the private sector and the state.

## 3.4 THE COMMERCIAL SEMI-STATE SECTOR

It is important for business managers and students alike to understand why the state intervenes in the commercial aspects of Irish business. As already mentioned, it is vital that strategically important aspects of the Irish economic infrastructure are well developed, efficient and affordable. This makes Ireland an attractive and competitive location in which to do business. This section analyses the semi-state sector in Ireland in the 1990s. In particular, it looks at the reasons why the state became involved in particular sectors of Irish industry. It also looks at the current commercial semi-state network and its performance in the first half of the decade. The various bodies are then analysed by sector.

As noted in Chapter One, the state has founded about 100 commercial enterprises for pragmatic strategic reasons. Many state-sponsored bodies are natural or legal monopolies and were set up to provide essential services, which were beyond the scope of private enterprise. Others were created to exploit natural resources or because their industries were of strategic supply importance.

Figure 3.2 shows the structure of the commercial semi-state sector. Activity is now centred on the three key areas of transport, communications and energy. Some of the enterprises cannot be classified as strictly commercial. For example, Coillte provides non-commercial assistance and grant-aid to the forestry sector.

*Figure 3.2: The Commercial Semi-State Network*

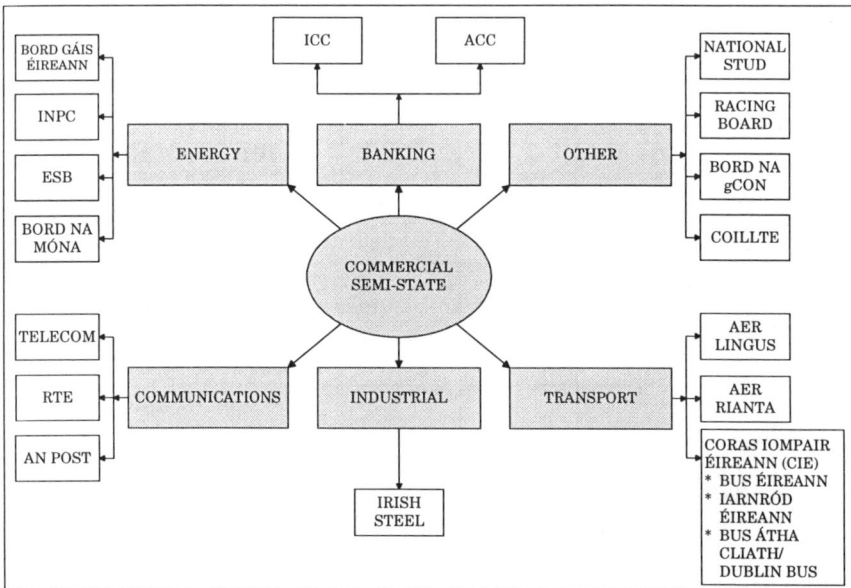

Table 3.1 shows the financial performance of the 17 semi-state enterprises between 1989 and 1993. In 1993, the combined

enterprises had sales of £4.22 billion, and a net loss after tax of
1.4 per cent or £60 million, with a net worth of £267 billion. In
addition, the state invested £1.21 billion in these companies between 1989 and 1993 and long-term debt was reduced by 36 per
cent to £4.95 billion, although this still remains a very high level
of gearing. It must be noted that 7 of these enterprises receive no
state equity, and therefore these figures might give an unfair
reading on the performance of individual enterprises.

It was originally expected that the state-sponsored commercial
enterprises would be self-financing and would generate an adequate return on government investment. In practice, performance
over the years has been uneven and, although important social
and strategic functions are served, on a strictly financial basis,
the returns to the state are low.

*Table 3.1 Performance of the Commercial Sector, 1989–93
(IR£ million)*

|                            | 1989   | 1990   | 1991   | 1992   | 1993   |
|----------------------------|--------|--------|--------|--------|--------|
| Turnover                   | 4,268  | 4,906  | 5,227  | 4,199  | 4,225  |
| Net Profit After Tax       | 93     | 228    | 231    | 169    | (60)   |
| Net Worth                  | 2,005  | 2,523  | 2,707  | 2,651  | 2,666  |
| Long-term Debt             | 7,706  | 8,572  | 8,401  | 4,559  | 4,946  |
| State Equity               | 5887   | 20     | 21     | 13     | 11     |
| State Subsidies            | 112    | 115    | 115    | 112    | 112    |
| Dividends/ Distributions   | 17     | 33     | 75     | 93     | 85     |
| Corporation Tax            | (19)   | (27)   | (32)   | (19)   | (18)   |
| Employment                 | 72,782 | 74,035 | 74,623 | 70,200 | 67,322 |

*Source: Business and Finance*, 27 October 1994, p. 13.

### 3.4.1 Energy

The state plays a key role in ensuring an effective energy infrastructure and a balanced portfolio of renewable and non-
renewable resources of energy for Irish business. The following

are the key drivers of change affecting the energy sector and the state's future position:

- Gas and electricity interconnectors to UK and Europe

- EU pressure: the need to improve competitiveness and increase competition

- Continuing dependence on too few non-renewable resources and the trends among large manufacturing businesses to install their own combined heat and power units (CHP)

- Potential volatility of the world oil market similar to the 1970s oil crisis

- The need to decrease pollution and conserve energy.

The continuing need for competitiveness and the need for renewable resources is having varying effects, including privatisation and semi-privatisation.

The **Electricity Supply Board (ESB)** is responsible for the provision of electricity services and the management of the electricity generating station network. It is by far the largest of the semi-states in financial terms with shareholders' funds of over £800 million. The ESB employed over 10,000 people in 1994, although this has been reduced considerably as a result of rationalisation. EU competition policy is demanding that the opportunity for private ownership in electricity generation be created, and the reconnection of the cross-border electricity interconnector with Northern Ireland will result in potential competition on a pan-European basis. This should have a positive effect on the energy infrastructure and result in more competitive supply to Irish business.

**Bord Gáis Éireann (BGE)** is responsible for the provision of natural gas-based energy throughout Ireland and particularly in the Dublin area. It employed over 800 people in 1994. The growth in importance of BGE is limited by the capacity of gas sources off the southern coast.

**Bord na Móna** is responsible for the development of the peat resources in Ireland and plays a key role in the economy of the west and midlands.

The **Irish National Petroleum Corporation Ltd. (INPC)** acquires crude oil, refines it through its subsidiary, Irish Refining plc, and supplies petroleum products to the Irish market.

### 3.4.2 Telecommunications

The quality of the telecommunications infrastructure is becoming a key factor in the business environment of all countries. The "global village" has become a reality and the way in which people communicate and transact business has changed dramatically. The emergence of Internet (E-mail), fax and computer technology is forcing these changes. Other key drivers of change in the tele-communications industry in Ireland are:

- EU pressure: as with energy, the need for competitiveness and competition

- The growth of global telecommunications enterprises and the commercial logic of transnational strategic alliances and part-nerships

- The growth of global courier networks concentrating on the business segment.

**Telecom Éireann** is responsible for the supply and development of telecommunications services in Ireland. In 1994, it employed over 13,000 people. As a result of major capital expenditure pro-grammes in the first half of the 1990s, Telecom Éireann was able to install a vastly improved telecommunications infrastructure. Telecom Éireann has many commercial subsidiaries, including Eircell (mobile telephone network) TÉIS (Terminal Equipment) and Eirtrade.

The telecommunications market is being opened up to com-petition in Ireland, and Telecom Éireann is now attempting to ensure that it remains competitive in this new environment. Telecom Éireann is already involved with many private-sector enterprises in joint ventures and strategic alliances (AIB, France Telecom, Crédit Lyonnais and Nynex), and the sourcing of a stra-tegic partner for future development would seem to be a natural progression from this.

**Radio Telefís Éireann (RTE)** is the Irish national broadcasting organisation for radio and television. It employs over 2,000 people directly and subcontracts an increasing portion of its production to an emerging and thriving independent production sector.

**An Post** is the state-owned national postal service which directly employs 8,000 people and employs another 3,000 indirectly through sub-offices. In addition to its general mail service, the key business services are SDS (Special Distribution Services) for parcel and document distribution, and EMS (Express Mail Service), the courier service. Multinational courier services such as TNT, UPS and DHL are now beginning to dominate business postal services worldwide and, indeed, are actively engaging in partnerships with many national postal services. This may be the case in Ireland in the future.

### 3.4.3 Transport

Because of Ireland's geographic position, a key factor in the attractiveness and competitiveness of Irish industry is an effective transport network. This is important for virtually all Irish industry which depends on exports and which has a high import requirement. At one level, the state has to ensure a developed road network to feed the export corridors and intracountry trade. At another level, it provides commercial carrier services by road, rail, air or sea. The key drivers of change affecting the state's role in the transport industry in the 1990s include:

- The EU "open skies" policy which deregulated the European airline industry and which continues to change the industry

- The opening of the Channel Tunnel between Britain and France

- The improvements in the rail network in the UK and Ireland

- Increased competition in all modes of transport from private sources.

**Aer Lingus** is a limited liability company providing airline services and airline-related ancillary services. It employs approximately 7,000 people. The first half of the 1990s has been a very difficult period for Aer Lingus in its attempts to remain competitive against larger global competitors on the transatlantic routes, and against smaller companies such as Ryanair, British Midland and Virgin on the Dublin to London route.

**Córas Iompair Éireann (CIE)** is the holding company for the state bus and rail services. The subsidiary companies of CIE include **Bus Átha Cliath/Dublin Bus**, which provides the bus services in the Dublin area, and **Bus Éireann**, which provides railway and road freight services throughout the country. There are approximately 11,000 people employed with the CIE group of companies.

**Aer Rianta** is the state-sponsored enterprise which manages the nation's airports. In addition, it manages the duty-free services in Ireland and now a number of duty-free services in other countries too. It also owns the Great Southern Hotel Group.

### 3.4.4 Other Areas of Commercial State Involvement

The other key areas where the state has an involvement in commercial activities include:

- **Banking**: The ICC and ACC were created in the 1930s at a time when there was a considerable lack of capital available for industry and agriculture, so a strategic requirement prevailed at the time. Since entry into the EC in 1973 the strategic importance of these institutions has been re-evaluated and much discussion and argument has taken place on their strategic importance today.

- **Manufacturing**: The state continues to be involved in manufacturing through its ownership of Irish Steel. Again, much discussion has taken place on the proper role of the state in this industry, and this is occurring in all countries involved in steel manufacturing in the EU.

- **Forestry**: The state is involved in the forestry sector in Ireland through Coillte, which is discussed in more detail in Chapter Four on Resource-based Industry.

- **Horse Racing and Greyhound Racing**: The state is involved in the horse-racing and breeding industry through the Racing Board and the National Stud, and the greyhound industry via Bord na gCon. Ireland is a significant global player in these areas, with sizeable exports, and the state intervenes to regulate the industry and to ensure that high-quality standards are met.

## 3.5 NON-COMMERCIAL STATE INVOLVEMENT

The state is involved in a number of areas related to the development of Irish business and in the provision of funding and assistance where deemed appropriate. The organisations that carry out this work are set up as non-commercial semi-state agencies. In this section, the state's involvement in these areas is examined. In particular, the focus is on the changes that have taken place in the restructuring of the development agencies since 1993.

There are five main areas of non-commercial state-agency intervention, namely:

- Business-policy development

- Financial assistance

- Marketing assistance

- Training and education

- Technical support.

There are some 20 non-commercial state-backed enterprises dealing directly with business development needs. In general, they have no commercial mandate and obtain the majority of their funding requirements directly from the Exchequer. The structure of the non-commercial state enterprise sector is summarised in Figure 3.3.

There are two general types of agency: business development agencies and functional-development agencies. It is difficult to classify some agencies — for example, Forfás is linked to many development agencies, as is Teagasc. In addition, the commercial state banks could be classified as financial agencies. Similarly, Coillte is involved in assisting private-sector forestry developers, as well as managing the state's forest resources.

At a local level, the County Enterprise Boards now hold the brief to support enterprise development in their counties. The

**Figure 3.3: Non-Commercial Semi-State Agency Structure**

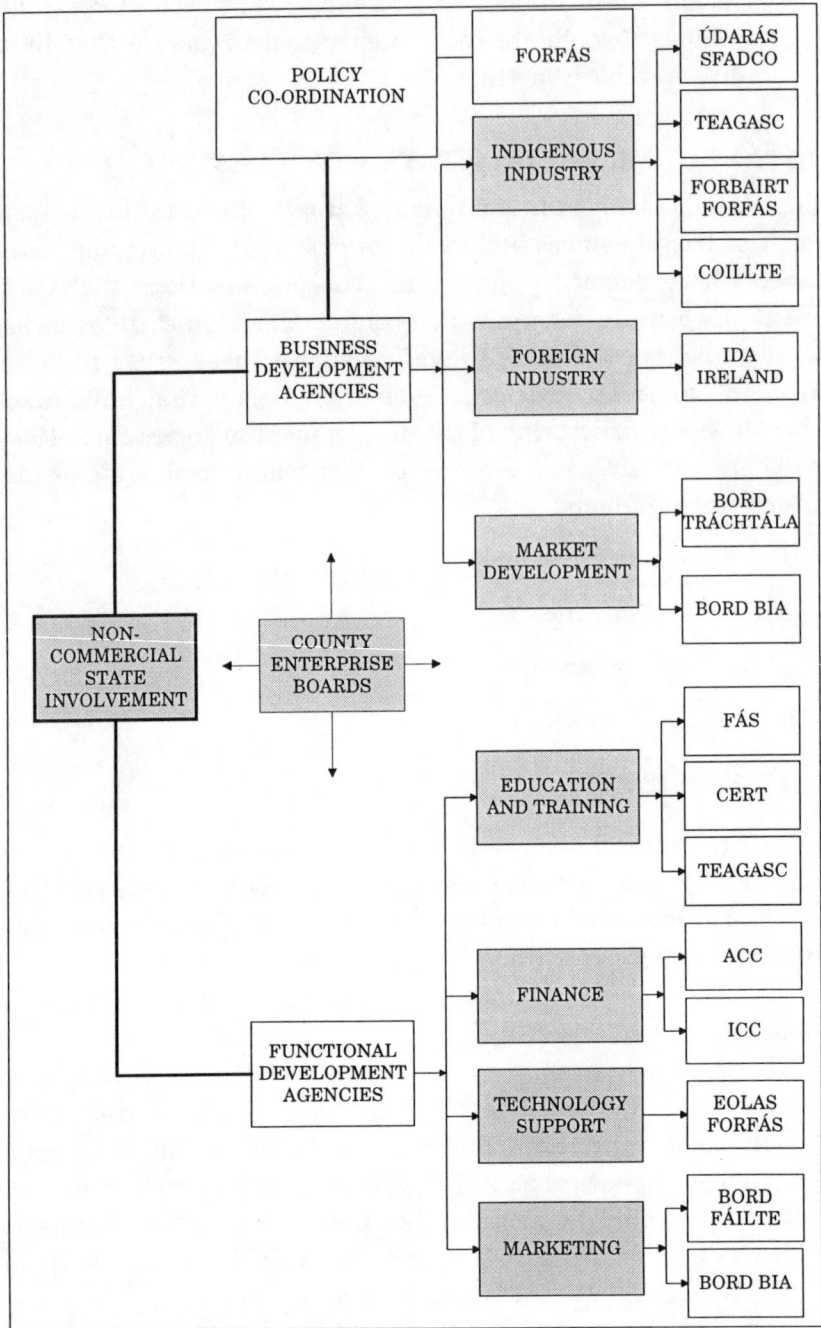

scope of the Enterprise Boards is broader than just industrial development. They can deal with all areas of enterprise at a local level, and in doing so can liaise with all the other state agencies, as well as with rural-development associations, many of which are funded by the EU LEADER Programme.

### 3.5.1 Forfás: The Policy Co-ordinator

Before examining the industrial development agencies, it is appropriate to analyse the nature and structure of Forfás as the co-ordinating agency and the role it now plays in business development in Ireland.

Forfás was established in 1993 as a result of the Culliton Review Group's recommendation for a more integrated approach to state-agency activities. Forfás is the policy advisory and co-ordination board for industrial development and science and technology in Ireland. It is the agency in which the state's legal powers for industrial promotion and technology development have been vested. Powers are delegated from Forfás to Forbairt for the promotion of indigenous industry and to IDA Ireland for the promotion of inward investment. The broad functions of Forfás are:

- To advise the Minister for Enterprise and Employment on matters relating to the development of industry in the state

- To advise on the development and co-ordination of policy for Forbairt, IDA Ireland, An Bord Tráchtála and such other bodies as the Minister may designate

- To encourage the development of industry and technology in the state

- To promote science and technology for economic and social development

- To encourage the establishment and development in the state of industrial undertakings from outside the state

- To advise and co-ordinate the functions of Forbairt and IDA Ireland.

### 3.5.2 Indigenous Development Agencies

*Forbairt*

Following the restructuring of the development agencies in 1993, Forbairt emerged as the agency responsible for the development of indigenous industry. It took over all of the indigenous activities from the old IDA, and in addition absorbed most of the activities of Eolas, the previous Science and Technology Agency. Forbairt, which commenced operation in 1994, offers a range of services to start-up and existing companies in the following areas:

• Small business

• International services

• Medium-sized and large Irish-owned industry

• Food and agri-business

• Science and technology.

Forbairt offers financial incentives in the form of grants for new capital equipment, training, feasibility studies, product development, loan guarantees and employment grants. The level of financial assistance depends upon the strength of the business plan submitted, the experience and calibre of the management team, and the prospects perceived for the market and the sector in question. The main programmes of Forbairt may be summarised as follows:

**Small Business**: This programme offers advice and financial incentives to small businesses employing not more than 50 people. In addition, it offers the Enterprise Development Programme, which is designed to attract experienced managers and professionals to set up their own businesses in manufacturing or internationally traded services. It also runs the Mentor Programme, which matches companies with business executives who act as part-time advisors in developing the business.

**International Services**: Financial and support services are available to service companies in many sectors which trade internationally, the largest being software and computer services. The National Software Directorate is concerned exclusively with the development and growth of the software industry and co-ordinates the activities of agencies and educational institutions providing support for the industry.

**Medium-sized and Large Irish-owned Enterprises**: These companies can participate in a variety of programmes aimed at enhancing their capabilities across all functional areas, from raw-material sourcing through world-class manufacturing processes, management development, marketing and exporting. The National Linkage Programme aims to maximise the amount of raw materials, components and services sourced in Ireland by all Irish companies and by the public-sector organisations. The Programme includes a specialist Electronic Linkages Team which aims to maximise the opportunities for indigenous companies to act as sub-suppliers to the overseas companies located in Ireland.

**Food and Agri-business**: This division is responsible for the development of both indigenous and overseas food, drink and agri-business firms. In addition to the usual grants and incentives, Forbairt provides specialist support in areas such as consumer foods and food ingredients. Representatives in New York, Düsseldorf and Tokyo are available to Irish companies seeking international business partners for joint ventures, subcontracting and technology transfer.

**Science and Technology Development**: Since 1994 the services formerly offered by Eolas have been merged into Forbairt. It now offers a range of science and technology programmes in the following areas:

- *Building Technological Competence*: This involves helping firms to achieve technical standards, install and improve quality systems, reduce costs and improve efficiency. It also helps in new product and process development, environmental protection and source funding. Programmes include the Techstart Programme, Technology Audit Programme and Technology Transfer Programme.

- *Technical and Consultancy Services*: These programmes are aimed at improving the competitive edge of manufacturing and service firms. The Programmes include Energy Management, Environmental Technology and Construction/Timber Technology, and World Class Manufacturing.

- *Laboratory Services*: These include areas such as meteorology, materials technology, electronics and industrial chemistry.

- *Programmes in Advanced Technology (PATs)*: Companies can access new technologies developed in selected niche areas including advanced manufacturing technology, biotechnology and advanced telecommunications.

### Shannon Development (SFADCo)

The brief of SFADCo (Shannon Free Airport Development Company) is broadly similar to that of Forbairt, but it is focused on the development of Shannon Airport, on the promotion of the town of Shannon as an industrial centre, and on the development of small businesses in the midwest region. SFADCo has a package of incentives similar to that of Forbairt, but it is more focused on small industry. It operates a business advisory service, provides training services managers, has built advance factories which permit low-cost accommodation for new or expanding ventures, has built the Plassey Technological Park, and works in close co-operation with the University of Limerick in many areas of science, technology and management.

### Údarás na Gaeltachta

This is again similar to SFADCo, but it is focused on the Irish-speaking areas of the country, and its brief encompasses virtually all aspects of sociocultural and business development in its areas. It is even more interventionist than SFADCo, as it takes equity holdings where necessary and provides more financial support in the incubation stages of new ventures.

### Teagasc

This is the agriculture and food-development authority, which provides advisory, research, education and training services to the agricultural and agri-food industries. Teagasc's priority is the education and training of young farmers, together with the provision of farm-management advice. It is heavily committed to and involved in undertaking research and in providing advice in all areas of farm development, rural development and in the development and marketing of all agricultural products. The National Food Centre, located in North Dublin, provides research, development and consultancy services on all aspects of non-dairy food products. The dairy industry is catered for by the National Dairy Products Research Centre at Moorepark in Cork.

### Coillte

This is the Irish Forestry Board, which manages the state's forestry and related activities. Coillte has a forest estate of some 1 million acres and harvests nearly 2 million cubic metres of timber per annum. Coillte works closely with the timber-processing sector and undertakes research and provides advice for the forestry sector in Ireland. It employs about 1,900 staff.

### 3.5.3 Overseas Industrial Development Agency

### IDA Ireland

The objective of IDA Ireland is to create employment in Ireland through encouraging foreign-owned enterprises to set up new businesses or expand their existing businesses in Ireland. IDA Ireland is successfully securing internationally mobile projects against increasing competition from other countries. It has a staff of 180 people and has offices in 15 countries.

The US is by far the largest source of investment. Japan and the Far East are very important in advanced technology, pharmaceuticals and financial services. Germany and the UK are the most important sources of mobile investment from Europe. Ireland now attracts nearly a fifth of all mobile greenfield US projects which locate in Europe and a third of all US electronics new projects in Europe.

IDA Ireland's main competitors in attracting international industrial investment during the 1980s and the first half of the 1990s were Scotland's and Spain's national development agencies. The competitive structure is now changing as certain industries are beginning to "cluster" in regions or countries, and Eastern Europe — in particular the Czech Republic — has emerged as a serious competitor.

### 3.5.4 Functional Development Agencies

In addition to its involvement in formulating policy and strategic direction in Irish industry, the state is also involved in helping to implement the overall policy through the provision of supports such as:

- Marketing assistance

- Training and employment services

- Technological support.

*Marketing Development Agencies*

**An Bord Tráchtála (ABT)** or the **Irish Trade Board**: This body was established in 1991 following the merger of the Irish Export Board/Córas Tráchtála and the Irish Goods Council. Its main objective is to assist Irish firms in developing sustainable markets at home and overseas. Bord Tráchtála has a head office in Dublin, regional offices in Cork, Limerick, Sligo, Waterford and Galway and 23 overseas offices. The wide variety of aids and incentives are for merchandise manufacturers and for firms providing certain internationally traded services. ABT also provides a range of services for overseas buyers and importers, and an information centre.

**An Bord Bia**: Established in 1994, it has responsibility for the promotion of Irish food and drink products, and for the development of both home and export markets. An Bord Bia encompasses the market development activities of a number of former agencies including Córas Beostoic agus Feola (CBF) — the Irish Livestock and Meat Board; An Bord Glas — the Horticultural Development Board; the food division of An Bord Tráchtála; and the market development and promotion activities of Bord Iascaigh Mhara (BIM) — the Irish Sea Fisheries Board.

**Bord Fáilte Éireann (The Irish Tourist Board)** is responsible for the development of the Irish tourism industry and for promoting Ireland in overseas markets. Bord Fáilte co-ordinates the activities of six regional tourism organisations in Ireland, and until 1994 engaged in market research, planning, sales promotion and publicity and offered a range of services and financial assistance to the tourism sector. In 1994 a strategic review of the role of Bord Fáilte was undertaken, with a recommendation that it be divested of its ancillary activities and concentrate on the promotion of tourism in Ireland. As a result, Bord Fáilte was going through a period of transition at the time of writing.

### FÁS — The Training and Employment Authority
The state has played an active role in supporting the training of people in Ireland since the 1950s. The organisation that has the responsibility for training and providing employment services is FÁS, the training and development authority, which was formed in 1988 with the amalgamation of An Comhairle Oiliúna (AnCO), the National Manpower Authority (NMA) and the Youth Employment Agency (YEA). The activities of FÁS include the following:

**Training in Industry**: This is supported through participation in the training of apprentices and through the provision — under the Training Support Scheme (TSS) — of financial support to firms to upgrade their skills base.

**Training for the Unemployed**: This focuses on the provision of skills training for unemployed people to help them to secure a job and return to employment. In the case of early school-leavers, the training focuses on the provision of basic skills.

**Employment Services**: This service is provided for unemployed people through a network of 60 employment service offices. It aims to provide unemployed people with information on available jobs and training courses.

**Employment Schemes**: Because of the very high levels of unemployment, it has not been possible to offer a place on a training course to everybody who is unemployed. However, the state does provide places on the Community Employment Programme for up to 40,000 people per annum.

FÁS has a staff of some 2,000 people who are distributed over 10 regions and a head office. It has a network of 12 training centres and 60 employment offices located throughout the country.

### Technological Support Schemes

As mentioned in Chapter Two, there has been a lot of criticism of
Irish industry in relation to its technological capabilities and its
investment in Research and Development. To help address these
shortcomings the state provides technological support through
the following organisations:

**Forbairt**: As already mentioned, Forbairt absorbed most of the
activities of Eolas, the previous Science and Technology Agency, in
1993. Forbairt is involved in helping firms to build their technological capability, and in doing so they provide technical and
consultancy services, laboratory services and a Programme of
Advanced Technology (PATs).

**National Microelectronics Application Centre (MAC) Ltd**:
MAC is located in Plassey Technological Park in Limerick. It supports firms through the development and application of advanced
technology in the areas of electronics, software, telecommunications and information.

**National Microelectronics Research Centre (NMRC)**: This
is located at University College Cork where its focus is on semi-
conductor and component manufacturing processes. In addition to
supporting industry through its research activities, it also has an
educational function, and awards postgraduate degrees.

**National Software Centre**: The centre was set up as a subsidiary of the IDA in 1984 and it now reports to Forbairt. Its brief
is to increase the technical capability of Irish software firms, and
to promote the image of Ireland as a centre for software development. Its main activities include software marketing and market
research, product development, advanced training courses, and
supporting Irish firms in the negotiation of joint ventures with
international partners.

### SUMMARY

This chapter focused on the important role that the state plays in
Irish business. The main points from the chapter may be summarised as follows:

- The state intervenes in Irish business for two key reasons: first, to maintain a competitive infrastructure in terms of strategically important services and raw materials, to ensure that Ireland is an attractive location in which to do business; second, to assist and support the development of the various sectors of Irish industry through state development agencies.

- State involvement in Irish business can be divided between commercial and non-commercial activities. In total, there are some 103 state-sponsored organisations of which 17 are commercial companies.

- Commercial semi-state companies are involved in many strategically important areas of Irish business, including energy, transport and communications. EU competition policy is encouraging a trend towards the privatisation of state-owned companies, as it insists on competition and consumer choice. While privatisation has worked, and will work, effectively in some areas, it is likely that partnerships and alliances with the private sector will work more effectively in many of the state companies in Ireland.

- The non-commercial organisations are, in general, involved in policy development in the provision of supports to business. There are two types of agencies involved: business development agencies such as Forbairt and IDA Ireland; and functional development agencies such as An Bord Tráchtála. The latter provide funding and assistance in the areas of marketing, technology, training and finance.

- The approach to industrial development policy changed in the late 1960s and has been radically updated during the 1980s and 1990s. Beginning with the Telesis Report in 1982 and up to the Industrial Policy Review Group's (Culliton Report) recommendations in 1993, Industrial Policy has become much more focused on the development of indigenous industry. In addition, there has been a movement away from a reliance on grant-aiding fixed assets. In the case of indigenous industry, there has been a move to support total-company development programmes through a combination of equity participation via preference shares and grants.

## FURTHER READING

Coonan, Clifford and Tom McEnaney, "Science: Trailing The Pack" *Business and Finance*, 11 August 1994.

"Employment through Enterprise" The Response of the Government to the Moriarty Task Force of the Culliton Report, Government Publications, 1994.

Forbairt, various brochures, annual reports and literature.

IDA Ireland, various brochures, annual reports and literature.

Industrial Policy Review Group, "A Time for Change — Industrial Policy for the 1990s", Report, Government Publications, 1993.

*IPA Yearbook and Diary, 1995*, Institute of Public Administration (IPA), Dublin, 1994.

McGee, John and Dan White, "Semi-States in Crisis", *Business and Finance*, October, 1994, pp. 12–16.

National Development Plan 1994–1999, Government Publications, 1994

National Economic and Social Council (NESC), various reports, Government Publications.

CHAPTER FOUR

# TRADITIONAL INDUSTRY

W hile the previous three chapters provided background details of the general business environment in Ireland, this chapter and the three that follow will investigate the main sectors of Irish business. The intention is to identify the practical considerations of strategy that apply to the firms operating in the four main business sectors. This chapter examines the nature of the traditional sector of business in Ireland and trends taking place worldwide. Following an overview of the traditional sector, the various subsectors are analysed in more detail. The driving forces that are changing the competitive environment are then reviewed. Finally, there is a review of the strategic implications of the analysis and the competencies that Irish firms must develop.

## 4.1 OVERVIEW OF THE TRADITIONAL INDUSTRY SECTOR

This section gives a general overview of traditional industry in Ireland. It begins by defining traditional industry and goes on to give a brief description of the activities involved. This is followed by an analysis of output and employment.

### 4.1.1 Definition and Description

The traditional sector comprises industries whose products in general are long established, labour-intensive and face mature or declining markets in many instances. They have tended in the past to face high import-penetration levels while making some contribution to exports. Some of the traditional industries produce non-traded goods, that is, Irish goods which incur high logistics costs and are not readily exported. As a result, location close to the market is a major competitive weapon, and this is why most exports in the past have gone to the UK. The most important traditional sectors include the following:

- Clothing and Footwear
- Paper, Printing and Publishing
- Textiles
- Plastic and Rubber
- Crafts
- Wood and Timber Processing.

Since traditional industries have a high proportion of their total costs in labour, they are subject to intense price competition from foreign manufacturers who can reduce labour costs by locating in low-wage countries or by achieving production economies of scale. This competition, from firms in both developing and industrialised countries and regions, reduced employment in these industries in Ireland in the 1970s and early 1980s, and led to low and sometimes negative profits or liquidation for many firms involved in traditional industries during this period.

In some traditional industries — printing and publishing, for example — technological advances have radically transformed the production process utilised, and, in turn, customer needs and requirements, to the point where it is almost impossible to compete without being in possession of new technology.

Many indigenous traditional-sector firms are small and are family run, and this may account in part for the sector's failure to respond adequately to increased competitive pressures. Established family firms are prone to certain kinds of internal weaknesses that make it difficult to adjust to change. Succession problems, difficulties with management development and conservative approaches are not conducive to the flexible strategic thinking needed to cope with change. On the other hand, the acquisition of one of these firms can provide a new entrepreneur with a vehicle for entry into an industry.

The traditional-industry sector generally has a two-tier structure. On one hand, there are small Irish-owned firms that sell mainly to the domestic market. On the other, there are large, mainly foreign-owned firms that focus on export markets — Fruit of the Loom in Donegal being one example. A small but growing number of indigenous firms have managed to develop strong competitive positions in exporting traditional products, but many are constrained by inferior design and product quality, or inadequate managerial or financial resources.

Traditional-sector enterprises in general produce consumer or industrial goods that are at the mature stage of the product life cycle (see Chapter Nine on marketing strategy for an explanation of this concept). Growth in these markets is largely determined by growth in consumer incomes, and this has, on average, been quite low in the 1980s and 1990s in Ireland as well as in the main exporting markets. It has thus been difficult for Irish firms to grow and to establish strong competitive positions.

It is, however, possible to compete successfully and to become profitable in traditional industries if the correct strategy can be defined and implemented. Companies can make good use of technology, human resources, marketing skills and financial strategy to do this, and these alternatives will be examined in more detail later in this chapter. The next section analyses in more detail the output and performance of the subsectors of traditional industry.

### 4.1.2 Output and Employment

Traditional industry has undergone a slow revitalisation in terms of output. This began in the late 1980s and has continued among most traditional subsectors through the 1990s. Table 4.1 gives a

*Table 4.1: Output and Employment in Traditional Industry*

|  | Output IR£ m | Employment 1992 |
|---|---|---|
| Paper, Print, and Packaging | 1,250 | 18,500 |
| Rubber and Plastic | 595 | 9,600 |
| Textiles | 451 | 7,300 |
| Clothing, Leather and Footwear | 415 | 15,800 |
| Timber and Wooden Furniture | 385 | 7,100 |
| Jewellery and Crafts | 40 | 6,000 |

*Source:* CSO, Irish Productivity Centre and authors' estimates .

brief overview of output and employment in traditional industries in the 1990s. As traditional-sector enterprises are usually labour-intensive, employment in this sector has also been growing slowly over the past decade, and there have been improvements in overall productivity. Growth in output was particularly high in the printing sector, primarily as a result of growth in the demand for computer manuals. During this time, a shake-out has occurred in the sector in terms of uncompetitive firms which have not invested in, or modernised, their production technology.

### 4.1.3 Value-Added and Productivity

Value-Added (VA) relates to the amount of value that is added to raw materials in the business transformation process. The labour intensity of traditional industries means that value-added per employee is low in comparison to modern industries such as computers, for example, where value-added is six times that in paper and print. Table 4.2 shows the trend in value-added in the traditional sector between 1988 and 1992.

*Table 4.2: Value-Added and Productivity in Traditional Industries, 1988–92*

| Sector | 1988 VA (IR£ m) | 1988 Adjusted VA per employee | 1992 VA (IR£ m) | 1992 Adjusted VA per employee |
|---|---|---|---|---|
| Paper, Print, Packaging | 378.9 | 39.08 | 520.9 | 54.43 |
| Rubber and Plastic | 221 | 43.42 | 235.5 | 41 |
| Textiles | 191.4 | 24.48 | 235.4 | 33.91 |
| Wooden Furniture | 121 | 25.81 | 129.6 | 25.93 |
| Leather and Footwear | 23.6 | 20.45 | 15 | 21.31 |
| Clothing | 114.3 | 15.73 | 101.7 | 14.96 |

*Source:* Irish Productivity Centre, 1995.

Value-added grew substantially in print and packaging, and, while it has declined in the rubber and plastics industry, it remains high in relative terms. In contrast, VA has declined in clothing and remains the lowest in comparative terms.

In comparison with modern industry, the value-added in traditional sectors appears to be extremely low. For example, VA per employee in 1992 in chemicals was £169,040 and it was £290,850 in office and data-processing equipment. This is nearly five times as much as in paper and printing. The much higher levels of value-added in the modern sectors reflect much higher levels of investment and borrowing in these sectors, all of which has to be remunerated from the value-added. Since most of the modern sector of Irish industry is in the hands of overseas companies, the higher levels of value-added can also reflect the use of transfer pricing by those companies to maximise profits in Ireland, which incur only a 10 per cent rate of profits tax.

## 4.2. ANALYSIS BY SECTOR

This section analyses in more detail the constituent parts of the traditional sector, in terms of output and employment, regional concentrations, the importance of foreign-owned companies and the importance of exports.

### 4.2.1 Clothing

Output in the clothing sector is approximately £415 million, representing over 2 per cent of total manufacturing output. The clothing industry in Ireland is quite labour-intensive and increases in output translate directly into job gains. Employment is approximately 16,000, representing over 8 per cent of total national employment. Table 4.3 below summarises the situation in the main subsectors within the clothing sector. Ladies' outerwear, at nearly £110 million, is clearly the dominant business area, accounting for nearly 40 per cent of all firms and over 25 per cent of all employment. This is followed by knitwear, children's wear, menswear and leisurewear. Both employment and output levels have been declining since the early 1980s, with productivity growing at a lower rate than the manufacturing average.

The clothing industry is concentrated in two regions: Dublin, which accounts for 50 per cent of companies, and over 40 per cent of both employment and output; and the North West, which

accounts for 10 per cent of the companies (including Fruit of the
Loom), 26 per cent of output and 22 per cent of employment.
Small firms predominate with 70 per cent of firms employing
fewer than 25 people. However, the 33 largest firms account for
over 55 per cent of the employment. The sector is primarily Irish-
owned, but the 30 or so foreign firms account for over 40 per cent
of both output and employment. The majority of firms rely on export markets to some extent, and one quarter of the firms export
50 per cent of their output. The leisurewear business, which is
dominated by Fruit of the Loom, is highly dependent on exports,
with 85 per cent of output being exported. The UK remains the
most important export market, accounting for 42 per cent of exports, followed by Germany (6 per cent) and the USA (4 per cent).
On the domestic market, import penetration is extremely high at
just under 80 per cent, primarily from UK sources.

**Table 4.3: Output and Employment in the Clothing and
Footwear Sector**

| Subsector | No. of Firms | Output (IR£ m) | Employment |
|---|---|---|---|
| Ladies Outerwear | 162 | 108 | 4,051 |
| Intimate Apparel | 12 | 13.6 | 832 |
| Knitwear | 98 | 37.8 | 1,580 |
| Childrens Wear | 44 | 35.7 | 1,486 |
| Menswear | 27 | 35.9 | 1,344 |
| Underwear | 10 | 16.7 | 795 |
| Shirts | 9 | 10.3 | 548 |
| Careerwear | 32 | 26.6 | 1,038 |
| Leisurewear | 19 | 77 | 2,500 |
| Other | 29 | 51 | 1,630 |
| TOTAL | 442 | 412.6 | 15,804 |

*Source:* FÁS/Clothing Industry Survey, 1991.

The range of firms varies from the large multinationals such as
Fruit of the Loom, to larger indigenous firms such as Loretta

Bloom, John A. Hickey, and Magees of Donegal, to a variety of smaller, more specialised indigenous firms such as Paul Costolloe, John Rocha and Simon Treacy.

### 4.2.2 Paper, Printing and Packaging

Total output in this sector was nearly IR£1,250 million in 1993. The sector consisted of 622 firms and they employed nearly 19,000 people. Table 4.4. below summarises the output and employment in the subsectors. Overall, the sector has grown more strongly than total manufacturing since the 1980s, influenced strongly by the demand for computer-manual printing for computer software firms.

*Table 4.4: Output and Employment in the Print, Paper and Packaging Sectors*

| Subsector | No. of Firms | Output IR£ m | Employment |
|-----------|--------------|--------------|------------|
| Packaging | 102 | 420.3 | 4,567 |
| Paper | 44 | 165.3 | 1,312 |
| Pre-Press | 85 | 35.9 | 819 |
| Printing | 281 | 330.5 | 6,540 |
| Newspapers | 46 | 217.6 | 4,163 |
| Services | 64 | 73.5 | 1,162 |
| TOTAL | 622 | 1243.1 | 18,563 |

*Source:* FÁS/Print and Paper Industry Survey, 1994.

The industry is concentrated in the Dublin region, where nearly 75 per cent of employment is based. Nearly 50 per cent of the firms in the sector employ fewer than 10 people. Over 90 per cent of firms are Irish-owned but these firms account for only 78 per cent of employment. The 30 foreign-owned firms are large and are concentrated in the packaging and printing subsectors. They account for 22 per cent of employment. Value-added averages around 55 per cent and the sector is highly reliant on imports (44 per cent of consumption). The domestic market accounts for 75 per cent of total sales, while UK exports at over £140 million represent 80 per cent of total exports.

### 4.2.3 Textiles

Output from the textile sector was valued at IR£451 million in 1993, but it has been declining slowly since the early 1980s. Employment was approximately 7,200 in 1993 and this has also declined considerably over the same period. Table 4.5 summarises the output and employment details in the various subsectors of the textile industry.

*Table 4.5: Output and Employment in the Textiles Sector, 1993*

| Subsector | No. of Firms | Output (IR£ m) | Employment |
|---|---|---|---|
| Yarns and Fibres | 17 | 158 | 2,262 |
| Woollen Fabrics | 16 | 21 | 536 |
| Other Fabrics | 15 | 107 | 1,676 |
| Carpets | 10 | 68 | 1,318 |
| Household Textiles | 9 | 20 | 498 |
| Industrial Textiles | 25 | 78 | 997 |
| TOTAL | 92 | 452 | 7,287 |

*Source:* FÁS/Textile Industry Survey, 1993.

There are almost 100 firms operating in the textiles sector in Ireland. Large firms (More than 100 employees) dominate in all the subsectors apart from woollen fabrics and industrial textiles where medium-sized companies (25–99 employees) predominate. Fifty per cent of the firms are Irish-owned, but these firms account for only 20 per cent of employment. The Irish textile industry is heavily dependent on the European market. Over 85 per cent of Irish output is exported, and 47 per cent of this goes to the UK. Other important export markets include Germany, France and Italy. Only the woollen fabrics, carpets and household textiles subsectors are dependent on the domestic market. The major firms in the fibre area include the foreign-owned Asahi and Unifi companies, while Longford Textiles is a prominent Irish firm in the yarn subsector, and Magees of Donegal dominates the wool and worsted area. In other fabrics, Schoepp Velours, Atlantic Mills and Klopmann are the key firms, while Lissadel is the major manufacturer of towels in the household textiles subsector.

### 4.2.4 Timber and Wood Processing

In 1993, the Forestry and Timber Industries in Ireland were estimated to have a value of £200 million and they provided employment for 12,000 people. This is a key growth area within the traditional industry sectors. Ireland is Europe's fastest-growing timber producer. This is the result of major investment in forestry start-ups and plantings in the 1950s and 1960s. Foreign-owned firms that have announced developments in Ireland include Medite of Europe, Masonite and Louisiana Pacific. The primary output of the timber industry is the larger logs or saw logs cut for use in house and building construction. Smaller logs, sawdust and residues from the sawmills are taken in by the board mills and turned into composite boards such as Oriented Strand Board (OSB), Chipboard, Medium Density Fibre board (MDF) and hardboard. Table 4.6 shows the projected output and employment figures for the wood-processing sector by the year 2000.

*Table 4.6: Projected Value and Employment in the Wood-Processing Sector to the Year 2000*

| Subsector | Volume (metres cubed) | Value (IR£ m) | Direct Employment |
|---|---|---|---|
| *Sawmilling* | | | |
| Sawn Timber Products | 93,000 | 103 | 1,200 |
| *Board Manufacturing* | | | |
| OSB (projected) | 350,000 | 80 | 125 |
| Chipboard | 90,000 | 16 | 170 |
| MDF | 300,000 | 57 | 208 |
| Hardboard (projected) | 120,000 | 60 | 330 |

*Source:* Forbairt, Statistics, 1995.

In the past, growth in the timber industry was confined to timber production and processing of solid timber into intermediate products or wood fibres. The industry is well developed in these areas. The next stage of growth will be in the more value-added areas of manufactured wood-based end products. The processing or manufacturing linkage being created through ventures such as Masonite is seen as vital for sustained growth in this sector In addition, it will be necessary to increase both product and market diversity, and to develop niche markets.

### 4.2.5 The Craft Industry

This sector comprises many small-scale artisan-based enterprises in clothing, jewellery, textile-weaving, pottery, wood-turning, furniture-making and other related arts and crafts. It is a very important area of employment in rural and coastal areas, and in other areas where there is little manufacturing. It is estimated that there are 6,000 people employed full-time in the craft sector, with a further 10,000 involved in a part-time or seasonal capacity. The majority of the enterprises are one-person operations, although business and marketing co-operatives and clusterings, such as that around the Kilkenny area, are becoming critical to growth in rural or disadvantaged areas. Seventy-five per cent of the output from the craft industry is either exported or sold to visiting tourists. Value-added is very high in crafts, and indigenous raw materials are generally used. Worldwide demand for exclusive and distinctive quality craftwork is on the increase. Marketing and market development, as in many other traditional subsectors, is crucial for the further development of the craft industry in Ireland.

### 4.3 DRIVERS OF CHANGE IN TRADITIONAL INDUSTRIES

This section identifies and examines the key forces driving change in the traditional sector, and their effects on the sector. Each major subsector is addressed specifically. However, there are a few key forces which affect each subsector to varying degrees, which require a change in business definition for many of the firms involved, and which have serious implications for strategy in these firms. They are:

- Technological change (internal and external)

- Environmental concerns

- Changes in industry and market requirements

- Shifts in world trade and world production.

### 4.3.1 Drivers of Change in Paper, Printing and Packaging Industries

*Technological Change and World Class Business (WCB)*

The trend towards World Class Business (WCB) and Total Quality Management (TQM) is creating new and improved uses for information technology within paper and printing, through improving management and production control, database management systems, telecommunications and publishing technology such as electronic publishing. In addition, technological change outside the sector itself, including imaging, CD-ROM and electronic communications such as EDI and electronic banking, will all decrease the demand for hard-copy business forms, security printing and print media. (see Chapter Ten on operations management for a more developed discussion of the concepts of WCB and TQM).

*Environmental Issues*

Push and pull environmental factors are affecting the paper and printing markets. The "push" of environmental legislation is aimed at reducing the amount of packaging waste, while the "pull" of consumer concerns will influence printers and packaging manufacturers in their choice of processes and materials The *Grüne Punkt* system used in Germany, which promotes and organises recycling activities, is one example of how environmental standards are being used as a competitive weapon to achieve differentiation.

*Changes in Market Requirements*

The emergence of CD-ROM and Internet in the computer software industry reduces the need for paper-based computer manuals. In addition, the educational and lifestyle changes among end-consumers are changing the market requirements, as consumers become more accustomed to technology, colour print, and multi-media.

These drivers are creating threats to traditional Irish printers and packagers, but at the same time they are also providing opportunities — for firms that change their business definition and strategy — to create new competitive advantages. Opportunities exist, particularly in export markets, in direct mail, electronic publishing and multimedia, eco-labelling, computer-labelling substitutes, and in non-traditional industry areas.

### 4.3.2 Drivers of Change in the Clothing Sector

#### *Technology and WCM*
Computer-Aided Design and Computer-Aided Manufacturing (CAD/CAM) are becoming increasingly important in the areas of sewing, design, cutting and knitting. Production systems are evolving, away from the traditional Progressive Bundle System (PBS) towards quality management systems. Examples include the modular systems similar to Kan-Ban, which involve a high degree of teamwork, and Unit Production Systems (UPS), which involve a high degree of flexibility. In addition, the growing use of EDI by major multiple retailers in Ireland and abroad for all their information flows will have important implications for Irish clothing firms. In the future, Irish firms will have to be able to provide a fast response service with short-run ranges, using efficient production systems, and will also have to be able to increase the barriers to entry via technology (see Chapter Eight on strategy for a discussion of barriers to entry). Irish firms such as John A. Hickey, Rowear, Polimic and Elena Models are all well advanced in the adoption of these technologies.

#### *World Trade Organisation*
Shifts in world production are occurring at a time of change in world trade through the newly-formed World Trade Organisation (WTO), formerly GATT. The removal of the European Multi-Fibre

Agreement (MFA) is increasing competition for companies seeking to compete solely or primarily on the basis of price. Competition is now coming from South Korea, Hong Kong, Sri Lanka and Malaysia, and also from the Central and Eastern European countries. However, areas of competence and competitive advantage still exist for Irish firms in the UK and European markets, where they can benefit from closeness to the markets, niche marketing, flexibility and fast response.

### *Demographic/Psychographic Changes*
Fashion and lifestyle factors are constantly changing and at different rates in the various market regions. Combined with an increase in the levels of disposable income, consumers are seeking individuality through fashion, and this increases the demand for variety. The demand for variety leads to new market niches, which in turn create opportunities for companies that understand the market and can respond quickly with appropriate designs and product ranges.

### 4.3.3 Drivers of Change in the Textile Sector
The drivers of change in the textiles sector are similar to those in the clothing sector. They include changing technology and production systems, changing world production and trade patterns, and changing market requirements. The industry is also affected by environmental concerns and legislation covering synthetic fibres, dyeing, treating and finishing. The textile industry, which is very internationally traded, is influenced to a great extent by European exchange-rate fluctuations — an uncertainty that has affected Europe at various stages in the 1990s.

### 4.4 STRATEGIC CONSIDERATIONS FOR TRADITIONAL INDUSTRY IN IRELAND
It is difficult to group all of the traditional subsectors and to discuss them as a whole because of the variety of sectors and their scope. However, it is evident that most of the sectors are being affected by similar threats, be they economic, investment, competitive, technological or skills-related. Following the analysis of the various subsectors within traditional manufacturing, and the

drivers of change that are affecting the competitive situation, this section considers the strategic implications for Irish firms, under the following headings:

- The key strengths of traditional Irish industry
- The Key Success Factors (KSFs) for the future
- The core competencies fuelling sustainable competitive advantage, and the need for benchmarking against overseas competitors
- The strategic options for Irish firms.

### 4.4.1 Strengths and Key Success Factors (KSFs)

Traditional industries — in particular clothing, textiles and printing — share many factors that are critical for competitive success: the so-called key success factors. The most important KSFs for the traditional sectors are discussed below.

### *Product/Market Positioning*

It is vital that the firm is positioned in its product/market where it is possible to sustain its competitive advantage *vis-à-vis* western and eastern European firms, as well as those from third countries (product/market positioning is discussed in more detail in Chapter Eight on strategy). It is important to view this positioning from a long-term perspective, as fixed capital costs are generally high in traditional industry, and this creates high exit barriers and minimises short-term strategic flexibility. This is crucial for Irish firms who wish to follow niche strategies in value-added markets. An example would be Bailey's positioning of its liquor products on the global market.

### *Quality*

Quality assurance and quality management in all their guises offer the traditional Irish firm an opportunity to differentiate itself from low-cost competitors in newly industrialised or re-industrialising countries. Marginal improvements in quality can produce significant improvements in competitiveness. High quality has now become an essential requirement in all product markets, as a result of technological change, the need for economic efficiency, and changing customer expectations.

### Cost-Minimisation and Control
This is now an important element in all generic strategies. For commodity products, cost control is essential in achieving a low-cost manufacturing status and in competing against firms with lower wage costs and/or cost of capital. For differentiated products in niche markets, price is still very important and cost control is essential.

### Fast Response and Flexible Manufacturing
Responsiveness has become a crucial form of competitive differentiation for Irish firms *vis-à-vis* low-cost competitors. Whether the firms are operating in industrial or consumer markets, they are, in the main, selling to customers who, in turn, must react quickly to their own customers' demands. Fast response varies by traditional sector and subsector from 24 hours to 8 weeks, but in all cases there is pressure to reduce the time.

### Customer Service
As product and production quality have become standard in most of the mature markets, and will do so in most developing markets before the end of the century, the quest for newer forms of competitive advantage is increasing, and none more so than increasing customer service and its quality. High levels of before- and after-sales service are a vital part of any relationship-marketing strategy for traditional Irish firms. Chapter Nine on marketing strategy provides a more developed discussion of relationship marketing, while Chapter Ten on operations strategy looks at service quality.

### Design and Marketing
Where the technology for producing a certain type of product is fairly uniform throughout the industry, to be successful, firms need to acquire either a substantial level of technical expertise or strength in marketing. This means understanding end-user requirements, and how these requirements are evolving, being able to design and tailor the product through product development,

and being able to push the product through the channels by means of effective communications and distribution.

### 4.4.2 Growth Forecasts in Traditional Manufacturing

According to the ESRI, a rapid increase in output is forecast for most of the traditional industries for the rest of the decade, although clothing is expected to remain under pressure from low-cost producer countries. Table 4.6 outlines the growth trends in output and employment for all traditional industry to the year 2000. Despite technology improvements and productivity gains, employment is expected to rise substantially in these sectors. To ensure this, Irish firms will have to address the strategic issues already discussed.

*Table 4.7: Growth Forecasts in Traditional Industry*

| Year | Output Change on Previous Year (%) | Employment (000) |
|------|-----------------------------------|------------------|
| 1995 | +10 | 110 |
| 1996 | +7 | 114 |
| 1997 | +5 | 117 |
| 1998 | +4.5 | 119 |
| 1999 | +4 | 120 |
| 2000 | +4 | 121 |

*Source:* ESRI, *Medium Term Review 1994–2000*, 1994.

### 4.4.3 Core Competencies and Strategy

Given the strengths of Irish firms and the key success factors discussed above, it is clear that some core competencies or capabilities need to be developed to survive in traditional industries. The required competencies include:

• Competencies in product design and market positioning

• Competencies in manufacturing excellence

• Competencies in marketing and in integrating design, selling and relevant technical know-how into the firm's marketing.

Figure 4.1 graphically illustrates these required competencies.

***Figure 4.1: Core Competencies for Traditional-Sector Irish Firms***

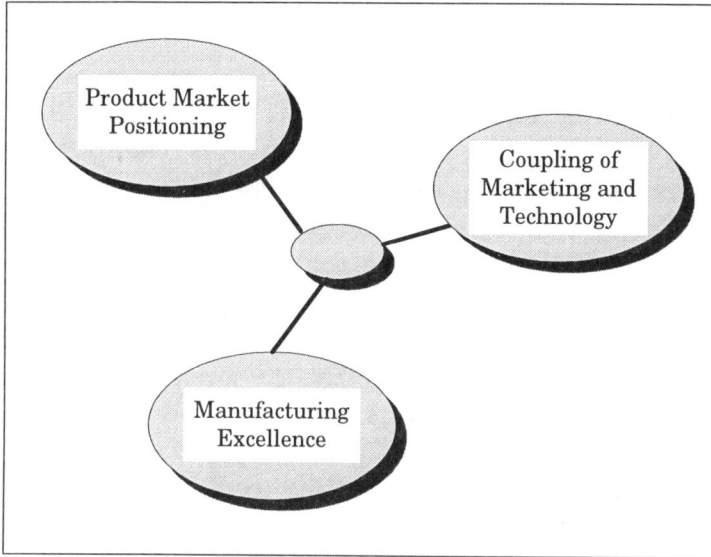

Firms within traditional industries require some level of competence in all of the areas, but in particular in the area of product/market development and positioning. As a result, three principal approaches to strategy will dominate traditional industries into the next century:

- An emphasis on market identification and the choice of strategic positioning within markets, coupled with an ability to respond with excellent product design

- A strong focus on manufacturing excellence aimed at providing excellent customer service with excellent quality at a competitive cost. This is important for all firms, but for producers of commodity-type products, as in most textile subsectors, it is vital.

- A strong focus on marketing excellence and related capabilities including product development, pricing, distribution, selling, promotion and customer service. This is vital in the case of companies manufacturing differentiated products, as in the case of most clothing subsectors.

For a more detailed discussion on strategy, see Chapter Eight.

## SUMMARY

This chapter has examined the traditional sectors of Irish industry, namely, Print, Paper and Packaging, Clothing, Textiles, Timber and Wood Processing, and Craft industries. Traditional industries in general are long established, are labour-intensive, face mature or declining markets and face high import penetration levels, while at the same time contributing to exports. Many traditional industries produce non-traded goods, and their location close to the market is their major competitive advantage. The 30 per cent of traditional firms that are foreign-owned, account for over 70 per cent of exports in these industries. The Irish-owned firms are generally small and family-owned.

The key drivers of change affecting traditional Irish industry in the 1990s include the following:

- **Technological Change and WCM**: The trend is towards the adoption of WCM and other technological changes within traditional industry.

- **Environmental Concerns**: Environmental legislation and consumer concern, particularly in the print, paper and packaging subsectors is changing both industry and consumer attitudes and is influencing the consumption of products.

- **Change in Market Requirements**: Technological and lifestyle changes, together with the use of information technology, are changing the way in which firms do business. This is having a profound effect on the print, paper and packaging industry where electronic media and Internet are replacing the traditional print media in some areas.

- **Shifts in World Trade and Production**: As international markets increasingly open up and become global under the influences of the GATT agreement, increased pressure is being placed on traditional Irish firms from low-cost producers in the

Far East and Eastern Europe. This has serious implications for policy and strategic development among traditional Irish firms.

The major threats to traditional industries include the lack of reinvestment, lack of scale economies, underinvestment in and underutilisation of technology, and the lack of skill resources compared with foreign competitors. Despite these threats, many traditional Irish firms possess some key strengths that can be developed and exploited as they strive to secure competitive positions in major European markets. The key strengths include:

- **Close Proximity/Fast Response/Flexible Manufacturing**: Closeness to the major export markets in Europe creates a competitive advantage in that Irish firms can compete through fast response. This, combined with new flexible manufacturing techniques, creates a potent competitive weapon, which it is difficult for low-cost producers from the Far East to match.

- **Design and Quality**: Many Irish firms in clothing and textiles in particular have developed high levels of design and quality, which are crucial for survival in their major markets. Included in this is the requirement for a high rate of product development to meet changing customer requirements. The next step will be for Irish firms to adopt the new production processes based on WCM and TQM.

- **Cost Minimisation and Control**: This has become essential even for niche market/differentiated products, and it is an area to which Irish firms have to pay particular attention if they are to become or remain competitive.

- **Marketing and Service Quality**: Many Irish firms have developed good skills in marketing and in customer service.

To prosper in the next century, traditional Irish firms will have to develop these strengths into the following core competencies:

- Competency in the development of new products required for the product markets addressed

- Competency in manufacturing excellence

- Competency in marketing and in integrating design, selling and relevant technical know-how into the firm's marketing mix.

---

## FURTHER READING

CSO, "Census of Industrial Production", Government Publications, 1992.

ESRI, *Medium Term Review 1994–2000*, Government Publications, 1994.

FÁS, Clothing Industry Sectoral Study Report, October 1991.

FÁS, Print & Paper Industry Sectoral Study Report, April 1994.

FÁS, Textile Industry Sectoral Study Report, Summer 1993.

CHAPTER FIVE

# RESOURCE-BASED INDUSTRY

*H* aving looked, in the previous chapter, at the changing role of traditional industry in Irish business, this chapter examines and analyses resource-based industries. This is a diverse area, covering not only the agricultural and agri-business system in Ireland, but also the areas of Forestry, Fishing, Mining, Turf and Natural Gas. As will be shown, by far the most important segment of this sector is food and drink. The following areas will be discussed with regard to resource-based industry:

- An overview of resource-based industries including an analysis of output and employment. A review of the agri-business system and the various agri-food subsectors, and an analysis of the Common Agricultural Policy (CAP)

- The Food, Drink and Tobacco (FDT) segment, including an analysis of output, employment, exports, imports and value-added in the FDT sector

- Other resource-based industries including forestry, fisheries, mining, turf and gas industries

- A review of the drivers of change in resource-based industries, including EU Policy on CAP/GATT; the effects of the Single European Market; Eastern Europe; the growing power of the multiples; technological innovation; environmental concerns and consumer trends

- The future for the food-processing industry and how to achieve growth, addressing issues such as marketing and distribution, product design and development, quality, technology, scale and finance.

[111]

## 5.1 OVERVIEW OF RESOURCE-BASED INDUSTRY

### 5.1.1 Definition, Output and Employment

Ireland has some significant natural resources which, in turn, provide the basis for further industrial development. These include:

- A climate favouring the production of milk and meat from grassland

- Sea fisheries and aquaculture

- Forestry

- Base metals in the form of lead and zinc

- Industrial minerals such as gypsum and barytes

- Turf from peat bogs

- Offshore natural gas at Kinsale.

The importance of these industries is summarised in Table 5.1.

*Table 5.1: Output, Employment and Exports in Resource-Based Industries in 1994*

| Sector | Estimated Output (IR£ m) | Estimated Employment | Estimated % of Output Exported |
|---|---|---|---|
| Agri-business (Agri-food Chain) | 6,237 | 200,000 | 60 |
| Fisheries | 149 | 15,470 | 85 |
| Forestry, Timber and Wooden Furniture | 378 | 7,580 | 15 |
| Mining | 95 | 776 | 85 |
| Turf | 276 | 4,388 | 10 |
| Gas | 140 | 1,029 | 0 |

*Source:* Authors' estimates.

It is evident from the figures above that agri-business is much bigger than any other natural resource-based areas in terms of national importance. For this reason, this chapter concentrates on the agri-business area.

### 5.1.2 The Agri-Business System
This section analyses the agri-business system in Ireland. It defines agri-business, examines the environment in which it exists, and looks at key aspects of the system, including food consumption, distribution, manufacturing and processing, farm production, farm inputs and supports.

### *Definition and Scope*
The term "agri-business" may be used to describe the food system from farm supplier to the ultimate consumer of food products. It was originally defined as " the sum total of all operations involved in the manufacture and distribution of farm supplies, production operations of the farm, and the storage, processing and distribution of farm commodities and items made from them". Defined in this way, agri-business represents a very important sub-system in the economic structure of virtually all countries. Globally, it employs 60 per cent of all the world's population, In the US, over 60 per cent of the total assets of all corporations and agriculture are invested in agri-business. The agri-business sector in the US accounts for about 25 per cent of employment, and consumers spend about 25 per cent of their expenditures on products produced by agri-business.

In Ireland, agri-business is the single most important sector of the economy, accounting for:

- 35 per cent of National Income

- 37 per cent of manufacturing industry output

- 30 per cent of exports

- 40 per cent of employment.

Although the agri-business system is an identifiable subsystem of the economy, it should be emphasised that it is totally integrated into the economy. A further important characteristic of the system is that it has its own political dimension, largely governed by the Common Agricultural Policy of the European Union.

In a very simplified form, the agri-business system may be portrayed as shown in Figure 5.1.

## *Figure 5.1: The Agri-Business System, 1994*

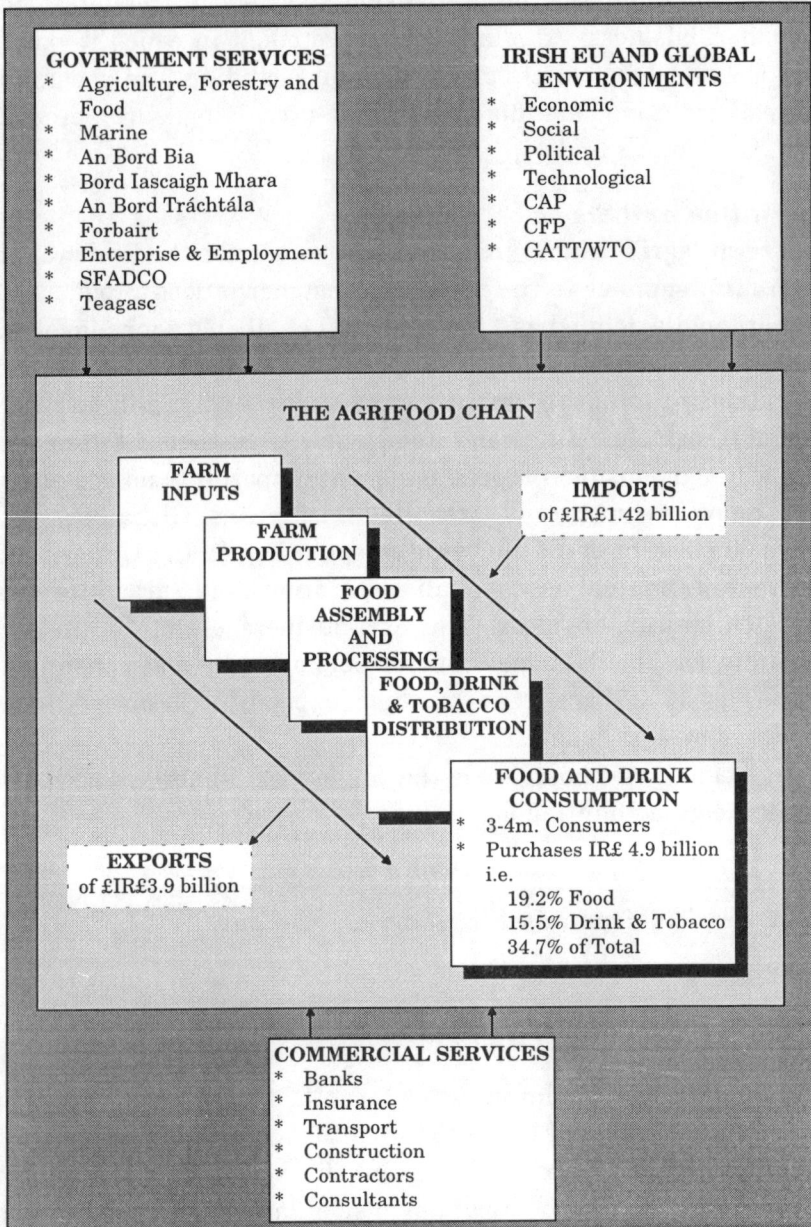

**GOVERNMENT SERVICES**
* Agriculture, Forestry and Food
* Marine
* An Bord Bia
* Bord Iascaigh Mhara
* An Bord Tráchtála
* Forbairt
* Enterprise & Employment
* SFADCO
* Teagasc

**IRISH EU AND GLOBAL ENVIRONMENTS**
* Economic
* Social
* Political
* Technological
* CAP
* CFP
* GATT/WTO

**THE AGRIFOOD CHAIN**

**FARM INPUTS**

**FARM PRODUCTION**

**FOOD ASSEMBLY AND PROCESSING**

**FOOD, DRINK & TOBACCO DISTRIBUTION**

**IMPORTS** of £IR£1.42 billion

**FOOD AND DRINK CONSUMPTION**
* 3-4m. Consumers
* Purchases IR£ 4.9 billion i.e.
  19.2% Food
  15.5% Drink & Tobacco
  34.7% of Total

**EXPORTS** of £IR£3.9 billion

**COMMERCIAL SERVICES**
* Banks
* Insurance
* Transport
* Construction
* Contractors
* Consultants

As can be seen, the central production function of the agri-business system is shown in the centre of the diagram, moving through the successive stages of transformation from inputs to food and drink consumption.

### The Broader Agri-business Environment

Because the Irish agri-business system exists within a broader framework, which encompasses the Irish national economy, the EU and the world economy, it is, therefore, greatly affected by the environmental forces that have their origins in these larger systems. Within the EU, the political economy of the agri-business system is dominated by the Common Agricultural Policy (CAP) and to a lesser extent by the Common Fisheries Policy (CFP). At a global level, trade in most food products is subject to trade agreements by the World Trade Organisation (WTO). The CFP relates to mechanisms to manage the supply and demand for fish within the EU. The CAP covers a much broader range of product areas of particular importance to Ireland. Within the EU, the CAP establishes the framework within which most agricultural products are produced and traded. It is, therefore, necessary for managers to understand the basic principles and aims of this policy. The CAP and the reform that is taking place are analysed below.

### Food Consumption

In Ireland, expenditure on food, drink and tobacco still represents a very significant proportion (almost 35 per cent) of total consumer expenditure, as shown in Table 5.2. While the overall demand for food is relatively static, it is evident that there are substantial changes taking place with regard to the variety and types of food consumed. As a result of a general tendency on the part of processors to enhance the convenience value of food through further preparation, most food products have a relatively short product life cycle, and this presents a continuing challenge for distributors and processors in the food chain.

### Distribution

The distribution of food and drink has become very concentrated in Ireland in recent years. Traditional wholesalers have become less important in the food chain — over 70 per cent of food is now distributed direct from the manufacturer to the retailer.

**Table 5.2: Personal Expenditure in the Food, Drink and Tobacco (FDT) Sector, 1985–92**

|                             | 1985   | 1989   | 1992   |
|-----------------------------|--------|--------|--------|
| Total Personal Expenditure  | 10,598 | 13,242 | 14,132 |
| Food as %                   | 22.7   | 19.4   | 19.2   |
| Drink as %                  | 13.1   | 12.4   | 11.9   |
| Tobacco as %                | 4.7    | 3.6    | 3.6    |
| Total FDT Ir£.              | 4,297  | 4,705  | 4,932  |
| Total FDT %                 | 40.5   | 35.4   | 34.7   |

*Note:*   Excluding Taxes.
*Source:*  FÁS, Food, Drink and Tobacco Sectoral Study Report, 1993.

Within the retail sector, the large multiples — Dunnes Stores, Quinnsworth, Superquinn, L&N and Roches Stores — control 55–60 per cent of grocery sales nationally. In Dublin, they account for 80–85 per cent of grocery sales. The multiples have not only concentrated the selling power in the chain, but as a result they have also acquired enormous buying power. This enables them to negotiate very favourable terms with suppliers/manufacturers and to squeeze margins and thus reduce prices paid to farmers and producers. Traditional independent grocery outlets have been put under pressure by the multiples, but many new small specialist-food retail shops are now emerging in areas such as delicatessen, health food, fruit and vegetables and confectionery, while the symbol groups such as Spar, Centra, Mace and Londis now control approximately 20 per cent of total retail sales.

This trend of multiple concentration is not unique to Ireland. As can be seen in Table 5.3, other European countries have similar trends, led by the UK with 80 per cent of retail distribution by the multiples. Such concentration of buying power presents Irish producers exporting to these countries with many problems of pricing and credit terms.

*Table 5.3: Percentage of Food Distribution by Type of Organisation in Europe, 1993*

| Country | Co-Op | Multiple | Symbol Group | Independent | Total |
|---------|-------|----------|--------------|-------------|-------|
| France  | 2     | 43       | 30           | 25          | 100   |
| UK      | 10    | 80       | —            | 10          | 100   |
| Germany | 5     | 40       | 50           | 5           | 100   |
| Ireland | —     | 55       | 24           | 21          | 100   |

*Source:* European Commission/Eurostat and National Statistics Offices.

### Manufacturing and Processing

Food processors, located in the middle of the food chain, have had a difficult time in recent years. Manufacturers, on the one hand, have been faced with the enormous purchasing power of the multiples and the continuous demands of consumers for cheaper prices; on the other hand, they have been faced with having to pay guaranteed prices to farmers for produce, much of which falls within the jurisdiction of the Common Agricultural Policy (CAP). The very large food companies such as Kellogg's, Heinz, Van Den Bergh and Nestlé have substantial bargaining power with the multiples in that they have well-established brand names which are demanded by the consumer. By comparison, most Irish food manufacturers are small, their branded products in general are limited to the Irish market, they do not have very strong brand equity and so do not have strong bargaining power with the multiples. Faced with the cost/price squeeze, Irish Food manufacturers have found it difficult to match their international competitors in investing in the necessary research and development to produce new products or to invest significant amounts of money in developing brands for international markets. Exceptions would include Kerrygold, Bailey's, and Poldy's.

### Farm Production

What makes the agri-business system particularly important to Ireland is that most of the raw material requirements are produced domestically. Table 5.4 shows that Irish expenditure as a percentage of sales is very high at 72 per cent.

**Table 5.4: Food, Drink and Tobacco Industry Expenditure, 1993**

|                                      | Total Food, Drink and Tobacco, 1993 | Change (%) 1987–93 | Change (%) 1992/1993 |
|--------------------------------------|:-----------------------------------:|:------------------:|:--------------------:|
| Wage Costs as % of Sales             | 9.0                                 | 3.5                | -2.4                 |
| Irish Raw Materials as % of Sales    | 47.2                                | 28.7               | 4.8                  |
| Irish Services as % of Sales         | 12.8                                | 43.5               | 10.3                 |
| Total Expenditure as % of Sales      | 72                                  | 28                 | 4.3                  |

*Source:* Forfás Irish Economy Expenditure Survey, 1993.

In the past, farmers typically sold their produce to processors on the open market. No prior contracts were made, and prices were negotiated on the spot. In response to the increasing need to co-ordinate supply and demand in the food chain, this old practice is now being replaced by contractual relationships between farmers and processors. In this system, prices are known in advance of delivery. Today, contractual relationships are the norm in the sugar beet, pea, potato, poultry, egg and mushroom industries. This trend has also seen the development of processors like Greencore through Comhlucht Siúcra Éireann in sugar, Monaghan and Walsh in mushrooms, and the Kerry Group in poultry.

This concentration of food processing has yielded larger processing firms with much greater purchasing power, giving them strong negotiating positions with farmers. In response, farmers have grouped together within their national organisations under commodity groupings, to negotiate prices with the processors. In the future, it can be expected that some very powerful groups will emerge to negotiate contracts and prices with individual processors.

### Farm Inputs
Farm inputs represent over 40 per cent of the sales value of farm

output, and thus play a very central role in the agri-business system. The major inputs are food, fertiliser, energy, seeds, agri-chemicals, veterinary products and various services. Advances in technology are yielding much improved farm inputs, and these can be expected to play a central role in further increasing the productivity of the system as a whole. Of particular relevance here are the developments in biotechnology, which are producing better products and more efficient conversion processes in a wide range of areas from better silage preservatives to specialist techniques in plant and animal breeding.

### Supports
The main production function of the food chain outlined in Figure 5.1 is supported by an array of government and commercial services. Many government departments are involved in the system and the agencies play a central role in providing development, training, education, advisory and scientific inputs. The key support agencies would include Forbairt, FÁS and Teagasc, in addition to the county development teams. An important programme in a rural sense would be the EU-funded LEADER programme, which promotes rural development, primarily in the areas of agri-food, crafts and tourism-related projects. Chapter Three gives a more detailed review of the state supports available to resource-based industries in Ireland.

### 5.1.3 The Agri-Food Sectors
Despite low levels of employment in agriculture, the Irish economy relies heavily on agriculture and its associated processing industries. The cattle and beef sector makes up nearly 40 per cent of total agricultural output, and the dairy sector over 30 per cent. The contribution of the Food and Drink sector to exports is very significant, accounting for 25 per cent of total exports in the early to mid-1990s. The largest segments in Irish agricultural export earnings are live cattle and beef, and dairy exports, both accounting for 5 per cent of total export earnings and 30 per cent of agricultural exports. Today, any agricultural economy is heavily dependent on low-cost production, and Ireland has a comparative advantage in that its climate and soil conditions are highly

conducive to inexpensive and efficient production of grass. However, this comparative advantage may disappear in the twenty-first century as East European countries become more efficient and South American producers gain increased access to the European market.

This section summarises the key output figures and trends for the following agri-food subsectors:

• Dairy

• Beef

• Pigmeat

• Sheepmeat

• Poultry and Eggs

• Cereals

• Horticulture.

### The Dairy Sector

The dairy area is a key agricultural segment not only within agribusiness but in the entire resource-based sector. One third (49,000) of the country's farms are involved in dairying. Over 60 per cent of milk producers have quotas of less than 20,000 gallons. Dairy cow numbers were 1.4 million in 1993, with an annual milk output of 5.26 billion litres and a raw material value in excess of £1 billion. The quota régime has reduced output by nearly 10 per cent since 1985. In addition, milk processing accounts for nearly 90 per cent of dairy output. This area has also been subject to change in that there has been a reduction in the number of milk processors during the 1990s, from 40 in 1990 to 34 in 1993. Today, the majority of manufacturing milk (70 per cent) is processed by the five largest firms: Kerry Group plc, Avonmore Group plc Waterford Foods Group plc, Golden Vale plc and Dairygold Co-operative. Butter manufacture now accounts for 64 per cent of manufacturing of whole milk, while the remainder is used mainly for the production of cheese, skimmed and whole milk powder, cream, butter oil and chocolate crumb.

## Table 5.5: Production of Irish Dairy Products, 1992–93

| Dairy Product | 1992 (000 tonnes) | 1993 (000 tonnes) |
|---|---|---|
| Butter | 133.6 | 127.5 |
| Cheese | 89.4 | 88.9 |
| Whole Milk Powder | 28.9 | 31.9 |
| Chocolate Crumb | 85.7 | 79.3 |
| Butter-oil | 8.4 | 8.8 |
| Cream | 15.6 | 15.8 |
| Skimmed Milk Powder | 126.3 | 131.6 |
| Casein and Caseinates | 40.1 | 35.5 |

*Source:* An Bord Bainne, 1994.

In addition to the problems related to the quota régime and the seasonality of supply, other problems include the following:

- Lack of scale which, through lack of financial strength, affects production costs, new product development and the ability to penetrate overseas markets

- Limited product range which can be readily stored and marketed over a period, resulting primarily from the seasonal supply of raw material

- Inefficient plant utilisation, again caused primarily by seasonality

- High milk assembly costs because of the structure of primary production

- Varying milk quality.

### The Beef Sector

As stated earlier, export earnings from live cattle and beef are significant in terms of total export earning and agricultural exports. The total cattle population in Ireland in the 1990s stands at approximately 7.2 million. The number of beef cows is

increasing (753,000 in 1992) to the detriment of dairy cows. The
sector directly employs nearly 4,900, not including contract
workers. The number of dairy cows is expected to drop to 1.28
million in 1999, while total cow numbers are expected to rise
slightly to 2.2 million over the same period. The production system is characterised by low output and low incomes. Direct
subsidies account for one third of the income of beef farmers, and
this dependence is forecast to increase with the CAP movement to
direct producer subsidies from product price support. Domestic
consumption at around 17kg per capita accounts for only 14 per
cent of net disposals, and the country has a self sufficiency ratio of
nearly 700 per cent. Cattle output is approximately 1.3 million or
38 per cent of gross agricultural output.

Beef production is highly seasonal, reaching peak during the
autumn. This seasonal pattern creates diseconomies at processing
and marketing levels. And this problem is being addressed
through the deseasonalisation premium. Much of the beef output
remains exported on the hoof or unprocessed. The processing of
beef is limited in the main to vacuum packing and basic freezing.
Mincemeat processing developments have been slow, as has
canning. Offal by-products are plentiful but also exported
unprocessed.

### The Pigmeat Sector

Pigmeat is one of the agricultural segments that has undergone
considerable change since the 1960s. From a predominantly
small-scale farmyard enterprise with many involved on a non-
intensive level, it has developed into a large-scale intensive
industry pursued by much fewer full-time operators. Approximately 85 per cent of production comes from around 6 per cent of
holdings. There are approximately 2,500 holdings with an average herd size of 400. The industry today has only 12 central
licensed slaughter plants, employing approximately 3,800 and
accounting for output valued at over £2,120 million in 1994, and
exports valued at nearly £190 million. Combined with the intensification and centralisation of the sector, much modernisation and
re-equipping has occurred: the primary processing sector now
holds a favourable competitive position compared to EU counterparts. In product terms, there has been a significant move away

from bacon production, which at one time predominated, towards pork and value-added processed products.

### The Sheepmeat Sector

Like other segments in agri-foods, sheepmeat production has grown rapidly in the 1990s in Ireland, from 64,000 tonnes in 1989 to over 100,000 tonnes in 1994. Ireland now accounts for approximately 9 per cent of total EU production. It is a particularly important form of agricultural production in disadvantaged areas. Approximately 53,000 farms are involved in sheep production, with total sheep numbers at 9.1 million head and ewe numbers at 4.6 million. Sheep output value has decreased in the 1990s from very high levels in the late 1980s (approximately 150 million in 1993). The processing industry comprises two distinct groups: the meat-export premises, licensed to slaughter for the export market and trade in fresh/frozen meat; and the domestic slaughter-houses, catering exclusively for the domestic market. Total slaughterings are approximately 4.4 million, with per capita consumption at 8.5 kg, which means that Ireland has a self-sufficiency ratio of nearly 350 per cent.

### The Poultry and Egg Sectors

Over the years, the egg segment has not grown as quickly as the poultry (fowl, turkey, ducks). Nevertheless, taken together in 1994, the value of poultry and egg output was approximately £130 million — or 4 per cent of gross agricultural output. This production is broken down as follows:

|             | %  |
|-------------|----|
| Fowl        | 51 |
| Turkey      | 27 |
| Eggs        | 18 |
| Ducks, etc. | 4  |

Total poultry numbers are nearly 12 million, while poultry volume output has grown much faster than value output, 60 million tonnes and £106 million respectively. Output of eggs is nearly 600 million and valued at £24 million. Exports of poultrymeat and live poultry account for 1.5 per cent of total agricultural exports. Consumption per capita is nearly 24kg, which is the highest in the

EU. There are 16 approved slaughterhouses, 6 approved cutting premises, and 18 approved export poultrymeat establishments in Ireland. The market has reoriented away from cooked product, which, in combination with the threat of imports, has shifted investment. As already mentioned, the egg sector has not grown as quickly as the poultry area. In addition, per capita consumption of eggs is the lowest in the EU. Today, the output of eggs is £600 million approximately, valued at £24 million, and while an egg-products processing plant in the early 1990s has allowed the development of a wide range of products for the catering and industrial sectors, with high hygiene and health standards, Irish producers have not succeeded in developing any sustainable presence in export markets.

### The Cereals Sector

Total cereal production is approximately 2 million tonnes and accounts for over 5 per cent of gross agricultural output and nearly 1.5 per cent of total EU cereal production. About 25 per cent of this is retained for farm feeding purposes. The remainder is used as follows

|                           | %   |
|---------------------------|-----|
| Compound Feeding-stuffs   | 33  |
| Exports                   | 20  |
| Food                      | 7   |
| Home Malting              | 7   |
| Industry and Seeds        | 3   |
| Intervention              | 30  |

Exports are valued at approximately £85 million. Twenty-three thousand farms are involved in cereal production, and 6 per cent of these own less than 10 hectares. The area sown to wheat, barley and oats in 1992 was 92,700, 211,200 and 16,800 hectares respectively. There was a 9 per cent reduction in the area sown to cereals between 1987 and 1992. There are 352 grain preparation and assembly points, 258 of which are owned by merchants or independent operators, the rest by co-operatives. The compound foodstuffs sector is highly fragmented, with 101 firms manufacturing compound foodstuffs, mineral mixtures and milk-replacers.

Thirty-three firms account for 85 per cent of production. There are 41 registered seed assemblers, based mainly in the traditional cereal-growing areas, although the smaller assemblers are being pushed out because of inadequate and outdated plant and machinery and insufficient storage facilities

### The Horticultural Sector

This segment includes fruit, vegetables, indoor crops such as tomatoes, lettuce and mushrooms, and also flowers and plants. Including potatoes, this sector accounts for 5.5 per cent of total agricultural output and is valued at nearly £185 million. This output is broken down as follows:

|                  | %  |
| ---------------- | -- |
| Fresh Vegetables | 54 |
| Potatoes         | 30 |
| Fresh Fruit      | 7  |
| Other            | 9  |

Output has increased dramatically in this sector in the 1990s, mainly as a result of the growth in mushroom exports to the UK. In addition, there has been significant growth in the re-exporting of fruits, mainly bananas. Total exports are valued at over £70 million and imports are valued at £242 million. Ireland's self-sufficiency in fresh fruit is only 15 per cent, although, as mentioned above, we are a major re-exporter. There are approximately 140 wholesalers servicing the retail trade, although this is dominated by a few firms, in line with retail domination by the multiples. Much of the soft-fruit production is destined for processing. Apart from the mushroom sector, grower organisation is quite weak, and greater emphasis needs to be placed on the concentration of supply, quality control and market servicing by producer organisations

### 5.1.4 The Common Agricultural Policy (CAP)

At the Stresa conference in July 1958, several proposals were put forward for a Common Agricultural Policy. These were later adopted in December 1960. The CAP is guided by three main principles:

- **Single Market**: The concept of the single market is intended to guarantee easy movement of goods within the Community, free of tariffs and other barriers. Associated with this is the concept of protecting this internal market from a flood of imports.

- **Community Preference**, in all market regulations, to members' products. Extra Community imports are controlled as necessary. Import levies and quotas ensure that the community imports few of those products which it can produce internally.

- **Financial Solidarity**: The Community must strive for financial solidarity and joint responsibility of members in undertakings in the agricultural sector. The cost of the policy must be borne equally by members.

In addition, all Community policy must honour its world trade commitments, such as those which exist under GATT via the WTO. The Community encounters a number of obstacles that must be overcome. Currency fluctuations have in the past militated against the objective of a single market. Furthermore, technological advances, particularly in the dairy sector, are resulting in higher productivity, and a trend towards more highly intensive milk production.

### Structure and Mechanism of CAP
In organising the CAP, the Commission is chiefly concerned with:

- Putting ceilings on the supply of agricultural products by member countries

- Supporting market prices in the Community, so that everything that is produced will be consumed, while farm incomes will not fall excessively

- Promoting reorganisation of existing structures where necessary to ensure a future inherent stability

- Financing these measures.

The large sums needed to pay for the above measures are sourced through the European Agricultural Guidance and Guarantee

Fund (EAGGF or FEOGA). This fund is allocated from the Community's total budget, and in 1993 the fund accounted for 54 per cent of the total Community budget, down from 72 per cent in 1985. The guarantee section of FEOGA comprises refunds on exports to non-member countries, intervention on the internal market (in terms of subsidies, premia and intervention buying), and payment of compensatory amounts which are temporary measures to create price parity of agricultural products when traded internally between member states. Two types of compensatory amount exist: accession compensatory amounts for newcomers to the Union, and Monetary Compensation Amounts (MCAs) including export levies and import subsidies.

The Guidance section of FEOGA administers Community funds for structural policy schemes. These schemes are mostly planned and implemented on a decentralised basis, in collaboration with the member states. As a general rule, the Community contributes 25 per cent of the expenditure for structural-policy measures. In special circumstances, and for the most disadvantaged areas of the EU, it can contribute up to 65 per cent of total expenditure. The milk quota system has been introduced to eliminate oversupply in the sector, which has occurred over the past 20 years because of increased productivity and intensification.

### Review and Outlook for CAP

In 1993, Ireland received £1,408 million from the FEOGA Guarantee and Guidance funds. This was equivalent to 5 per cent of GNP in 1993. In response to the continuing problems of overproduction of the major farm commodities, and the increasing cost of financing surplus production, the CAP has been subject to significant reform. Upper limits have been set on the CAP budget and milk quotas are now established, and other surplus areas are being addressed. The trends in EU funding are shown in Table 5.6 below.

The main aim of CAP reform has been to replace the different régimes for arable crops with a more unified framework of supports. Emphasis is placed on lowering product prices to world market levels, compensating producers for price reductions by per hectare payments, penalising larger producers, and finally controlling supply by means of set-aside and manipulation of price compensation. Two million hectares have been taken out of production, out of the 40 million hectares in grain and oil seeds, mostly from the 35 million hectares in cereals. The main member states to be affected by set-aside are France, Germany, Denmark and, to a lesser extent, the UK.

**Table 5.6: Trends in EU Funding, 1987–93 (ECU million)**

|                | 1987   | 1990   | 1993   |
|----------------|--------|--------|--------|
| Total Budget   | 43,990 | 57,241 | 52,410 |
| Agriculture    | 26,860 | 28,860 | 28,040 |
| % of Total     | 61.1   | 50.4   | 53.5   |

Source: *Ireland: A Region of the European Commission,* European Commission, 1994.

## 5.2 THE FOOD, DRINK AND TOBACCO SECTOR

### 5.2.1 General Description, Output and Employment

This section analyses in detail the Food, Drink and Tobacco (FDT) sector. As shown in Figure 5.1, the FDT sector is part of the agri-food chain. The FDT processing sector accounts for 37 per cent of the total output of the manufacturing industry, and food and drink exports represent 27 per cent of total exports., The breakdown of output indices in the food industry by product area between 1990 and 1993 is shown in Table 5.7 below. It is clear that major growth in output has occurred in three areas, meat products, chocolate/confectionery and other foods, which would include cola concentrate, fish and fruit and vegetables.

Table 5.8 shows the trend in employment between 1987 and 1993. Between 1987 and 1992, output growth came about as a result of increased productivity, reducing employment, resulting in increased efficiency. Since 1992, employment has been growing substantially in certain sectors, mainly fuelled by a growth in demand for exported Irish produce.

There are a few very important points to be made relating to the figures in Tables 5.7 and 5.8. First, the meat and dairy sectors

**Table 5.7: Output in the FDT Sectors, 1990–93 (1985 = 100)**

| Products | 1990 | 1991 | 1992 | 1993 |
|---|---|---|---|---|
| *Food Products:* | *130.9* | *136.5* | *149.1* | *156.7* |
| Meat Products | 134.4 | 151.3 | 156.7 | 151 |
| Dairy Products | 100.4 | 99.6 | 102.8 | 105.4 |
| Sugar Chocolate and Confectionery | 125.1 | 129.5 | 137.6 | 131.1 |
| Bread, Biscuits and Flour | 76.9 | 72.5 | 70.1 | 70.4 |
| Grain Milling and Animal Feed | 111.1 | 115.1 | 123.4 | 129.3 |
| Other Food | 174.2 | 182.4 | 212.9 | 237.3 |
| *Drink* | *124.7* | *130.1* | *128.1* | *130.1* |
| *Tobacco* | *86.9* | *94* | *99.3* | *90.7* |

*Note:* Other Food includes Cola Concentrate, Fish, Fruit and Vegetables.
*Source:* CSO Statistics.

**Table 5.8: Employment in the FDT Sectors, 1987–94**

| Products | 1987 | 1992 | 1993 | % Change 92/93 |
|---|---|---|---|---|
| *Total Food* | *37,019* | *35,900* | *37,100* | *3.3* |
| Meat Products | 9,578 | 11,700 | 11,600 | -0.85 |
| Dairy Products | 7,532 | 7,100 | 6,900 | -2.8 |
| Sugar Chocolate & Confectionery | 4,326 | 4,400 | 4,000 | -9.1 |
| Bread, Biscuits and Flour | 6,677 | 5,300 | 5,500 | 3.8 |
| Grain Milling and Animal Feed | 3,025 | 2,700 | 2,500 | -7.4 |
| Other Food | 5,881 | 4,700 | 6,600 | 40.4 |
| *Drink* | *5,381* | *4,600* | *5,600* | *21.7* |
| *Tobacco* | *1,745* | *1,300* | *1,200* | *-7.7* |
| Total FDT | 44,145 | 41,800 | 43,900 | 6 |

*Source:* CSO Statistics.

combined account for over 55 per cent of total output and almost
49 per cent of food employment. Second, the areas which have
shown any significant increase in volume output since 1990 are
meat, drink and "other foods", which includes cola concentrate
produced by Coca-Cola in Drogheda and Pepsi Cola in Cork. The
cola concentrate is by and large exported. Third, employment is in
decline in nearly every sector, with the exception of bread, other
foods and drink.

## 5.2.2 FDT Exports and Imports

An examination of FDT trade statistics in Table 5.9. shows that
the major export sectors are meat and meat products (live and
processed), dairy and drink sectors. Other sectors of the food industry are primarily focused on the domestic market.

*Table 5.9: Irish FDT Trade Statistics, 1992 (IR£ m)*

| Products | Exports | % of Total | Imports | % of Total | Balance of Trade |
|---|---|---|---|---|---|
| Meat and Meat Products | 1,026 | 26.2 | 112 | 7.9 | 914 |
| Dairy Products | 1,003 | 25.6 | 73 | 5.2 | 930 |
| General Food | 893 | 22.8 | 104 | 7.3 | 789 |
| Drink | 339 | 8.7 | 160 | 11.3 | 179 |
| Fish and Fish Products | 175 | 4.5 | 48 | 3.4 | 127 |
| Coffee, Tea, Cocoa, Spices | 141 | 3.6 | 113 | 8.0 | 28 |
| Cereals and Preparations | 101 | 2.6 | 209 | 14.8 | -108 |
| Sugar and Sugar Preparations | 69 | 1.8 | 78 | 5.5 | -9 |
| Fruit and Vegetables | 70 | 1.8 | 242 | 17.1 | -172 |
| Animal Foodstuffs | 55 | 1.4 | 228 | 16.1 | -173 |
| Tobacco | 37 | 0.9 | 46 | 3.3 | -9 |
| Other | 4 | neg. | 2 | neg. | 2 |
| Total | 3,913 | 100 | 1,415 | 100 | 2,498 |

*Source:* CSO Trade Statistics.

It is clear that the main resource base of the Irish FDT industry exists in the meat and dairy sectors, and to a lesser extent in the drinks and fish sectors. Despite being limited in volume terms by EU policy, the dairy, meat and fish sectors offer the best opportunities for further development through increasing the amount of value added to the basic commodity products. It should be pointed out, however, that there are some examples of brand names that are well known internationally: Kerrygold Butter, Cadbury's Chocolate, Guinness Stout, Bailey's Irish Cream Liqueur, Bushmills and Jameson Whiskey, for example.

### 5.2.3 Value-Added in the FDT Sector

In Ireland, gross value-added per employee in food processing is significantly below the European average, and well below the average in other Irish manufacturing sectors, in particular modern industries. This reflects the fact that the Irish food industry is still very much at a commodity stage of development. This is particularly true in the case of major product areas such as meat, dairy and fish. Commodity products would include Skimmed Milk Powder (SMP), sides of beef and block frozen mackerel, whereas value-added examples would be ambient ready meals, packaged soups, yoghourts and fromage frais.

There are many reasons why these sectors have depended mainly on commodity products, and these must be understood prior to discussing the need to add more value to the basic raw materials. The best focus for this discussion might be a comparison of the factors which favour the production of commodity products with those which simultaneously militate against added value or consumer-ready products (see Table 5.10 below).

It is obvious from the list in Table 5.10 that there are some very compelling reasons why Irish food processors have remained primarily in commodity products. The relatively low cost of being a commodity producer, combined with the considerable support mechanisms for commodity products in the past, has resulted in the Irish food sector being characterised as one using low-tech inputs in the production of commodity-type products, sold to other processors outside Ireland, in wholesale or international markets, and earning relatively stable, if low, profit margins. In addition, the concentration of purchasing power of multiples in Ireland, the UK and Europe means, as explained earlier, that only well-financed producers can penetrate these markets. Finally, the competition for shelf-space in Europe's multiples is intense, particularly from multinational firms like Unilever, General Foods, Heinz and Nestlé.

*Table 5.10: Factors Facilitating Commodity Production*

| Factors Facilitating Commodities | Factors Militating Against Value-added |
|---|---|
| Peak seasonal supplies resulting in longer-term storage requirements | Requires year-round production to serve year round markets |
| Small size of Irish market means 80–90% of output is exported | The Irish market is very small to support significant investment |
| Export markets are very large and relatively stable for most commodity products | Market segments tend to be small, specialised and not as easy to serve. |
| Markets are easier to serve | Marketing costs are generally high |
| Markets are very flexible | Markets once chosen are not flexible |
| Markets are not very disciplined | Markets are very disciplined |
| Processing costs are low | Processing costs are high, requiring substantial investment |
| Products have been supported by EU policy in the past | Products could be sold into intervention in the past |
| Strong political support for farmers' incomes via prices for commodities | Much less political support for value-added products and processing in general |
| Management knows this business | Management does not know this business very well |
| Profits have been all right | Profits are riskier |

## 5.3 OTHER RESOURCE-BASED INDUSTRIES

This section looks beyond the food and drink sector and analyses the other key resource-based industries in Ireland. The industries to be analysed are:

- Forestry

- Fisheries

- Mining

- Turf

- Gas.

### 5.3.1 Forestry
In Ireland, some 5 per cent of the land — or nearly 1 million acres — is covered by forest. Seventy-seven per cent of the forests consist of softwood such as Sitka spruce and lodgepole pine. Ninety per cent of these forests are owned by the state through Coillte Teo, the semi-state agency. In fact, Coillte is the most asset-rich of all the semi-state companies, with assets of IR£803 million in 1993. Government Policy, with European Union assistance and pension-funds investments, has resulted in new private plantations being developed at a rate of 8,800 acres per annum (1994). Most of the hardwood forests, consisting of oak, elm and ash, are privately owned.

In 1993, the output of timber was 1.85 million cubic metres, of which 0.56 million cubic metres consisted of wood suitable for construction and some joinery, and boxwood which is used to manufacture pallets and crates. Further downstream, processing in forest products is conducted by Medite of Clonmel and by Louisiana Pacific in Co. Galway.

As a result of significant post-war planting and downstream investment, Ireland is close to becoming a net exporter of timber, and it is estimated that some £40 million of the £100 million of timber imports can be replaced by home-grown produce.

### 5.3.2 Fisheries
The sea-fishing industry is governed by the EU Common Fisheries Policy (CFP), which, in its efforts to manage the scarce supplies of fish, has imposed quotas on the various species that may be caught by individual member countries. There are nearly 15,500 people employed either full-time or part-time in the Fishing industry (see Table 5.11) with nearly 50 per cent employed in

Fishing Vessels. However, most of the fleet is small in scale and old. The recent addition of the *MV Veronica*, with an ability to process off-shore 3,500 tonnes of fish, is a welcome development. Approximately 255,000 tonnes of sea-fish are currently landed by Irish vessels, valued at approximately £100 million. Herring and Mackerel account for some 76 per cent of the volume of fish landed, and 35 per cent of this is simply block frozen and exported. Prime fish such as sole, plaice and whiting are available for processing only after the fresh market has been satisfied. Some shellfish such as prawns and crabs are processed, but in most cases, such as lobster, the premium market is the fresh market.

**Table 5.11: Employment in the Fishing Industry**

| Sector | Number Employed |
|--------|-----------------|
| Fishing Vessels | 7,700 |
| Aquaculture | 2,610 |
| Fish Processing | 3,400 |
| Ancillary | 1,760 |
| Total | 15,470 |

*Source*: Department of the Marine, "Ireland: Facts about Fishing", 1994.

The fish processing industry consists of some 120 firms including fishery co-operatives. They are mostly small and concentrated in Donegal, Dublin and the Wexford/Waterford area. The output of the processing industry is about £178 million and some 85 per cent of this is exported, mainly as commodity products. Most of the value-added processing consists of smoking. Letts and Co. in Wexford has developed consumer-ready recipe-type fish products for export to the UK and France and Italy. France is the most important export market for Irish products (29 per cent) followed by Spain (21 per cent) and Germany (11.2 per cent).

Ireland's western coastline is very suited to aquaculture, and the ceiling on fish supplies as a result of EU quotas has triggered significant investment in salmon-arming off the west coast. The output of aquaculture is in the region of 30,000 tonnes, valued at nearly £41 million. This represents significant growth from 1980, when volume production was only 5,753 tonnes, valued at £1.9 million. A large investment by Carrolls plc in the 1980s helped to develop a market, particularly for smoked salmon. However, its takeover by Rothmans brought with it a divestment away from aquaculture.

### 5.3.3 Mining

Ireland has significant deposits of base metals in the form of lead and zinc. Between 1956 and 1970, some 25 million tonnes of lead and zinc ore were mined at Tynagh, Silvermines and Gortdrum before the limited resources were exhausted. In 1970, a significant deposit of lead and zinc was discovered at Navan and mined by Tara Exploration, which is controlled by a Finnish mining company Otokompu. The concentrates are exported for smelting. It should be noted that it was not economically viable to establish a smelter in Ireland because of worldwide overcapacity and planning objections on environmental grounds. In 1986, a further deposit of lead and zinc concentrates was discovered at Galmoy in Co. Kilkenny by Conroy Exploration, now Arcon plc. Planning permission was given to proceed with a mining operation in 1994.

In addition to the base metals, Ireland also has some deposits of industrial minerals. Gypsum is mined in Cavan by Gypsum Industries, a subsidiary of British Plaster plc, and is used in the manufacture of plasterboard, plaster of Paris, cement and fertilisers. Silica is mined in Cavan for the manufacture of glass. Quartz is also mined in small quantities in Achill, and Calcite, which is used for ornamental chippings, is mined in Clare.

### 5.3.4 Turf

Ireland is one of several countries that possesses significant resources of peat bog. Other countries include Russia, Finland, Scotland and the USA. They are a major national resource, which to date has been used primarily as a source of fuel for the generation of electricity, which accounts for over 45 per cent of peat output. Bord na Móna, established as a semi-state in the 1930s, is responsible for the development of Irish peat bogs and has

220,000 acres of bog under its control in 19 centres, employing nearly 2,500 people. A further 16,000 acres are harvested by private sources. The ESB takes just under 3 million tonnes of milled peat for electricity generation, 482,000 tonnes are manufactured into briquettes, and 1.1 million cubic metres of moss peat is produced for the horticultural industry, the bulk of output being exported. In addition to Bord na Móna, private bog developments contribute over 660,000 tonnes of sod peat, mainly for domestic consumption.

While the exploitation of peat in the midlands has contributed substantially to the economic development of the area, peat became uneconomic as a primary source of fuel for electricity generation. However, Bord na Móna has proposed to develop a new high-tech peat-fired power station, subject to government approval. It has developed value-added horticultural and environmental products, such as briquettes and, in particular, peat moss for use in nurseries and gardens. By the end of the century, some 20,000–30,000 acres of cutaway bog will be available for other use — all the peat having been removed. Much work remains to be done to determine the optimum use of this resource. Possible uses include forestry, pastureland, nursery stock, vegetables and biomass.

### 5.3.5 Gas

To date, only two commercial finds of natural gas have been discovered in Ireland. The most recent discovery was made in 1971 by Marathon, 30 miles offshore in 300 feet of water off Kinsale Head. Gas reserves have been estimated at 1.5 billion cubic feet. The gas was brought ashore in 1978 at a cost of £250 million, and some 75 per cent of the reserve has now been utilised. Natural gas now supplies about 25 per cent of Ireland's energy needs and is worth over £250 million to the country's balance of payments. Under an agreement with the state, Marathon sells the natural gas to Bord Gáis Éireann, which takes over the responsibility for the supply once it is onshore. BGE serves the major urban regions of Dublin, Cork, Waterford, Carlow, Dundalk Drogheda and Limerick, and is steadily moving into the rural areas. It also sells gas directly to some major industrial users, including the ESB, NET,

Irish Distillers, Irish Biscuits, Guinness and Cement Roadstone plc. The second smaller gas field was discovered in 1988, also by Marathon, in Ballycotton, Co. Cork. However, it is expected that the reserves of both fields will be exhausted by the end of the century. BGE has planned for this eventuality by constructing a pipe line to the UK, thus connecting into a natural-gas grid that covers most of Europe.

## 5.4 DRIVERS OF CHANGE IN RESOURCE-BASED INDUSTRIES

The Irish agri-business macro business system is influenced by worldwide driving forces. This section looks at the forces driving change, with a focus on the changes affecting the agri-business sector. The main drivers can be grouped as follows:

- EU policy on CAP /GATT

- Effects of the Single European Market

- The emergence of Eastern European producers

- The growing power of the multiples

- Technological innovation

- Environmental concerns

- Consumer trends.

### 5.4.1 EU Policy on CAP and GATT

The Irish food industry has traditionally been overdependent on the intervention system and the export refund mechanism of the CAP, particularly in the beef and dairy industry sectors. Ireland is much more dependent than any other EU country on CAP. This situation is unlikely to exist in the medium term, with the continual demand for CAP reform. The MacSharry reforms of 1991 were one of the main forces driving CAP reform in the 1990s. The objective was to ease budgetary pressure and reduce dependence on intervention.

The main thinking behind the reform of the system was that as it stood it tended to encourage intensive and efficient production

(20 per cent of farmers producing 80 per cent of output) of large quantities of unrequired foodstuffs. The overdependence on price support is being broken and replaced with income supplements targeted preferentially at smaller farmers, in combination with a set-aside policy. Agriculture in Ireland is far less intensive than in the UK, France and Germany, and therefore not affected as much by set-aside. The main changes in price and quota support as outlined in the MacSharry reforms are outlined in Table 5.12.

*Table 5.12: EU Quota and Price Support Changes*

| Sector | Change | Main Effects |
|---|---|---|
| Cereals | Reduction in price by 29 per cent | Cost of animal feeds reduced — knock on effects |
| Milk | 1% p.a. Quota reduction to 1994<br><br>2.5% price reduction to 1994 | Reduced Flexibility<br><br>Increased Competition |
| Beef | 15% reduction in price between 1993/96<br><br>Lowering of intervention safety net<br><br>Direct payments for less intensive production | Forecast net prices lower by 30 per cent in 1995 than in 1992.<br><br>Low-quality product taken off the market |
| Sheepmeat | Direct payments for less intensive production | Low-quality product taken off the market |

There is no doubting that the system which has evolved has to be changed further. Nevertheless, a reformed system, which ultimately supports extensive rather than intensive farming, and which penalises efficient high-quality production, will have a long-term detrimental effect on the Irish food-processing industry. It is imperative that the Irish food industry invests in developing value-added products. Future competitive advantage for Irish agri-business lies in successful development of products for the commercial and final-consumer markets.

## 5.4.2 Effects of the Single European Market

The open borders and open access of the EU are resulting in increased competition as food companies extend the scale and geographical scope of their businesses. This push towards scale economies has accelerated the number of acquisitions, mergers and alliances occurring in Europe. Many multinational companies have acquired Irish-based concerns including:

- Irish Distillers (Pernod Ricard)

- Irish Biscuits (BSN)

- HB Ice Cream (Van Den Bergh/Unilever)

- Rowntree Mackintosh (Nestlé)

- Poldy's Foods (Northern Foods)

- Emmett's Cream (Grand Metropolitan plc).

In addition, the major Irish food PLCs and Co-ops are all involved in acquisition activity, in particular in Europe, the UK and Northern Ireland. The Kerry Group is buying food ingredients companies like DCA in the USA. Avonmore acquired a processing plant outside Budapest in Hungary, Golden Vale acquired Leckpatrick Dairies in Northern Ireland and Volk in Holland, and Waterford Foods purchased Heald in Manchester in the UK. Scale allows companies such as these to achieve economies in many areas, including manufacturing costs, new product development, logistics, brand development, information technology and bargaining power with buyers and suppliers. It can be reasonably assumed that consolidation and globalisation of the food industry will continue in Ireland, as it will in other European countries. However, the dependence on commodity products still remains a problem.

## 5.4.3 Emergence of Eastern European Countries

As mentioned in Chapter Two, Eastern European countries are forecast to become major low-cost producers in agri-business, as new economic and farming systems replace the inefficient systems of collective farming. This has serious implications for the Irish Food Industry, which is overdependent on low value-added production. In the long term, as the economic well-being of these countries improves, substantial new markets for Irish produce will open up. However, it appears that the European food multi-nationals, and not Irish firms, are in the best position to avail of these opportunities.

### 5.4.4 Growing Power of the Multiples

The trend towards consolidation in the European food-processing industry is being paralleled in the retail industry. Independent retailers are being pushed out of the market by the larger mul-tiples and the symbol groups. In addition, trans-European buyer groups (such as Spar) are being formed to concentrate purchasing power when dealing with the multinationals such as Nestlé and Unilever (Van Den Bergh). Moreover, own-label and private-label growth like Cott's of Canada, imitating Coca-Cola in Europe, diminishes brand equity and increases retailer power in Europe and the USA. The electronic exchange of information, fuelled by EPOS and EDI will become a requirement for business dealing in the future. The overall effect will be: increased relative power over manufacturers; increased pressure on supplier margins; in-creased retailer control over forward stocks; and increased in-volvement of retailers in manufacturers' sales and marketing strategies.

### 5.4.5 Technological Innovation

The focus on World Class Manufacturing (WCM) and Total Quality Management (TQM) affects the food industry in terms of innovation and advancement in raw-materials testing, quality control and process, and packaging efficiency. The effect of this is potential value added, a wider variety of goods, and increases in capital investment for those who embrace technology or those who can afford or who have access to it.

### 5.4.6 Environmental Concern and Legislation

Linked to the increased emphasis on WCM and TQM is the focus on the environment, waste reduction and recycling. Current en-vironmental pressure, mainly through EU legislation, but also from lobby groups and political parties like the Greens, is focused

on minimising the material content of packaging, maximising re-
cyclability, increasing product traceability through the food chain
and managing effluent control. For example, it is difficult selling
into German supermarkets such as Aldi unless the product is
marked with the *Grüne Punkt* (the green dot) showing that 80 per
cent of the packing material is recyclable. These pressures have
serious implications for both large and small-scale food producers
in Ireland, but also provide opportunities to exploit Ireland's
"green" image.

## 5.5 THE FUTURE OF THE FOOD-PROCESSING INDUSTRY

As explained earlier in the chapter, the food-processing sector has
undergone radical reorganisation in the 1980s and the first half of
the 1990s. However, there is still spare capacity in the industry.
Some further rationalisation and consolidation can be anticipated
to the turn of the decade. According to the ESRI, the volume of
agricultural output will only grow marginally through the 1990s
(see Table 5.13) as a result of CAP reform.

*Table 5.13: Forecast Growth in Food Processing
Manufacturing, 1993–2000*

| Year | Output<br>% Change per Annum | Employment |
|------|------------------------------|------------|
| 1993 | 5 | 38,000 |
| 1994 | 6 | 35,000 |
| 1995 | 2 | 34,000 |
| 1996 | 2 | 34,000 |
| 1997 | 2 | 33,000 |
| 1998 | 2 | 32,000 |
| 1999 | 2 | 32,000 |
| 2000 | 2 | 31,000 |

*Source:* ESRI, *Medium Term* Review, 1994.

The ESRI forecasts output growth to stabilise at less than 2 per cent per annum after 1995, with employment decreasing by 2 per cent per annum thereafter. Thus, the supply of raw material for food processing in the future is effectively fixed. Increased output in the industry can only occur through increasing value added. As already mentioned, Irish firms have not been successful in the past, mainly because of the continued attractiveness of inter- vention markets, and the question still remains — can the Irish food processing industry meet the value-added challenge?

Despite the current and historical attractions of a low-tech commodity-type business, it is generally agreed that the future of the Irish food industry rests on supplying the high-tech, high- value product at the upper end of the market both at retail and end-user level. The reasons for this include:

- Markets, and in particular, consumer markets, are increas- ingly demanding further-processed food products in packs that are convenient and ready to consume, whether as fresh, chilled, frozen or ready meals.

- Retailers who previously purchased commodity products, such as meat, now require the processors to supply these products in a form that is ready for sale — for example, consumer packs of fresh meat, vegetables, fish-based products such as Donegal Catch and ready meals, either as branded or as private brand/ own-label.

- Suppliers who stick with pure commodities will be limited to supplying other processors, will miss out on significant oppor- tunities to add value, and will earn decreasing returns.

- The supports for commodity products will decrease over time as supply/demand balances are restored.

- There is more certainty for all concerned in the food chain when there is stronger integration among all the elements from retailers back to farmers.

### 5.5.1 Achieving Growth in the Food Industry
The food industry in Ireland is a strategically very significant one because of its natural resource base. Despite the fact that the

major products such as beef, milk and fish are controlled by quotas, there are significant opportunities to add further value to the basic commodity products through further processing. If the full potential of the food industry is to be realised, it is evident that many issues need to be resolved and many programmes put in place by industry and government. Major issues and required actions in the resource-based sectors are shown in Figure 5.2 and are discussed thereafter.

*Figure 5.2: Key Success Factors in Resource-Based Industries*

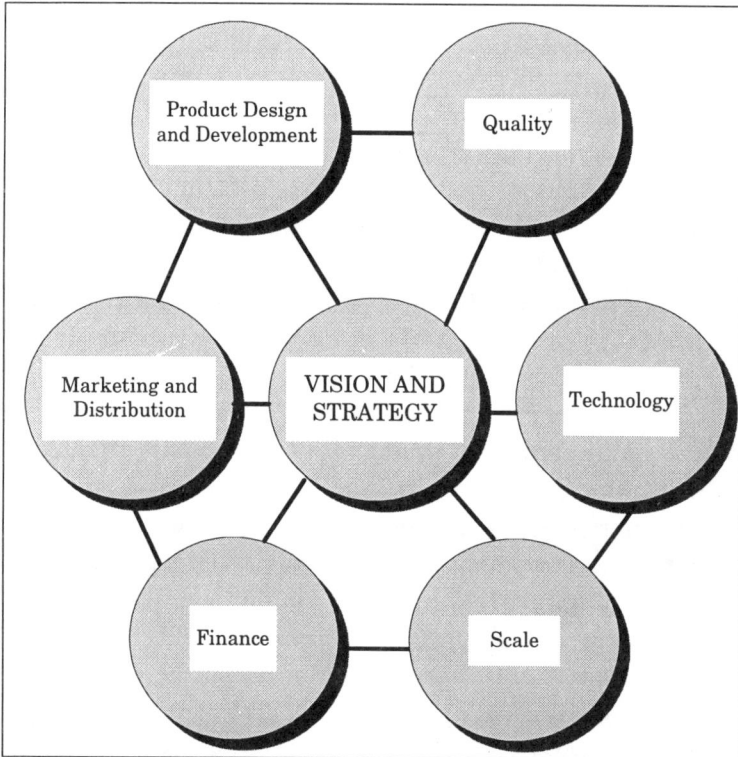

## 5.5.2 Agri-business as opposed to Food-Processing Strategies and Policies

Food processing is but one step in the food chain which begins with consumer needs and wants and ends up with farmers producing the right products for manufacturers to process. Future strategies must recognise the interrelated nature of the components of the system, and also the interdependencies among product areas such as dairy and beef, and cereal production in poultry and/or pig production. Ireland should not be caught in a situation where the demand for beef is quite buoyant, with well-managed and well-equipped factories, but where the supply of beef cattle is the limiting factor.

### 5.5.3 Marketing and Distribution

Emphasis will have to be placed on marketing and market developments as opposed to selling. While commodity products can always be sold on world markets, the necessary movement away from commodity products to value-added products will place a premium on marketing. So, the emphasis must be on understanding individual markets, selecting target markets and developing appropriate marketing strategies. Marketing structures and distribution systems must be put in place to address specific markets, and adequate budgets must be allocated to support products with the necessary promotion.

Given the current policies of the EU with regard to food and agriculture, the primary markets for Irish food should be in EU countries, and this is where the greatest opportunities will lie.

It is clear that value added does not necessarily mean consumer-ready branded products. Value-added products also include intermediate products sold to other processors such as speciality ingredients based on casein, mozzarella for pizza topping, or filleted herring or mackerel sold to German factories for smoking or canning. The production of high quality intermediate products can be a very profitable enterprise and will inevitably account for a substantial proportion of output where supplies of the basic commodities are large.

Beyond the intermediate product stage, firms have choices of focusing on catering markets. The growth in catering markets is providing substantial opportunities for firms that may not have the necessary scale or resources to create or develop their own brands. Own-label business can be very attractive for firms whose cost structures are optimised and who can thus earn reasonable margins without having to invest heavily in developing and supporting their own brands. It can also be an important learning experience for firms that may ultimately want to develop their own brands.

While many Irish food firms have developed brands for the Irish market — Galtee, Ballyfree, Kilmeaden, for example — the investment required to launch these brands successfully in the UK and other markets can be prohibitive, even for the larger firms. This leads to the conclusion that branded food products from Ireland can be developed when:

- Individual firms have the necessary scale and resources to do the job.

- The necessary distribution arrangements are in place in the target markets.

- It may be done via a joint venture with a firm that already has the distribution and marketing knowledge.

- It is limited to supplying smaller niches in the market or is limited to smaller geographic areas, which will not be as demanding on resources.

### 5.5.4 Product Design and Development
The traditional focus on commodity products has meant that the Irish food industry has not developed much by way of competence in new-product development, speciality products or recipe products. This competence must be acquired (developed and/or bought in) as it is an essential ingredient in the development of further value-added processed products. It highlights the very important role of the state and individual firms in increasing investment in R & D.

### 5.5.5 Quality
The importance of quality cannot be overemphasised, and relative product quality has become a major basis on which firms can develop a substantial competitive advantage. It is important also to understand that for consumers to get quality products, attention to quality must be extremely high at all stages of the food chain. Retailers or manufacturers cannot enhance the quality of a raw material supplied by the farmer or other primary producer.

### 5.5.6 Technology

The movement from a commodity system based on the utilisation of low-tech inputs to a system based on higher-tech inputs in the production of further processed value-added products implies the need for significant investment in technology. This investment will be required at all stages of the food chain, but in particular at processing and farm-production levels. The manufacturing processes required in the production of consumer food products are radically different from those used for commodity products. Management and worker skills and attitudes required are also radically different. While some Irish firms have successfully made this transition — Poldy's, Galtee, Dawn Foods and Rye Valley, for example — others have a long a way to go.

Furthermore, biotechnology is developing many new products and processes capable of greatly enhancing food production, processing and shelf-life. Biotechnology can be very important in brewing, cheese and yoghourt manufacturing, and in plant and animal production, where Ireland has a competitive advantage.

### 5.5.7 Scale

Two dimensions are important and very relevant in the food industry. The first relates to the scale of the manufacturing and being the right size in terms of throughput and technology to be competitive in terms of the cost per unit of output. The second relates to the scale and size of the firm required to undertake the necessary marketing and distribution activities to be competitive in the market place. In terms of value-added products, scale is particularly important as regards new product development, distribution and promotion. In terms of export market development, Irish firms should consider developing or acquiring the necessary marketing scale through purchasing distribution companies engaging in joint marketing activities with other firms.

### 5.5.8 Finance

Virtually all of the issues and requirements outlined above have major implications in terms of financial requirements. Finance will be required to develop strategies, product development, licensing, processing and distribution, as well as for brand-building and promotion. This is over and above funding requirements for fixed assets plant and equipment.

## 5.6 SUMMARY

Ireland's natural resource-based industries account for nearly £7 billion of output, they employ over 250,000 people and 50–60 per cent of the output is exported, thus generating significant over-seas revenue for the country. Agri-business is dominant in the resource-based sectors and the two major components of agri-business in Ireland are the beef and dairy sectors, which account for 60 per cent of the output, and the food-processing sectors.

Resource-based industry produce has traditionally been sold or marketed in commodity form. This is beginning to change because of developments by the agencies and by many of the food PLCs and co-ops. The available resource base does, however, provide very significant opportunities to create further wealth and em-ployment in Ireland through further processing and adding value to the available raw materials. In this respect, the priority areas for attention include meat, dairy, fish, timber and turf.

In moving from commodity products to further processed value-added products, very careful consideration must be given to: developing, planning and competitive strategies that recognise the interrelatedness of the sectors; developing firms that are the right size to be internationally competitive; acquiring the neces-sary technology through licensing or joint ventures; securing dis-tribution through purchase or joint ventures; ensuring the availa-bility of finance both in equity and special loan packages; develop-ing the necessary management skills; and ensuring that state and government support is focused on the priority areas and is well co-ordinated.

---

## FURTHER READING

Agriculture and Food Policy Review Group, The, *Agriculture and Food Policy Review*, Government Publications, December 1990.

Bord Bainne, An, Annual report and accounts, 1994.

Bord Glas, An, *Achieving Growth in Agriculture, Development Plan 1994–1999*.

CSO, Various Statistics, Government Publications Office.

Coillte, Annual report and accounts.

Department of the Marine, National Development Plan 1994–1999, Allocations for the Marine Sector, October 1993.

Economic and Social Research Institute, *Medium-Term Review, 1994–2000*, No. 5, April 1994.

European Commission, *Ireland: A Region of the European Union*, Office of Official Publications of the European Union, Luxembourg, 1994.

European Commission/Eurostat, *Eurostatistics: Data for Short-Term Economic Analysis*, monthly, 8–9, 1994

*Ireland: Facts about Fishing*, Department of the Marine, September 1994.

FÁS, The Food Drink and Tobacco Sectoral Study Report, 1993.

CHAPTER SIX

# MODERN INDUSTRY

*T*his chapter addresses the importance of modern industry in Ireland, in particular the role that foreign-owned multi-national companies have played in the development of the modern industry sector. Specific growth sectors are discussed and the global drivers of change are identified. The exporting difficulties for Irish-owned modern industry firms are then discussed and the National Linkage Programme is reviewed. Finally, the future of the modern sector in Ireland is discussed, focusing on the strategic issues involved and the key success factors for development.

## 6.1 OVERVIEW OF MODERN INDUSTRY IN IRELAND

As noted in Chapter One, modern industries in general produce products that embody a high level of knowledge and technical infrastructure, and thereby add a great deal of value to the raw materials and labour used in production. Typical modern Irish industries would include electronics, chemicals, pharmaceuticals, health care and precision engineering.

The key characteristics of the modern sectors of Irish industry may be summarised as follows:

• Output was £12.5 billion in 1994.

• Employment was 86,000 in 1994.

• The key growth areas are electronics, software development, chemicals, pharmaceuticals and health care.

• Modern industry in Ireland is dominated by foreign companies.

• The National Linkage Programme, run by Forbairt, plays a

[149]

key role in developing indigenous industry in the modern sector.

• The key to growth for indigenous firms is exporting.

The modern sector of business in Ireland has been the fastest growing of all sectors in the 1990s. Output reached approximately £12.5 billion in 1994 and was growing at over 11 per cent per annum in the early to mid-1990s. Total employment in modern industry was over 86,000 in 1994, growing at a much slower rate of 1.5 per cent per annum, reflecting gains in productivity in the sectors. Tables 6.1. and 6.2. show the output and employment trends from 1981 to 1994.

### Table 6.1: Output in Modern Industries, 1985–94 (£ m)

|                              | 1981    | 1985    | 1990    | 1994*    |
|------------------------------|---------|---------|---------|----------|
| *Chemicals*                  | *958.7* | *1,774.2* | *2,456.0* | *3,511.5* |
| Basic Industrial Chemicals   | 253.3   | 486.3   | 454.0   | 466.9    |
| Pharmaceuticals              | 441.0   | 914.5   | 1,471.2 | 2,438.9  |
| Other Chemicals              | 264.4   | 373.4   | 530.8   | 605.7    |
| *Engineering*                | *2,143.2* | *4,178.2* | *6,253.6* | *9,019.0* |
| Preliminary Metals           | 68.5    | 133.1   | 189.3   | 105.8    |
| Metal Articles               | 383.5   | 465.6   | 662.0   | 454.0    |
| Mechanical Engineering       | 208.3   | 357.3   | 494.0   | 467.4    |
| Office and Data Processing   | 519.0   | 1,576.7 | 2,075.9 | 3,501.9  |
| Electrical Engineering       | 447.7   | 986.4   | 1,911.7 | 3,550.1  |
| Motor Vehicle Parts          | 202.0   | 107.6   | 140.9   | 105.8    |
| Other Transport              | 113.4   | 143.4   | 235.1   | 123.5    |
| Instrument Engineering       | 199.8   | 408.1   | 544.7   | 710.5    |
| *Total*                      | *3,101.9* | *5,952.4* | *8,710.0* | *12,530.5* |

*        Estimated from CSO monthly production indices
*Note:*   Other Chemicals includes health-care products, paints, varnishes etc. Electrical Engineering includes telecommunications equipment, electrical consumer goods and domestic appliances.
*Source:* National Development Plan (1994–99), 1994.

It is clear that some subsectors, including basic chemicals, primary metals, mechanical engineering and basic metal fabrication and motor vehicle parts, have been in decline in Ireland. However, there are five main growth areas within modern industry in Ireland, namely:

- Electronics (telecommunications, computers etc.)

- Software Development (covered in Chapter Seven on services)

- Chemicals

- Pharmaceuticals/Health Care

- Precision Engineering.

*Table 6.2: Employment in Modern Industries, 1981–94*

|  | **1981** | **1985** | **1990** | **1994*** |
|---|---|---|---|---|
| *Chemicals* | *12,277* | *11,719* | *13,587* | *15,900* |
| Basic Industrial Chemicals | 3,123 | 2,859 | 2,606 | 2,300 |
| Pharmaceuticals | 3,321 | 4,305 | 6,220 | 8,000 |
| Other Chemicals | 5,833 | 4,555 | 4,761 | 5,600 |
| *Engineering* | *66,082* | *58,737* | *67,693* | *70,300* |
| Preliminary Metals | 2,380 | 1,869 | 1,744 | 1,500 |
| Metal Articles | 16,656 | 11,972 | 12,612 | 12,100 |
| Mechanical Engineering | 8,232 | 7,947 | 8,460 | 8,700 |
| Office and Data Processing | 4,996 | 6,071 | 7,423 | 7,300 |
| Electrical Engineering | 15,934 | 17,279 | 22,081 | 23,500 |
| Motor Vehicle Parts | 5,987 | 3,105 | 3,082 | 2,700 |
| Other Transport | 5,486 | 3,788 | 4,388 | 5,100 |
| Instrument Engineering | 6,411 | 6,706 | 7,903 | 9,400 |
| *Total* | *78,359* | *70,456* | *81,280* | *86,200* |

\*       Estimated from CSO monthly production Indices.
*Source:* National Development Plan (1994–99), 1994.

Apart from slow- and fast-growth sectors, the modern sector of Irish manufacturing industry can be divided into indigenous and foreign components, each of which has very different dynamics and strategic imperatives. Of the 86,000 employed in modern industries, over half are in overseas firms. The overseas firms have in the past tended to be purely manufacturing assembly plants set up to service export markets — sometimes not serving the Irish market at all. Overall, foreign firms export 82 per cent of their output, as against 34 per cent of output exported by Irish-owned firms.

Output in modern industry in Ireland, and particularly in the high-technology sectors, is seriously affected by the flow of mobile foreign investment into the country. This flow has been substantial in the 1980s and 1990s, for the following reasons:

- The attractive corporate tax régime of 10 per cent up to the year 2010

- The supply of skilled labour

- The relatively lower wage levels for skilled labour compared with most countries in the EU.

As a result, overseas firms have found modern industry to be very profitable in Ireland. Much of this profit is, however, repatriated to their home countries, and much of the expenditure consists of services bought in from the parent company. In other words, many of these plants are not true stand-alone businesses, in that major functions such as marketing or R & D take place elsewhere. In the past, there has been little natural linkage between the overseas companies and the Irish economy, other than in employment and locally purchased services. Hence the establishment of the National Linkage Programme in 1985 (see section 6.4). Strategies for these operations are determined outside Ireland, and a worldwide operations perspective is generally held. An example would be Packard Electric (Ireland) Limited of Tallaght, which assembles car wiring harnesses for General Motors European car plants. This plant is one of a number of identical GM sub-assembly plants in Europe, which also include Champion Spark Plugs of Naas, which makes some spark-plug components.

The technology of the development and production processes determines the scale that is necessary to be profitable. In the traded sector of modern industry, this scale is generally much greater than the Irish domestic market can absorb. For example, Keytronics, a Dundalk-based firm which makes keyboards for the computer industry, exports virtually all of its output. Thus, strategies for indigenous modern industry firms must revolve around creating and maintaining viable positions in export markets. For some indigenous companies, the industrial policy of attracting foreign industry provides an opportunity for sub-supply, which can offset the disadvantage of location in a small market. For example, a vibrant precision metal fabrication sector has developed on this basis. Typical of this sector is Computer Fabrication (Silverview) Ltd. of Tallaght, which makes computer cabinetry to exacting standards for MNCs.

## 6.2 ANALYSIS OF GLOBAL GROWTH SUBSECTORS

This section analyses the main growth subsectors of modern industry in Ireland. It examines the drivers of change in the respective global industries and the implications of these trends for the industries in Ireland.

### 6.2.1 Computers and Electrical Components

The computer and electrical components sector has been a key growth area of modern industry in Ireland following global developments. Output in 1994 was approximately £3.5 billion, and at least 15,000 people were employed. Key Irish firms include Power Technology and Lake Electronics. Ireland has been extremely successful in attracting foreign direct investment in terms of new companies and expansions of existing operations. Recent arrivals include Gateway 2000, AST Research, Sun Micro Systems and Dell Computers. Over 6,000 people are employed in the electronics sub-supply industry base in Ireland, and the Electronic Linkage Programme run by Forbairt is bidding to increase output and employment in this area to 9,000.

The global computer industry is in a period of change in the mid-1990s, fuelled primarily by joint ventures and strategic alliances between traditional rivals. A price war is expected in the mid- to late 1990s in the main-frame and mini computers markets with heavy competition between IBM and Digital. Computer hardware production is forecast to be concentrated among a few large, mainly American, firms. In the components industry, the "power PC"-chip joint venture between IBM, Apple, Hewlett Packard and Motorola threatens to break Intel's hold on the market with its Pentium product. Similarly, a joint venture between Apple and Motorola aims to counter the dominance of Microsoft and IBM in operating systems. One key trend in computer technology is the connection of PC area networks by radio waves or "wireless technology", in addition to the massive growth in usage of Internet and/or E-Mail.

This sector will experience continued growth between 1995 and 2000 as it will benefit from the gradual merging of electronics and telecommunications technologies

### 6.2.2 Electrical Engineering

The electrical engineering sector includes telecommunications equipment and domestic appliances. Output in this sector in Ireland was over £3.5 billion in 1994, an average growth rate of over 21 per cent in the 1990s. However, employment rates were less inspiring at 1.6 per cent per annum, and stood at 23,500 in 1994. The key growth area is in telecommunications equipment as the use of digital mobile-phone networks expands rapidly internationally. A key technological development in the mid-1990s is the use of radio waves linking houses to the normal phone network. As in computers and component manufacture, joint ventures and strategic skills-pooling are occurring more frequently within the telecommunications industry. Another key area within electrical engineering is domestic appliances, where Glen Dimplex is now a major company internationally.

### 6.2.3 Industrial Chemicals and Agri-Chemicals

Growth in chemical output in Ireland throughout the early 1990s has not been matched by employment gains, which dropped by nearly 3 per cent per annum on average, caused primarily by restructuring and productivity improvements. Irish output is dominated by multinationals such as Bayer, BASF, ICI and Rhône Poulenc Rorer. Other players include Hoechst, Du Pont, Dow and Ciba Geigy. Irish firms competing in this market include Clonmel Chemicals, which produces generic products for the human health-care market and Barclay Chemicals, which produces branded off patent agri-chemicals for the Irish and European agri-chemical market.

The European market for bulk chemicals in the mid-1990s is in decline, resulting in many job losses and significant restructuring. Among the key factors are:

- World production of bulk commodity chemicals is now moving towards low-cost plants in Taiwan, Pakistan and China. In addition to becoming key producers, the Asian countries have now become key growth markets for chemical products.

- Chemical manufacturers in Europe are now concentrating their strategy on the production of speciality chemicals.

- Environmental lobbying and legislation have forced countries to reduce Chlorofluorocarbon (CFC) production to 25 per cent of its 1986 level, and it is due to be ceased completely by the end of 1995.

- The European Directive on environmental control is forcing firms to reduce significantly their water, air and solids waste in the mid- to late 1990s.

### 6.2.4 Pharmaceuticals and Health Care

This has been a significant growth area for both employment and output in the 1980s and 1990s in Ireland. In pharmaceuticals, some 8,000 people are employed, and an additional 2,000 are employed in toiletry preparations and health care. The main firms in the world of pharmaceuticals include Merck, Glaxo, Bristol-Myers Squibb, all having sales of $5–7 billion. They are followed closely by firms such as Smith Kline Beecham, Hoechst, Pfizer and Johnson and Johnson, all having sales of $3–5 billion. Merger and acquisition activity is high in the mid–1990s — for example, the acquisition of Warner Lambert by Smith Kline Beecham. Companies such as Merck and Pfizer are beginning to diversify forwards into the retail sector. A key growth channel for the future is direct marketing, as opposed to going through the pharmacist channels.

## 6.3 DIFFICULTIES FOR INDIGENOUS MODERN INDUSTRY

The key to long-term survival in modern industry is having innovative and high-quality products for the export markets. Unlike many of the traditional sectors, which can only hope to export a small percentage of output — and often do not need to in order to maintain viability — the indigenous modern industry sector can achieve viable export positions, and indeed for many companies exporting is mandatory if survival is to be assured. An example of a firm that succeeded in doing this would be P.J. O'Callaghan Ltd., of Dublin, which makes point-of-sale credit-card imprinting machines for the major credit card companies. All of P.J. O'Callaghan's output is exported. There are, however, great difficulties in developing exports successfully.

Direct exporting creates costs and managerial problems of a kind and scale different from those of operations in the domestic market. Ireland's geographic remoteness creates inherently higher costs of transport and communications, adding again to the general problems of exporting. The main difficulties faced by exporters include:

- The expense and technical difficulty of obtaining adequate information on how foreign products/markets are structured

- The scale of resources required to develop a suitable product, launch it in a foreign market and maintain adequate support services

- The inadequate resources — technical, managerial and financial — of Irish would-be exporters.

The demands on management are also significant and include the following:

- Selling modern goods to export markets requires a world perspective on the product/market, and generally speaking it is costly to obtain the necessary information. A very close focus on a small number of foreign markets reduces the cost but the limitation of scope could be critical to success.

- Modern industry sectors tend to undergo rapid change, and this implies that business environment and technology monitoring become a permanent managerial function (and a further demand on resources) — for example, MDS of Dublin, which designs and exports telecommunications products, continually operates this kind of market surveillance.

- The rate of change in these industries leads to constant repositioning among competitors and among substitute products. The need for constant decision-making can lead to a blurring between tactics and strategy and also leads to frequent organisational and structural changes.

- Generally speaking, modern industry needs to interface more closely with customers, to align products with requirements, and to develop new products in co-operation with customers. Marketing and product development must be integrated and sophisticated. An example is the industrial adhesives market where Loctite will tailor-make adhesives and packaging to individual customer requirements throughout Europe.

- In modern industry, technology management — a wider concept than R & D — has to take place on a continuous basis. This places demands on management, first to develop the capability by hiring and/or training people, then to maintain it by holding onto the people (in the face of higher salaries abroad). Because it is difficult to do this well, successful innovation management can, itself, be the basis for a sustainable competitive advantage (e.g. Lake Electronics).

- Funding can present great challenges to managers in modern high-technology firms. The pervasiveness of state aid agencies has almost led to the development of a special management function — that of grant applicator. A good deal of managerial skill is required to achieve effective linkages with sources of capital and state development agencies. Financial projections and controlling finances require particularly close management attention. Obtaining finance for export projects —

especially working capital to fund debtors and launch costs —
can be very difficult. State aid through An Bord Tráchtála's
Targeted Marketing Consultancy (TMC) Programme, which
provides certain firms with financial assistance to increase
their export market base, helps small and medium-sized companies to make the transition to exporting less painful.

- The management of a foreign-based sales force or, alterna-
  tively, the logistics of running the export marketing from a
  domestic base impose heavy demands on marketing management.

- Many modern industry products require a new approach to
  production management, because the production process often
  has to be continually re-engineered as process improvements
  change the industry cost structure, and as new products have
  to be produced. Some examples of these include:

  ◊ The advent of Just-In-Time (JIT) techniques, World
    Class Manufacturing (WCM) and Total Quality
    Management (TQM).

  ◊ The increasing use of adhesives to replace welding pro-
    cesses.

  ◊ The introduction of Flexible Manufacturing Systems
    (FMS) in the metal fabrication sector. For example,
    Thermo King of Galway employs FMS in the manu-
    facture of vehicle refrigeration units.

- The most crucial demand on management ability occurs at the
  level of strategic integration. For a first-time exporter there is
  usually only one chance to achieve a foothold. Everything has
  to go right the first time, as the resource commitment is very
  great.


## 6.4 THE NATIONAL LINKAGE PROGRAMME

A growing recognition that the large overseas-based sector was
inadequately integrated into the rest of the economy led to the
establishment of the National Linkage Programme (NLP) in 1985.
The primary objective of the NLP is to maximise the amount of

raw materials, components and services sourced locally by manufacturing industry, in particular by the foreign multinationals.
The NLP works with over 200 MNCs and large Irish companies in
all major manufacturing sectors to identify new business opportunities for local suppliers and to analyse the barriers that prevent
linkage business from being developed. The NLP also helps to
develop the sub-supplier base, through assisting in the development of operational management and control, quality systems,
finance and marketing.

Between 1985 and 1993, the NLP generated over £400 million
of new business for supplier companies in Ireland. For the companies involved in the NLP supplier base, the benefits include:

- Quality assurance systems increased from 15 per cent to 85
  per cent of the total

- Sales increased by 83 per cent

- Employment increased by 33 per cent.

A key component of the NLP is the Electronic Linkage Programme (ELP) run by Forbairt. This was established in 1992 to
increase employment in the electronic sub-supply base from 6,000
to 9,000 over the period to 1997, and to increase the output from
£300 million per annum to £600 million. The key areas of strategic development include:

- Scale/Networking: increasing the size and scale of Irish sub-
  suppliers creating a larger network of small specialised suppliers

- Enhancing capability in customer service, world class manufacturing and product/process technologies

- Import substitution and market development.

Irish supply companies are encouraged and supported in developing supply contracts, not only with the local overseas companies
but also with the parent company and its operations in other
overseas markets — for example, with corporate or other overseas
operations of Irish MNCs. Examples include:

- Industrial Print supply Thermo King worldwide

- Nypro supply Verbatim.

Output in the companies participating in the ELP has increased by £65 million per annum in the mid–1990s, with employment increasing at a rate of nearly 500 per annum.

Originally seen as an import substitution opportunity, the sub-supply market is perhaps better viewed as an indirect export market, which may provide a practical route into direct exports at a later stage. The imports that these products replace are not in any case for consumption by the domestic market, and import volume is a function of external demand for the finished goods of which these are components. By servicing these companies, Irish suppliers have an entrée into world markets for their products, via the world market share of the MNC customers, without having to go outside Ireland. Even more importantly, the MNCs on the NLP offer a relatively cheap opportunity to learn how MNC procurement, quality and financial policies operate. This experience is invaluable for the future development of direct exporting.

Although the advantages of developing a thriving sub-supply market are obvious, the fact remains that few Irish suppliers are prepared to invest to meet the high technical and quality standards demanded by the MNCs. However, this situation also offers a strategic opportunity to firms that can overcome the barriers by thorough planning, deep knowledge of customer requirements and by adequate and appropriate investment in technology. A high level of managerial competence and experience is needed to do this successfully, and the National Linkage Programme can ease the process of developing this competence.

## 6.5 THE STRATEGIC CHALLENGE FOR MODERN INDUSTRY IN IRELAND

The ESRI has forecast sustained growth in output and employment in modern and high-technology manufacturing late into the 1990s (see Table 6.3), mainly as a result of growth in world activity. The rate of growth will settle down to a more modest growth rate of 6 per cent in output and 2–4 per cent in employment after the year 2000. This lower rate of growth caused by an expected increase in competition for mobile investment from Central and Eastern Europe and Asia.

It is clear that indigenous Irish firms trying to develop modern industry exports have to overcome major obstacles posed both by technology and by the nature of the export markets themselves. The difficulties emphasise the overriding importance of careful and comprehensive strategic planing long in advance of major resource commitments. In addition, there is often a requirement for innovation in the development of strategy in modern industries.

*Table 6.3: Growth in High-Technology Manufacturing*

| Year | Output<br>% change per annum | Employment |
|------|------|------|
| 1993 | +6 | 88,000 |
| 1994 | +7 | 90,000 |
| 1995 | +12 | 94,000 |
| 1996 | +7 | 97,000 |
| 1997 | +2.5 | 101,000 |
| 1998 | +6 | 102,000 |
| 1999 | +6.5 | 103,000 |
| 2000 | +6 | 104,000 |

*Source:* ESRI, *Medium-Term Review*, 1994.

Flexible innovative strategies are needed to cope with the high rate of change in technologies, products, processes, consumer needs and competitive actions. The strategic ramifications of this include the following:

- Some modern industry products are developed in advance of markets, and demand-arousal activities may be necessary. MDS of Dublin, for example, developed a unique small PABX/ Security system combination for sale in markets that were only just relaxing restrictive controls on the sale of such equipment, and had to invest in helping to stimulate demand in the market.

- For both existing and new products, innovation in distribution channels may be a key to competitive success. Irish TV viewers are now exposed to advertising for products that can be ordered by telephone. Minitel, and more recently Internet, are becoming established sales and distribution channels, and it may be desirable, or even necessary, to collaborate closely with a key supplier or customer to share some aspect of the cost burden, such as R & D or marketing. In general, the more complex the product development/production/marketing processes, the more opportunities there are for a firm to develop synergistic relationships with suppliers, customers and sometimes competitors. These relationships demand high-quality management attention.

- Managing high rates of change requires close attention to appropriate organisation design. Even small companies can contain a great deal of complexity where many highly specialised tasks have to be integrated. In situations like this, bad communications or a distortion in the responsibility/authority set-up can have a devastating effect on company performance.

Although these difficulties sound intimidating, it is possible for small companies to formulate strategies with good chances of success — for example, focusing initially on successful sub-supply as a means of achieving direct export positions at a later stage.

The Strategic Planning Institute in the US launched a study called Profit Impact of Market Strategy (PIMS), which identifies the most important marketing variables affecting profit, including market share and product quality. From his study of the PIMS database, Charles Carroll has derived a concise analysis of the general strategic position of Irish firms *vis-à-vis* their export markets. The PIMS data indicate that relative positions on three critical variables account for a great deal of profitability. In relation to their immediate competitors, high-profit firms in the PIMS database tend to have a high market share, high product quality and relatively low investment intensity. Relative to close competitors on export markets, Ireland's indigenous exporting industries hold an unfavourable position on the variables identified as being important. The PIMS data also suggest some strategic approaches to counteracting these disadvantages. The recommendations of relevance to small Irish companies include:

- Attempt to obtain a dominant position in a small number of product/market niches, defined by product sector, region and narrowly targeted market segments. Consolidate carefully and take time to build a secure base for further expansion. One implication of this strategy is to secure dominance of the Irish market before attempting exports.

- Offset the inability to establish a dominant market position by aiming for modest positions in markets with characteristics that make market share less important. Generally speaking, these are markets where economies of scale of various kinds are not very great. Some examples of these are markets with:

   ◊ Industrial and institutional products, which are less marketing-intensive

   ◊ Own-brand distributors, which are also less marketing-intensive

   ◊ Standardised products and regular purchases, which allow good capacity utilisation

   ◊ High differentiation possibilities, which allow improved relative product quality

   ◊ Products where technology does not require high integration, which is also less capital-intensive

   ◊ Sector growth potential that is moderate rather than high, which requires less working capital

   ◊ Moderate growth in mature sectors, where less R & D is needed

   ◊ Customised products, which allows differentiation

   ◊ Buyers that are unlikely to integrate backwards

   ◊ Suppliers that are unlikely to integrate forwards

   ◊ Products that can secure a small position in naturally concentrated markets where large firms don't react too strongly to small firms

- Constantly work on improving relative product quality, that is, increasing the value of a product's quality. This means increasing the value of a product to a buyer either by lowering the cost or by raising the perceived benefits, or by both.

- Carroll points out that the planning and implementation of these kinds of closely targeted niche strategies require sophisticated marketing skills operating from a wider background than that provided by the traditional marketing concept, which focused mainly on satisfying the consumer. What is now required is the strategic skill to understand and identify appropriate targets for attack, and to unite and align the other functions into manageable units.

## 6.6 SUCCESS IN EXPORT MARKETS

Some general strategic factors that make for success in export markets can be identified. A firm must have a sustainable competitive advantage over its close competitors — its products must either be cheaper than competitors, or provide better value to buyers for the same price. Competitive advantage of some sort is a prerequisite to obtaining market share, and the competitive positions of other actors in the market must be understood and nullified. Of the various ways in which competitive advantage can be maintained, most involve considerable financial resources. For many Irish firms the best approach, therefore, will be through developing and maintaining proprietary knowledge — of products, process technology and market requirements — in conjunction with operating close and mutually beneficial linkages with customers, suppliers and other manufacturers. For example, Oglesby and Butler of Carlow have developed gas-burner technology for portable soldering irons and have gained export sales based on continuing technical innovation of this proprietary product called the Portasol.

A firm must have developed a detailed strategic plan that goes beyond the market-entry strategy right up to the stage of a consolidated position in the export market. The plan should anticipate and monitor competitor reaction and technology developments. It should focus on the maintenance of competitive advantage and on delivering this to the marketplace. This kind of planning requires sustained high-calibre managerial ability.

Innovation of business practices, such as integrating or de-integrating part of the production process, opening up new distribution channels, or the effective use of infrastructural technology, can change the cost structure, and may itself be the basis for competitive advantage. The distribution costs of bread and milk in the Dublin area were reduced by changing the deliverers from employees into independent, self-employed subcontractors.

The marketing strategy must recognise that the firm is operating in a context in which it is very small compared to competitors. This implies that it should maintain relatively low marketing expenditures (since there are economies of scale which cannot be achieved by the small-market-share firm). Promotion activities should be very closely targeted, and market research activities should be directed at obtaining a deep understanding of the narrowly defined segment. General Paints of Celbridge, which manufactures a wide range of high-quality paints, initially focused its UK marketing effort on the tennis-court coatings market.

The firm should adopt a policy of permanent search for ways to improve its competitive advantage. The structures of modern industries are very dynamic — that is, there are entries and exits from the industry, the industry definition is frequently altered by developments in technology, and suppliers and customers are changing as needs are redefined. To function effectively in such conditions of flux, management must understand that the only constant thing is change; and the only way to live with it is through constant monitoring and constant repositioning. In effect, for success, the rate of change inside the firm must be greater than the rate of change outside the firm.

The costs of an export campaign are often underestimated in plans, particularly the "hidden" costs of working capital and foreign exchange management. The planning process must address these issues directly, and the plan should not be initiated until adequate resources can be secured.

## SUMMARY

This chapter has discussed the importance of the modern-industry sector in Ireland. The main points of the discussion may be summarised as follows:

- Gross output in modern industry was £12.5 billion in 1994 with employment at approximately 86,000. Very high growth levels were experienced in the 1980s and early 1990s. This growth is forecast to increase up to the turn of the century albeit at slower levels of 5–6 per cent.

- The key growth areas in modern industry are electronics, software development (covered in Chapter Seven on services), chemicals, pharmaceuticals and health care.

- Modern Industry in Ireland is dominated by overseas companies. Indeed the overall growth of the modern sector is dependent on the flow of mobile investment into the country. This flow has been substantial in the 1980s and 1990s, because of an attractive corporate tax régime, attractive set-up grants and incentives and the supply of skilled labour and competitive wage levels.

- At a global level, the electronics industry is being affected by joint ventures (e.g. Apple and Motorola) and alliances, which are threatening the traditional dominance of Intel in electronic components and Microsoft in operating systems.

- The rate of flow of mobile investment into Ireland over the next decade will be threatened by fierce competition from other European countries, and from Eastern Europe in particular.

- The global commodity and bulk chemicals industry is in decline, with consequent job losses and restructuring. Much world production is moving towards South East Asia which is becoming both a key producer and a consumer of chemical and agri-chemical products.

- The National Linkage Programme was set up in 1985 to maximise the amount of raw materials, components and services sourced locally in Ireland by foreign-owned manufacturing companies. It continues to play a key role in developing indigenous modern industry, and in achieving growth in output and employment.

- The forces driving change in modern industry require Irish firms to overcome major strategic and operational obstacles. Innovation and exporting are crucial for growth.

---

## FURTHER READING

"A Time for Change — Industrial Policy for the 1990s", Report of the Industrial Policy Review Group, Government Publications, 1993

"Employment through Enterprise" The Response of the Government to the Moriarty Task Force of the Culliton Report, Government Publications, 1993

ESRI Medium Term Review 1994–2000, Government Publications, 1994

National Development Plan 1994–1999: Government Publications, 1994

Various National Economic and Social Council (NESC) Reports.

CHAPTER SEVEN

# SERVICES INDUSTRIES IN IRELAND

*T*his chapter analyses the growing importance of the services industries in Ireland. Services now account for 60 per cent of total employment, and 80 per cent of all small businesses. Following a brief description of the services industries, the trends in output, employment and exports are analysed. The various subsectors are then reviewed in more detail, followed by an analysis of the drivers of change which are influencing the services sectors in the 1990s. The chapter concludes by examining the strategic issues that arise in the light of the changes taking place in the environment.

## 7.1 OVERVIEW OF SERVICES INDUSTRIES IN IRELAND

This section gives a general description of the service-based industry in Ireland. It begins by describing the scope and definition of services, the key subsectors involved and the importance of service-based industry from a job-creation point of view. This is followed by an analysis of the sector in terms of output, employment and exports.

### 7.1.1 Definition and Description

Services have been defined as "any act or performance that one party can offer to another that is essentially intangible and does not result in the ownership of anything. Its production may or may not be tied to the production of a physical product." The services sector plays a vital role in job- and wealth-creation in most developed countries including Ireland. Between 1980 and 1993, service employment grew rapidly in Ireland, but not as fast as in other developed countries, and as a result, unemployment

[169]

grew faster than the OECD average. Employment in services grew by 113,000 between 1980 and 1993. Thanks to the additional jobs in market services, total employment has been able to approach its previous peak of 1980, despite the declines in employment in industry and agriculture. Growth in services employment is a worldwide phenomenon, resulting primarily from increased specialisation, a focus on core business, the growth of information technology and the labour-saving nature of technological change in other sectors. When compared to other developed economies, the growth in services employment in Ireland is less than might have been expected, because economic growth has focused on exports and not on domestic demand. The relative shortfall in the growth of services jobs in Ireland is a major contributory factor to Ireland's disappointing employment performance.

There are five key subsectors of the service sector:

- **Professional services**, including services in education, health, accountancy, legal services and consultancy, and advertising

- **Personal services**, including hotels, restaurants, hairdressing, private domestic services, etc.

- **Financial services**, including banking, stockbroking and insurance services on a national and international level

- **Transport, communications and distribution**, including all aspects of the distribution sector (retailers, wholesalers, freight forwarders, etc.), post and parcel services, telecommunications and warehousing services

- **Public administration and defence**, including all of the public services sector, the Army and the Garda Síochána.

Table 7.1 gives a brief overview of output and employment in the key services subsectors according to activity.

These sectors may be further divided into **internationally traded services** (includes financial services, transport and communications and professional services) and **domestic market-based services**.

## Table 7.1: Overview of Services Industries

| Industry | Employment | % of Total |
|---|---|---|
| Retail | 96,000 | 14 |
| Tourism | 90,000* | 13 |
| Construction | 75,000 | 11 |
| Transport | 70,000 | 10 |
| Banking, Insurance and Building Societies | 36,000 | 5 |
| Security and Defense | 31,000 | 4.5 |
| Computer Software | 8,000 | 1 |
| Civil Service and Public Administration | 249,000 | 36.5 |
| Miscellaneous | 33,000 | 5 |
| TOTAL | 688,000* | 100 |

\*      Includes an estimate for part-time employment in tourism.
*Source*:  Authors' estimates.

The Government's Task Force on Services report on jobs in the service sector, published at the end of 1993, highlighted the emphasis placed in the past by many of the state agencies on manufacturing and agriculture as opposed to services, in terms of their policies for job creation and job maintenance. The reasons for this, according to the Task Force, are as follows:

- Many service areas are manifestations of a strong industrial base (the "real" economy), and a perception exists that jobs will automatically follow if industrial policy is catered for.

- The majority of jobs in services are perceived to be "non-traded" and not contributing to the balance of trade.

- The market services sector is particularly diffuse, from financial services to distribution to tourism. This makes it difficult to prescribe in an overall way.

- Many jobs in services are perceived to be low-paying or part-time in nature.

- In the past, public-sector services have accounted for a very high share of the total sector, and employment growth was constrained or reduced because of restrictive financial policy in the late 1980s and early 1990s.

The public sector accounts for a large proportion of service sector employment as it includes the civil service, defence forces, Garda Síochána, local authorities, education, health and semi-state bodies. A public-sector cap on employment in the late 1980s and early 1990s limited the overall growth in the public sector in Ireland compared to other developed countries over the same period. However, it now seems that the freeze on public sector employment has been terminated in the mid-1990s.

### 7.1.2 Output, Employment and Trends

The Task Force on jobs in services reported that the output from services in 1992 was estimated at nearly £14 billion. As such, it represents over half of the country's total output. As can be seen from Table 7.2, this represents a significant growth through the 1970s and 1980s. In discussing the services sector, it must be noted that certain activities which were previously classified as manufacturing or agricultural in nature have been rationalised, and parts of them have been reclassified as services — as opposed to new services necessarily being created. This phenomenon is known as "outsourcing".

*Table 7.2: Output in Services, 1975–92*

| Year | IR£ m | % of GDP |
|------|-------|----------|
| 1975 | 1,599 | 42.1 |
| 1980 | 4,358 | 48.4 |
| 1985 | 7,352 | 51.4 |
| 1990 | 12,886 | 54.4 |
| 1992 | 13,925 | 53.0 |

*Source:* Government Task Force on Services, December 1993.

As already mentioned in Chapter One, approximately 60 per cent of the Irish workforce is now employed in service-related activities

— approximately 660,000 in total. In relative terms, this is low compared to most developed economies. For example, 70 per cent of the American workforce is now in services. Services employment has been increasing by 10,000 on average in the 1990s but it has not resulted in an overall gain in employment because of the decrease in employment in agriculture.

Despite the marked rise in public sector employment in 1993/1994, employment increases in the 1990s have been concentrated in three sectors: financial services, professional services and personal services. Employment generated by tourism revenue, which cuts across many of these sectors, was estimated at 90,000 in 1993. As already mentioned, "outsourcing" accounts for much of the employment created. Table 7.3 shows the growth in employment in both public and private sectors.

*Table 7.3: Public and Private Sector Services Employment*

| Year | Public Services Employment 000 | Net Gain/Loss | Private Sector Employment 000 | Net Gain/Loss |
|---|---|---|---|---|
| 1989 | 269.3 | -1,600 | 351.7 | — |
| 1990 | 273.1 | +3,800 | 364.9 | +13,200 |
| 1991 | 270.7 | -2,400 | 376.3 | +11,400 |
| 1992 | 272.8 | +2,100 | 387.7 | +11,400 |
| 1993 | 276.8 | +4,000 | 393.5 | +5,800 |
| 1994* | 280 | +3,200 | 399.4 | +5,900 |

*Source:* Government Task Force on Services, December 1993, *Business and Finance*, January 1995, and authors' estimates.

Public services employment covers the Civil Service, Defence Forces, Garda Síochána, Local Authorities, Education, Health and semi-state bodies. Although the public sector accounts for over 40 per cent of all services employment, the private sector has been the driving force behind job creation in recent years.

### 7.1.3 Exports of Irish Services

Exports of Irish services amounted to approximately £2.3 billion in 1992, which represented 12 per cent of total Irish exports. This figure has been increasing gradually since 1988, the main growth area being in "other services" — that is, services other than transport and tourism. This area now accounts for 28.5 per cent of total services exports, up from 15.8 per cent in 1986. Examples of this would be companies involved in software development, financial services, and engineering, architectural and management consultancy services.

*Table 7.4: Exports of Irish Services, 1992*

|                           | Exports (IR£ m) | % of Total |
|---------------------------|-----------------|------------|
| Tourism and Travel        | 947             | 41.4       |
| "Other" Transport         | 321             | 14.0       |
| Passenger Fare Receipts   | 281             | 12.3       |
| International Freight     | 87              | 3.8        |
| "Other" Services          | 653             | 28.5       |
| Total                     | 2,289           | 100        |

*Source*: Government Task Force on Services, December 1993.

## 7.2 ANALYSIS BY SUBSECTOR

This section looks at the key subsectors within service-based industry, in terms of growth prospects and jobs potential. As already mentioned, these key growth subsectors are predominantly internationally tradable. The key subsectors to be analysed are:

• The Retail Sector

• International Services

• Tourism and Catering

• Construction

• Film Industry

• Transportation and Distribution.

### 7.2.1 The Retail Sector

The retail sector is an important sector in employment terms, accounting for over 11 per cent of total employment, and equivalent to nearly 60 per cent of all those employed in manufacturing. According to the FÁS/ESRI occupational forecasts, the retail sector is expected to account for 18 per cent of total employment growth between 1990 and 1996. According to the 1988 Census of Services, there were over 21,000 retail outlets in Ireland, 45 per cent of which were food outlets. Output in that year was nearly £5 billion. Trends in the retail sector have a major effect on the marketing strategies of many indigenous firms in Ireland, in particular for firms in the agri-food sector.

*Table 7.5: Employment in Retail Services, 1994*

| Sector | Employment Full Time 1994 | Employment Part-time 1994 | Total Employment 1994 |
|---|---|---|---|
| Grocery | 20,738 | 16,294 | 37,032 |
| Other Food | 6,090 | 3,137 | 9,227 |
| Department Stores | 1,442 | 1,835 | 3,277 |
| TSNs | 3,236 | 1,983 | 5,219 |
| Clothing/Footwear | 8,163 | 7,238 | 15,401 |
| Chemist | 3,649 | 801 | 4,450 |
| Household Goods | 5,479 | 1,730 | 7,209 |
| Other Non-Food Goods | 10,381 | 3,647 | 14,028 |
| Total | 59,178 | 36,665 | 95,843 |

*Source:* FÁS/Goodbody, Retail Sectoral Study, 1993.

The retail sector is experiencing a period of structural and technological change in Ireland and in Europe in general. This is the result of growth of the larger stores and multiples, the increased penetration in the market by foreign-owned outlets, and the increased use of information technology and systems. Demand factors will continue to determine the structure of the retail sector of the twenty-first century.

As consumer requirements evolve in terms of lifestyle, the type, location and range of retail services required will change. The following trends are expected to occur:

- **Increased dominance by the multiples.** The larger multiples now account for 60 per cent of grocery sales nationwide (85 per cent in Dublin) and this trend is set to continue. Table 7.7 shows the Irish retail structure in 1993.

*Table 7.6: Retail Outlet Numbers by Trade Sector, 1977–93*

| Outlet | 1977 | 1983 | 1988 | 1991 | 1993 |
|---|---|---|---|---|---|
| Multiples | 141 | 161 | 149 | 154 | 160 |
| Symbol Groups | 1,802 | 1,715 | 1,134 | 999 | 1,015 |
| Independents | 11,832 | 9,694 | 9,387 | 9,119 | 8,494 |
| Total Outlets | 13,775 | 11,570 | 10,670 | 10,272 | 9,669 |

*Source:* A.C. Nielsen, "Retail Census", 1994.

- **A split between functional and leisure shopping.** Functional shopping will be increasingly price- and convenience-driven, particularly in terms of self-service and discount shopping. Leisure shopping will be increasingly location-driven with close proximity to other consumer services such as restaurants, cinemas, etc. being a prime requirement.

- **Greater segmentation of the retail market.** Outlets in each sector will increasingly offer a continuum of product/ service/price options from the low-priced/small-range/low-services end to the high-quality/broad-range/high-services end. An example of this would be the low-price warehouse operations or discount clubs versus the traditional multiple operations.

- **Growth in specialist stores.** Small specialist stores should experience a revival in both the food and non-food sector during the anticipated period of economic growth.

- **Growth of chains/franchises.** Chains will continue to dominate the market, moving into smaller urban areas, having the advantage of flexibility and speedy response to changing customer requirements.

- **Increase in co-operation among independent retailers.** In order to compete against the multiples and benefit from cost and efficiency savings, independent firms will have to unite to act like voluntary and trading groups.

Other trends affecting the structure of the retail sector include the growth in self-service outlets, increasing competition from cheap and cheerful discount stores, and increased localising or tailoring of stores to local market demands. A more long-term trend will be the emergence of teleshopping in Ireland, as consumers become more accustomed to computer trading and as the interface becomes more user-friendly.

The second major driver, along with the changing retail structure, is the increased use of information technology. Information technology is having a tremendous effect on cost-efficiency in retail outlets, as well as improving the level and type of customer service offered. IT affects all levels of retail organisational activity, from logistics planning to functional support analysis (manufacturing, marketing, finance, inventory management) and transaction systems. Just-in-time (JIT) management relationships between suppliers and retailers require a developed IT infrastructure. Combined with the presence of Electronic Point Of Sale (EPOS), Management Information Systems (MIS) and Electronic Data Interchange (EDI), complete "back to front" information systems are now available, which allow inward and outward stock to be monitored, with automatic reordering and up-to-the-minute information on what is selling. Direct product profitability allows constant monitoring, and up-to-date sales information allows minimum stock holding and JIT as mentioned above. The adoption of IT in the retail sector will be concentrated on, although not confined to, the larger retailers.

### 7.2.2 Internationally-Traded Services
The internationally-traded services sector is one of the fastest

growing areas of the economy, albeit from a relatively low base. The following are the main international services promoted for their job potential:

• Data processing and software development

• Financial services

• Telecommunications

• Others, including technical and consultancy services.

Employment in these areas stood at over 11,000 in 1994 — an increase of 50 per cent over the 1990s. A key point to remember here is that employment created in this area has a high graduate and post-graduate content, and involves a high degree of value-added in most cases.

### *Computer Software*
Computer software is one of the strongest growth areas within the internationally-traded services sector. It is now among the top five exporting sectors in Ireland, resulting primarily from the presence of key international firms such as Microsoft, Lotus, Ashton Tate, Claris and Borland. A country's software capability is emerging as an essential ingredient in the development of a modern economy, as it determines competitive advantage of a whole range of products, and as the strategic initiative in information technology moves from hardware into software. Approximately 8,000 people — most of them graduates — are employed in the software industry in Ireland. Apart from being an important base for the activities of many key multinational firms in the area, Ireland possesses a vibrant indigenous software base of some 300 companies, focused on areas such as regeneration, translation and first-generation software development. Examples of Irish firms would include the CBT Group, which is now quoted on the American NASDAQ Stock Exchange, and the Software Vineyard, which specialises in the insurance sector.

The National Software Directorate (NSD) was established in 1991 and has responsibility for the development and growth of the software industry in Ireland. The main objective of the NSD is to develop measures which will have the support of the industry, stimulate growth and exploit the industry's potential fully. The NSD anticipates that the software industry is capable of growing from its current level of 8,000 employees to 12,500 by 1996 and eventually to 20,000 by the year 2000. In 1992 the National Software Directorate completed and published a strategic review, from the points of view of the industry, in terms of indigenous and non-indigenous firms. The key factors underpinning the software industry in Ireland were outlined as follows:

- Growing market opportunities, particularly in Europe

- High level of skills of Irish software personnel

- Competitive operating environment in Ireland

- Trend of electronic hardware companies to develop the software side of their business

- Localisation opportunities

- Opening up of new internationally-traded sectors such as telemarketing and remote data processing

- The increasing use of Internet by business and personal users

- Emerging new technologies which are broadening the scope of the software, such as imaging technology, multimedia, electronic data interchange (EDI) and optical technology.

The National Software Directorate supports the development of the competitive capability of indigenous firms by:

- Addressing the opportunities provided by the introduction of new technology by Irish public institutions

- Servicing the growing software-support needs of the non-indigenous companies based within Ireland and elsewhere in Europe

- Developing, selling and supporting innovative products in Europe in niche markets such as Computer Application of Software Engineering (CASE) Tools, graphic user interfaces, open systems, downsizing, client/server computing and development methodologies.

The National Linkage Programme (NLP) attempts to build strong, capable and competitive sub-supply and subcontracting sectors and is a key element in developing the overall industry. However it is particularly important in the electronics and engineering areas where software development is playing an increasingly important role. (See Chapter Six on Modern Industry for a developed discussion of the NLP.)

The Software Applications Development Initiative administered by the National Software Directorate is aimed at exploiting state-of-the-art products or solutions in industries where Ireland is a major international player, such as aerospace, print/packaging or telecommunications. The primary focus is to turn the better service firms into product firms, thereby adding value and, in addition, increasing the transfer of new technologies into the industry.

The Development Capital Fund for the Irish Software Industry has been developed between the Department of Enterprise and Employment, the National Software Directorate and the ICC as an independent fund manager. The fund will focus on companies whose products have clear potential and where investment for marketing and development purposes is required.

It is important that job creation in both indigenous and non-indigenous firms in Ireland be focused on first generation value-added software applications. Being the second highest producer of software material in the world after the US means very little if the software is merely being translated or modified.

### The International Financial Services Industry
Since the establishment of the International Financial Services Centre (IFSC) in Dublin in 1987, internationally-traded financial services have become an important growth area in Irish services. In 1994, a total of 147 companies along with 90 agencies were operating in the centre, employing 1,729 people, although the original projection was for 7,000 jobs. The companies which have set up in the IFSC are involved in the following financial areas:

- Mutual fund management
- Treasury services
- Insurance and reinsurance

- Asset financing

- Portfolio management

- Accounting and administration.

Multinationals which have set up treasury operations in the IFSC include IBM, GrandMet, Volkswagen, and Black and Decker. In the area of asset financing and leasing, some key Japanese firms such as Orix Leasing, Ito Chu and Nissho Iwa have set up. Chase Bank, Morgan Grenfell, Bankers Trust and PFPC have set up accounting and administration operations, while key German re-insurance firms such as Aachen Re, Hannover Re and Cologne Re have all set up operations in the IFSC.

### The Telecommunications Industry

Telecommunications is now the fastest growing industry in global terms, and Ireland is creating a competitive base in both tele-communications and telemarketing. It is estimated that 5,000 people work in the telecommunications industry (equipment pro-viders, software houses, maintenance houses, etc.) in addition to the 13,000 people who are employed in Telecom Éireann. ESAT, a new entrant to the Irish market, in conjunction with Sprint in the USA, provides international telecommunications services to busi-nesses. As the European industry is deregulated, opportunities are opening up in international and European markets for E-Mail and videoconferencing services. It is now widely accepted that telecommunications is a critical component of the infrastructure of a country, and is required for competitiveness. National Econo-mic and Research Associates (NERA), in a report entitled 'The Impact of Telecommunications on the Irish Economy", suggest that an additional 9,000 jobs could be created as a result of a sound telecommunications investment strategy. As the tele-communications industry worldwide expands in importance, many new opportunities will open up for Irish firms in this area.

A growing area of opportunity within the telecommunications industry is telemarketing. Three major multinationals set up European telemarketing centres in Ireland in 1994. They were Best Western (hotel reservations centre), Korean Airlines (Airline reservations) and Kao Infosystems (telemarketing).

### Other Internationally-Traded Services

Apart from the key areas of computer services, financial services and telecommunications, there exists a group of consultancy service-based firms that are experiencing growth on an international level. These would include strategic and engineering/ technical consultancies offering their services to nations and multinationals abroad. An example of this would be ESBI, a subsidiary of the ESB, which provides technical and engineering services. In addition, the Trade Development Institute (TDI) and the Industrial Development Institute (IDI) offer strategic and management consultancy services to the EU, the World Bank and individual developing countries worldwide.

### 7.2.3 Tourism

Tourism plays a very important role in the Irish economy of the 1990s in terms of value-added created from both overseas and domestic tourists, the contribution it makes to the balance of trade, and the major part it plays in creating employment in all geographic areas of the country. Like the crafts industry, tourism employment is particularly important in rural and disadvantaged areas. Approximately 91,000 people were fully employed in tourism and related activities in 1993. This represented an increase of 24,000 since 1988, accounting for half of the total increase in net national employment in Ireland in that time. In 1993, 6.9 million fee-paying visits by domestic and overseas visitors were made to visitor attractions, as outlined in Figure 7.1.

Tourism is particularly important to Ireland in terms of foreign exchange earnings. These earnings are mostly home-produced, so the multiplier effect is quite high in terms of national income. The import content of tourism is low at 10 per cent, therefore 90 per cent of foreign earnings are retained. Tourism's share of GNP rose from 5.8 per cent to 7 per cent between 1988 and 1993. Tourism activity in general tends to be seasonal in nature, which creates problems in terms of full-time employment. The new focus of tourism will be on activity-based holidays for the international market — for example, the number of Italians visiting Ireland has increased five-fold over the past few years.

**Figure 7.1: Visits to Tourist Attractions by Visitors to Ireland, 1993**

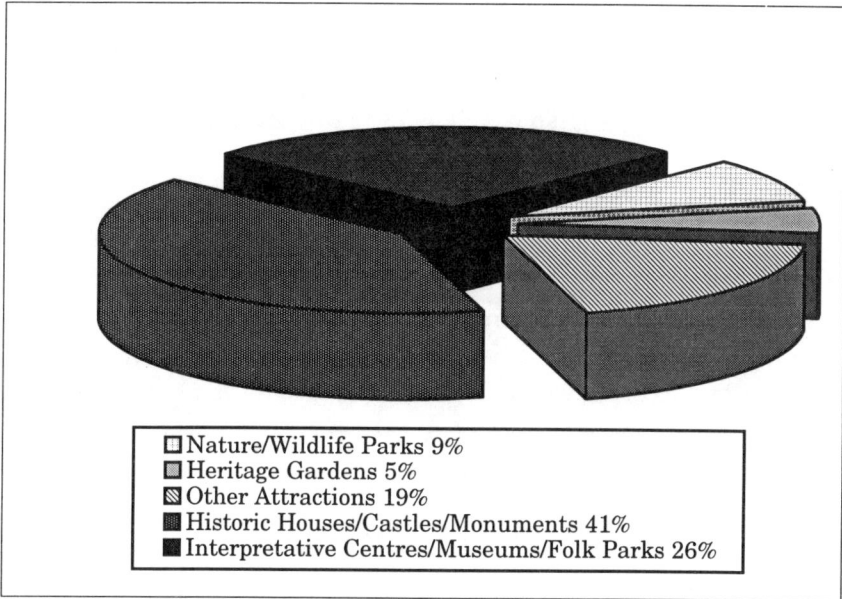

☐ Nature/Wildlife Parks 9%
▨ Heritage Gardens 5%
▧ Other Attractions 19%
▦ Historic Houses/Castles/Monuments 41%
■ Interpretative Centres/Museums/Folk Parks 26%

*Source:* Department of Trade and Tourism, 1994

In the Operational Programme for Tourism 1994–1999, which is part of Ireland's Community Support Framework Agreement with the EU, the following objectives have been created up to the end of the century:

- To achieve foreign exchange earnings of £2,250 million per year by 1999.

- To create an additional 35,000 full-time jobs over the period, including 17,250 in direct tourism employment, 6,000 in construction and the remainder in direct and induced employment in the economy.

- To concentrate growth in the off-peak periods so that by 1999 75 per cent of visitors will arrive in Ireland outside the July/August season, compared with 70 per cent at present.

- To continue to expand, develop and market the Irish tourism product.

- To improve the quality of service with high-quality training.

This means a large expansion in marketing activities, further product development, major improvements in the conference, angling, and culture and heritage products, and an expansion in the range and scale of training. It is clear from all of the above that the tourism industry will play a very important part in the development of the Irish economy over the next 5–10 years.

### 7.2.4 Construction

The value of construction output was estimated at £3.9 billion in 1994. Output in the construction sector showed growth rates of 7 per cent and 15 per cent in 1989 and 1990 respectively, both in employment and output, fuelled by EU funding and overall economic growth. Output in construction is totally dependent on the growth in public and private investment in the economy. Figure 7.2 shows the change in construction output between 1988 and 1994.

*Figure 7.2: Change in Construction Output, 1988–94 (percentage change per annum)*

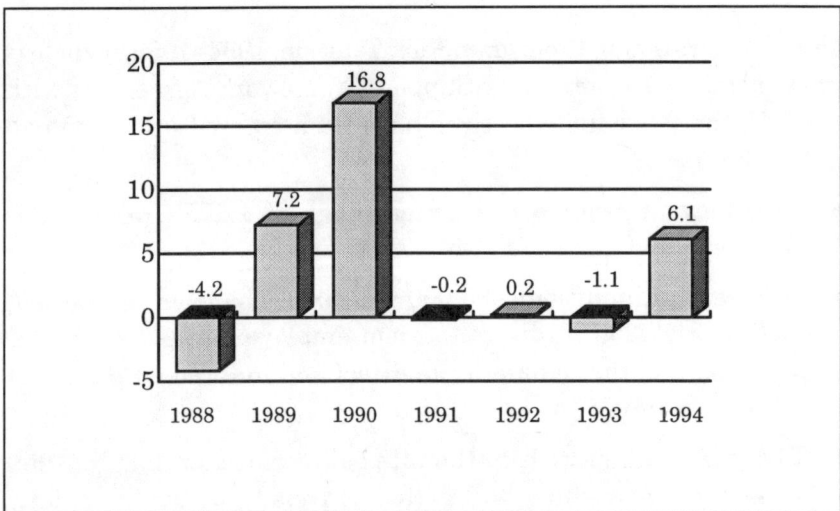

*Source:* Department of the Environment, 1995.

The stagnation occurred primarily in the privately funded areas of construction, including private residential, industrial and commercial sectors. The latter two sectors experienced the largest decline in output. Public-sector programmes were most stable during this time in terms of roads and water services, etc. Direct employment in construction averages between 70,000 and 75,000, with an estimated additional part-time workforce of 25,000. The planned level of investment helped by EU funding and the forecasted upswing in private business investment and private housing augurs well for the construction sector to the end of the 1990s.

### 7.2.5 Financial Services

Apart from internationally-traded financial services, domestically-based financial companies are one of the main employment areas in services. Approximately 35,700 people are employed in Banking, Insurance and Building Societies. The key employers include the Allied Irish Bank (AIB), Bank of Ireland (BOI), Irish Life and Ulster Bank. Table 7.7 shows the asset and employment situation in the top ten financial institutions in Ireland in 1994.

Other key employers in the financial area would be TSB Bank (995 employees), The Hibernian Group (929), the GRE/PMPA group (856) and National Irish Bank (850).

*Table 7.7: The Top Ten Financial Institutions in Ireland, 1994*

|  | Assets 1994 (IR£ 000) | Employees |
|---|---|---|
| AIB | 21,036 | 15,492 |
| Bank of Ireland | 17,126 | 12,196 |
| Irish Life | 5,814 | 2,177 |
| Ulster Bank | 5,662 | 4,015 |
| Central Bank of Ireland | 5,432 | 616 |
| GPA | 4,960 | 190 |
| Banque Nationale de Paris | 3,292 | 76 |
| Irish Permanent | 2,711 | 1,060 |
| First National Building Society | 1,752 | 678 |
| Woodchester | 1,440 | 866 |

*Source:* Adapted from *Business and Finance*, "Top 1,000", January 1995.

## 7.2.6 Transportation and Distribution

Apart from being a key area in terms of employment (68,000 in 1992), the transport, distribution and storage sector of Irish industry is a key link in the overall business-activity chain. The transport system provides access for people and freight to and from Ireland. It also provides internal transport in the country, by air, road and rail. In addition to the physical movement of people and goods, it relates to the warehousing of goods and the general area of logistics as a defined business function. The key sub-sectors in transport and distribution would be road freight and freight forwarding, travel agents, storage and warehousing, courier services and passenger transport. The key employers in the distribution sector in 1994 were Iarnród Éireann (5,539 employees), Bus Éireann/Dublin Bus (5,400 combined), Irish Continental Group (1,274), the Pandoro group (1,000), and the Jones Group (500).

The key factors influencing this sector in the 1990s include the development of JIT systems between suppliers, manufacturers and retailers; the growth in usage of Electronic Data Interchange (EDI), which improves general efficiency in the overall logistics chain; and the development of global distribution companies such as TNT/Skypak, DHL and UPS, which provide international services to international clients and are increasingly becoming involved in joint ventures with national postal services in Europe. In addition, the cost-effectiveness of using the central (Dublin/Dún Laoghaire to UK) and southern (Cork/Waterford/Rosslare to UK) sea corridors, as opposed to the Northern corridor via Larne, will remain an important issue for small to medium-sized exporters in particular.

## 7.2.7 The Film Industry

The Irish film industry is growing in importance, primarily because of the success of Irish films and Irish producers over the past 10 years and as a result of the introduction of an attractive tax-based financial package in the Budgets of 1993/1994 and enshrined in section 35 of the Finance Acts. Ireland is becoming a cost-effective and attractive location for international producers from the US and UK. Eighty per cent of production budgets are sourced from abroad. In 1990, for example, the industry had an output of £20.6 million and contributed £20.1 million to GNP. From a norm of 2–3 films per year completed up to 1992, the number jumped to 12 in 1993. In 1994, up to 18 feature length films and 11 major drama series for TV were commenced or completed in Ireland. The industry is labour-intensive, with the equivalent of 48–50 man years of employment created for every £1 million spent on film and television production. The Irish Film Board provides financial support for both pre-production and production activities.

## 7.3 STRATEGIC ISSUES IN SERVICE-BASED INDUSTRY

This section analyses the strategic issues that arise within service-based industry. The issues of globalisation are addressed in terms of their importance to Irish service firms. This is followed by a discussion on the importance of benchmarking, quality management and the World Class Business concept as it relates to services industry. The section concludes with a discussion on the future for services industries in Ireland.

### 7.3.1 The Globalisation of Services

A key driving force in this sector is the increasing globalisation of many services. This is most evident in distribution, where firms such as DHL, TNTSkypak and UPS are genuinely international service firms and are playing a major role in reinventing commercial postal networks. Another typical example of a globalised service firm is McDonald's, which offers a worldwide franchise network providing a globally consistent product/service mix. Other areas of services where these trends are apparent include:

- **Media and Television**: The media industry is, of necessity, becoming global. Vast empires have been created over the past 20 years, by individuals such as Rupert Murdoch, companies such as CNN and NBC, and potentially the BBC/Pearson alliance. In Ireland, Independent Newspapers is developing in the same way with interests in the UK, Australia and South Africa. The latter part of the 1990s will see an expansion of these trends, with the emergence of telecommunications companies using their networks to channel TV broadcasting.

- **Advertising**: The advertising industry has been a global one for many years as it served various multinational companies which required a high standard of advertising service in each of the countries in which they operated. One example of a global advertising firm would be Saatchi and Saatchi.

- **Telecommunications**: Telecommunications companies such as AT&T, Cable & Wireless and Bell, British Telecom and France Telecom are all becoming global companies. This is being accomplished mainly through a series of strategic alliances, but in some cases it will also include acquisitions and joint ventures.

A major reason for the globalisation of services is that manufacturing firms are becoming global and other service firms expect a similar standard or level of service in each country. Hence the opportunity arises for the firms to "internationalise" with the manufacturing firms. In the future, most services will become increasingly traded and Irish service firms can expect increasing competition from service firms in other countries. At the same time, however, this provides future opportunities for Irish firms to grow into international businesses. In a sense, this means Irish firms taking business from foreign firms.

Naturally, the trend towards globalisation creates many threats as well as opportunities for Irish firms. Many opportunities arise for Irish firms to extend their market boundaries. However, Irish-based firms that cannot meet the high standards of international firms may lose out or be taken over. Therefore, it is vital that service firms benchmark themselves against global service firms in order to create competitive advantage.

### 7.3.2 World Class Business and Competitive Advantage through Services

As can be seen in Chapter 10 on Operations Management Strategy, the World Class Business (WCB) concept is growing in importance for Irish manufacturing firms as they attempt to compete against the Newly Industrialised Countries (NICs) and East European counterparts and benchmark themselves against world leaders in business. However, the WCB concept is applicable not just in manufacturing, but also in services. And indeed the services content of manufacturing output is a key source of competitive advantage in manufacturing. It could be that quality in production will eventually become standard in industry, and one of the only ways to differentiate will be through quality service content. Service quality is addressed in more detail in Chapter Nine.

### 7.3.3 The Future for Service-Based Industry

In essence, it can be said that the business system over the past 200 years has gone through three generation phases of revolution, namely:

- First Generation — the revolution and flight from agriculture and agricultural production to the newly emerging manufacturing industrial sector

- Second Generation — the revolution and flight from manufacturing to the services economy

- Third Generation — the current revolution, being the growth and development of services .

The fourth generation is currently evolving. However, as already mentioned, growth in the long term is dependent on the strength of the manufacturing and wealth-producing base of an economy. In the short term, one economy may be able to secure service-based activity from another economy — internationally-traded services — but in the end, all services have to be paid for from the wealth created in the economy. The economy cannot exist without services, and services cannot act as a substitute for manufacturing in terms of employment creation.

It is difficult to forecast the nature of the fourth generation of revolution in the business system. However, it is clear that it will be technology-based, information-based and will most likely revolve around small enterprises or a fragmentation of larger enterprises. It could also be concluded from this that the age of the large corporation is diminishing and that the true age of the entrepreneur is about to begin with a larger amount of small firms of self-employed people feeding the core manufacturing and service companies.

Table 7.8 describes the forecasts for growth in service-based industry projected by the ESRI. Output in construction is expected to grow slowly in comparison to market services such as distribution, transport and communications. Highest growth is expected from other market and personal services, including software development and tourism.

*Table 7.8: Forecast Growth in Output in the Services Industries to 2005*

| Services Sector | 1990–1995 (% p.a.) | 1995–2000 (% p.a.) | 2000–2005 (% p.a.) |
|---|---|---|---|
| Construction | 1.1 | 1.2 | 1.2 |
| *Market Services:* | *3.2* | *4.7* | *4.5* |
| Distribution | 3.2 | 4.3 | 3.9 |
| Transport and Communications | 2.7 | 3.4 | 3.2 |
| Other Market Services | 3.5 | 5.3 | 5.1 |
| *Non-Market Services:* | *1.6* | *2.4* | *1.2* |
| Health and Education | 2.2 | 2.3 | 0.5 |
| Public Administration | 0.5 | 2.5 | 2.5 |

*Source*: ESRI, *Medium-Term Forecast*, 1994.

From a national development and policy perspective, it must be remembered that the needs and support requirements of services-based enterprises are different from those of manufacturing firms, as their competitive advantage lies in skills and not in fixed assets. In supporting a significant expansion of firms in the service sector, a higher emphasis will need to be placed on "softer" supports such as advice, knowledge and information.

## SUMMARY

This chapter reviewed the growing importance that service-based industry plays in the modern Irish economy. Service-based industry now accounts for 60 per cent of total employment, and 80 per cent of all small businesses. The main points that emerge from the chapter include the following:

- Output from services stood at £14 billion in 1992, representing a high percentage of GNP and showing significant growth since the 1970s. Employment in services grew by 113,000 between 1980 and 1993, to a level of 659,000.

- The five main subsectors are financial services; transport, communication and storage; public administration and defence; professional services (education, health, accountancy, legal services and consultancy); and, finally, professional services (hotels, restaurants hairdressing, etc.). These sub-sectors may be further subdivided into internationally-traded (primarily financial services, transport and communications, and professional services) and domestically-based services. Internationally-traded services represent the main areas for future growth within the overall sector.

- In the past, there has undoubtedly been an emphasis placed by government policies on manufacturing and agriculture to the detriment of services. This has occurred for a variety of reasons including the perceptions that services are non-traded, they result from having a strong industrial base, are too diffuse to be managed effectively, and are low-paying or part-time in nature.

- Service-based industries in the future will compete increasingly on an international level. This is occurring already in many service areas including telecommunications, software development, banking and finance, and advertising, where global firms are matching the global needs of their customers.

- For Irish service firms that want to grow, their future will lie in developing international markets for their services. While this creates opportunities for these firms, it also creates threats for Irish firms as international firms will penetrate the Irish services market.

- State supports for service-based industry are not well developed in Ireland. In contrast to manufacturing-based firms, which benefit greatly from "hard" supports, service firms require a softer assistance package, involving supports for advice, information provision and skills development.

---

**FURTHER READING**

A.C. Nielsen, "Retail Census 1994", Dublin, 1994.

*Business and Finance*, "Top 1,000", January 1995.

Central Statistics Office "1988 Census of Services", Government Publications, January 1992.

Department of Trade and Tourism, "The Operational Programme for Tourism 1994–1999", Government Publications, 1994.

Department of the Taoiseach, "Report of the Task Force on Jobs in Services", Government Publications, December 1993.

ESRI, "Medium Term Review, 1994–2000", April 1994

FÁS/Goodbody Economic Consultants "Retail Sectoral Study" 1993.

Forfás/Datanet Limited, "Telecommunications in Ireland", August 1994.

Services Industries Research Centre, University College Dublin, "Irish Retail Sectoral Study", May 1992.

# CHAPTER EIGHT

# STRATEGY

O ver a long period of time, the factor that distinguishes successful from unsuccessful companies is ability of general managers to formulate appropriate strategies and to implement them successfully. Strategy may be generally defined as the intended relationship between the organisation and its environment, together with concrete suggestions as to how this will be brought about. A business strategy is a broad picture of how to get from one business situation to another, more desirable one. The strategy is focused by having an objective (or set of objectives), and is underpinned by rational analysis of the forces at work in the situation, including personality aspects of the strategist. Where several paths present themselves, one must be chosen and then implemented correctly. In small businesses, this strategy-formulation process may take place in the head of the owner/manager, and its only objective existence is inferred from the performance of the company. However, larger businesses, because of their complexity, have a need to formalise this process, and the demand for formality has resulted in a wide body of theory, which has yielded some practical tools for management. The smallest one-man business has exactly the same need for a strategy as the largest corporation on earth — you have to know where you are going (otherwise you go nowhere), and you have to take deliberate steps to get there (otherwise the environment makes all the decisions).

This chapter outlines current thinking on the strategic planning process, in the hope that even a brief outline will help to structure analysis, and also will serve as an introduction to the subject.

[193]

## 8.1 STRATEGIC PLANNING AND STRATEGIC MANAGEMENT

*Strategic Planning — or Strategy Formulation — is a process (that is, a succession of ordered human activities) whereby management develops a definition of what its business mission is, derives specific objectives from this definition and from interpreting the situation of the firm in its environment, and chooses a strategy.* Where the process is carried out formally, a detailed strategic plan document is generated. In the implementation phase, information is generated to provide feedback to the next formulation phases, and the process is usually seen as perpetual, incremental and irregular. What seems to be especially important is that the process by which strategy is formulated, implemented and evaluated be itself deliberately managed as part of the strategic vision. We turn now to describing how strategy might be formulated, bearing in mind that strategy formulation and strategic planning are part of a holistic process, unlikely to be of much use unless accompanied by truly strategic attitudes and thinking.

Increasing rates of change and increasing competitiveness in the business world suggest that strategy should be dynamic, accommodating itself to events as they unfold. To maintain a continuously adapted strategy requires more than a strategic plan; the firm's management must become strategic in outlook and thinking as a matter of routine. Strategic thinking focuses on understanding the forces that influence business success. It questions present assumptions and poses "what if?" questions. Strategic management is constantly scanning the environment, monitoring resource deployments, evaluating activities, looking for opportunities and problems, communicating strategy and working creatively with people to achieve it. Strategic management has a clear-eyed view of the world as it actually is, and is prepared to change direction if necessary.

Figure 8.1 illustrates the conceptual tasks that have to be accomplished — what is done rather than how to do it, which is addressed in the next section.

Before looking at the components more closely, several general points should be made. One issue is where the cycle begins. This is a false issue in the sense that the components are highly

**Figure 8.1. Steps in the Strategic Planning Process**

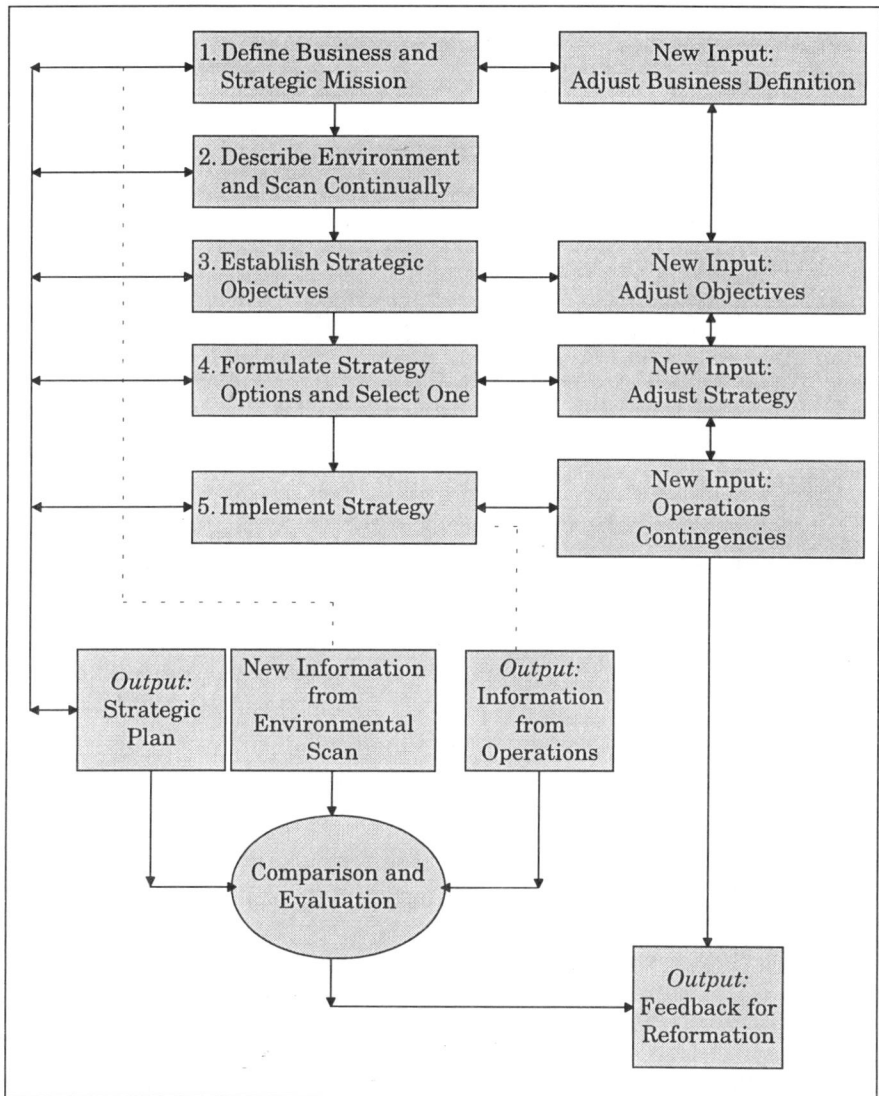

| | |
|---|---|
| 1. Define Business and Strategic Mission | New Input: Adjust Business Definition |
| 2. Describe Environment and Scan Continually | |
| 3. Establish Strategic Objectives | New Input: Adjust Objectives |
| 4. Formulate Strategy Options and Select One | New Input: Adjust Strategy |
| 5. Implement Strategy | New Input: Operations Contingencies |

*Output:* Strategic Plan

New Information from Environmental Scan

*Output:* Information from Operations

Comparison and Evaluation

*Output:* Feedback for Reformation

interdependent and an initial position will always exist, because the original entrepreneur will have formulated it, usually based on identification of an opportunity. Given an initial position, strategy generally evolves in a gradual, incremental manner as the firm interacts with its environment. On occasions, there are larger, more abrupt, changes as the environment shifts or as the

firm makes crucial strategic decisions. Formulation and implementation of strategy are deeply intertwined, and they evolve
together as the firm performs activities to cope with and thrive in
an environment of constant change. When the process is formal-
ised, a detailed strategic plan is produced, but not all of strategy
is concentrated into this single document. There are always actions in progress, verbal agreements, and organisational policies
and procedures that have not been formally recognised; these
influence the strategic outcome, and are part of the ongoing adaptation in the strategic response to change.

A second general point is that the conceptualised process of
strategic planning illustrated above is intended to apply to any
business, or indeed to any organised activity. The techniques used
to structure and analyse the strategic planning process are also
generally applicable. These are used to derive a situation-specific
analysis, unique to each firm, within its own, unique environment. The quality of a strategic plan is measured by the achievement of objectives. The quality of the strategic planning process is
measured in the long term by the firm's survival and growth.
Even though helpful analytical techniques exist, the major decisions required by strategic planing are highly judgmental — because even the best information can only go so far — and actually
formulating strategy options is a creative as well as an analytical
process.

The content of the strategic plan must address and provide
answers to four major areas of managerial concern:

1. How to anticipate and respond to change

2. How to obtain and allocate resources

3. How to obtain and maintain a viable competitive position

4. How to manage functional units to achieve objectives.


## 8.2 MAJOR COMPONENTS OF THE PLANNING PROCESS

Strategic planning starts with the most basic and most important
questions: What business are we really in? What do we really

want to achieve in this business? And how do we begin to develop a plan to get us from where we are to where we want to be?

### 8.2.1 Business Definition

Identifying correctly what business you are in establishes a solid ground in which to root objectives, strategies and operations. It is often difficult in practice to frame a good definition of the business mission and of strategic purpose, because there are several ways in which a business can be defined, and each will lead to different strategic emphasis. The statement should not be phrased too broadly, but should focus concretely on the fundamental who, what, and how questions:

* **Customers and Markets (Customer Groups)**: Who are they, what wants and needs of theirs are satisfied by our product or service? What specific target product/markets are we aiming at?

* **Products and Services (Customer Needs)**: What bundle of values do we produce for our customers? What is the scope of our activities in the industry? Are our activities dominated by specific inputs or processes?

* **Operations (Alternative Technologies)**: What is the basis for our competitive advantage? Are we dominated by technology? What is our geographical scope?

This may be described graphically on the "Tri-Polar Model", which charts the position of a firm in its business domain as shown in Figure 8.2.

SKF, the Swedish ball-bearing manufacturer, defines its business mission as "easing" the friction of mechanical movement, which helps it select the direction of technological development. In strategy formulation, the current business definition is first established, and then, through detailed analysis and decisions of judgment, a new statement describing the desired position of the firm in the future is developed.

*Figure 8.2: The Tri-Polar Model*

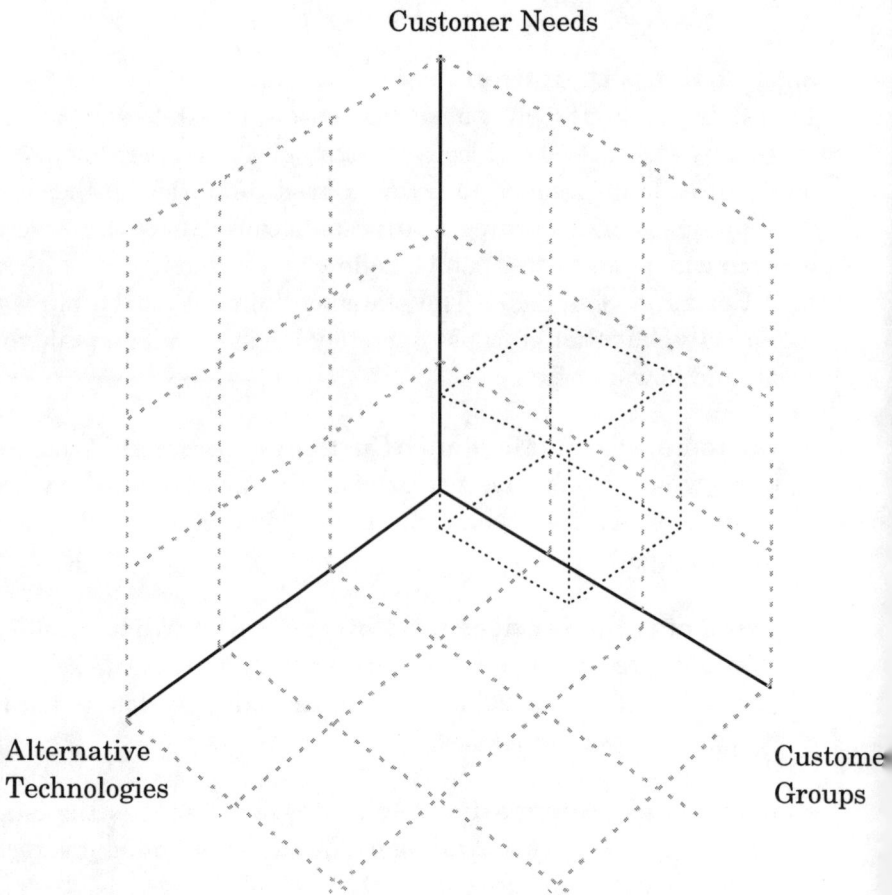

Customer Needs

Alternative
Technologies

Custome
Groups

## 8.2.2 Establishing Strategic Objectives

Strategic objectives quantify the mission statement in terms of specific, measurable results that are to be achieved within the timescale of the strategic plan. They are a summary of priorities, functional responsibilities, and authority to allocate resources. The strategic-plan document will contain a cascade of objectives, as the broad strategic objectives are defined in more and more detail down through the hierarchy of operating management. An example of layered objectives is shown below:

Mission Statement (part): "Become the 2nd largest company in industry"

Strategic Objective: "Achieve faster than market growth of 5 per cent for the next three years"

Marketing Objective: "Sell 100,000 units at £7 each during year one"

Operating Objective: "Allocate sales to the four territories and individual salesmen. Devise appropriate marketing support activities".

In this way, the strategic objectives help to provide focus for describing the deliberate steps that have to be taken to get from where you are to where you want to be.

There are five criteria by which the quality of an objective may be judged. Good objectives:

1. Deal with a single topic

2. Are expressed in terms of results, not activities

3. Are measurable, that is, stated in quantified terms

4. Specify a time deadline

5. Are challenging, but achievable.

Strategic objectives are not just derived from the mission statement — they have to be formulated within the realities facing the firm. Competitive factors, industry structure, and larger economic conditions set upper limits on what the environment will allow in terms of performance. The firm's own resources, both current and obtainable ones, also place an upper limit on what objectives can reasonably be attempted. Finally, the timescale must be realistically aligned with the firm's ability to implement the detailed functional and operational strategies.

### 8.2.3 Formulating Strategy

This area of the strategic planning process requires a great deal of analysis and a quite sophisticated understanding of business demands. Some of the practical techniques are described in the next section, and two issues will be dealt with here: (a) the nature of the broad determinants of strategy, and (b) the different levels of strategy formulation.

The inherent purpose of strategy is to enable a firm to control the interaction between it and its external environment so that the firm continues to survive and grow. There are, therefore, two sets of determinants of strategy: an internal set specific to the company itself, and an external set that is partly specific to each company, and partly shared with other companies in the immediate competitive and industry environments, and in the still broader general economic environment. The firm can be visualised as embedded in its environments (see Figure 8.3), which interact with the firm and with each other. How these environments can be analysed is dealt with in the next section.

The broad socio-economic context in which the firm operates produces opportunities and threats that impinge upon the choice of strategy. Political events, consumption trends, demographic changes, legal constraints, economic conditions and technological developments all play a part in defining what it is possible for a firm to do. Chapter Two outlines some of these factors as they apply to Ireland.

The industry environment consists of the market for the firm's product, along with the firms that supply inputs to the industry, and the firms (existing and potential) that compete for the market. It is possible — although with some difficulty — to describe the structure of an industry in such a way that strong suggestions for strategy can be derived from the analysis.

Most of the firm's interactions take place in the context of a competitive situation. Michael Porter of the Harvard Business School has pioneered the theory and practical analysis of industry structures and competition, and this work forms the basis for the competitive and industry analysis in the next section. The competitive situation describes the battlefield where firms fight for position, using strategies and counter-strategies to try and gain competitive advantage over rivals and potential rivals.

The final determinant of strategy concerns characteristics unique to the firm itself. The main internal elements are the business the firm has defined itself to be in, the firm's strengths and weaknesses (which form, or fail to form, its distinctive competence) and its relative competitive position. In addition to these more-or-less quantifiable characteristics, there are

**Figure 8.3: The Firm's Embedded Environments**

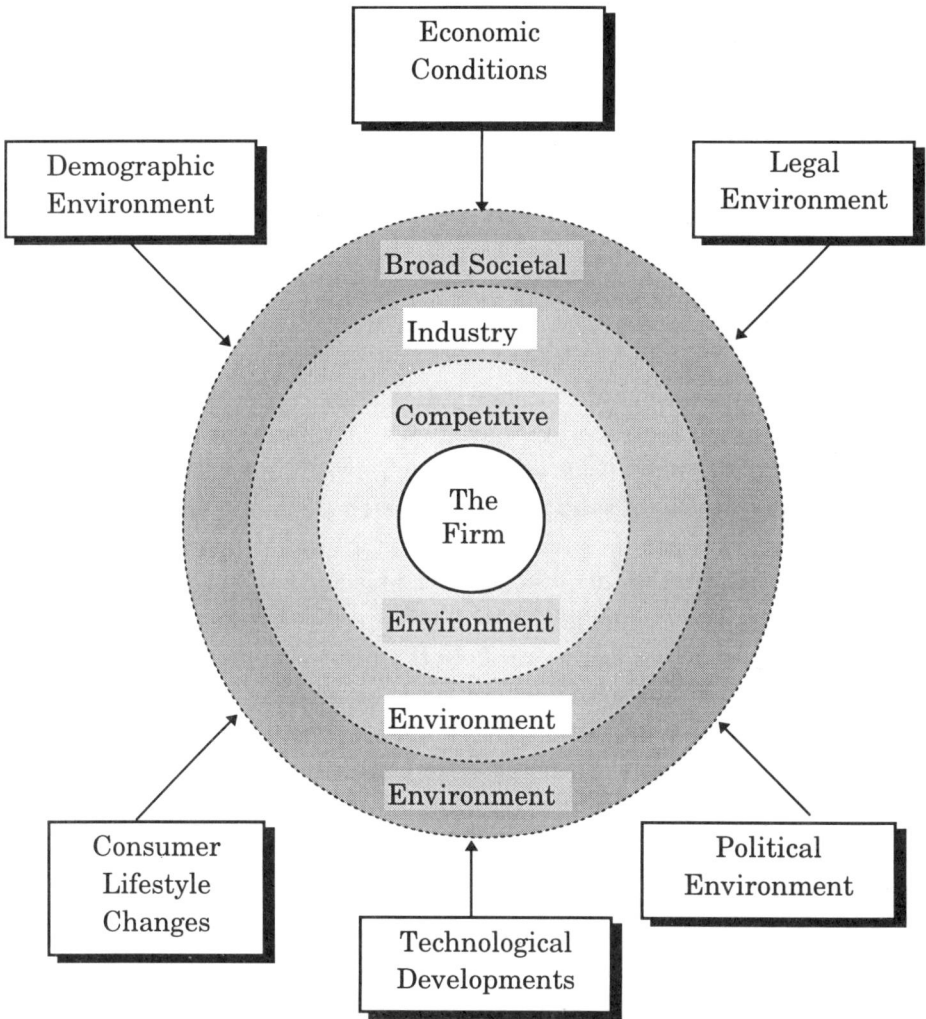

personality inputs into the final selection of strategy. The actual personalities and perspectives of the decision makers, especially the chief executive, can make a big difference to the strategy selected. Similarly, the cultural "personality" of the organisation, which is embedded in management values and workforce attitudes, can be very important, both as an influence on the kinds of strategies considered and in their implementation. The strategic planning process attempts to change the firm's activities, building on strengths and minimising weaknesses in order to exploit opportunities and avoid threats.

In the same way that there is a hierarchy of objectives, there is a hierarchy of strategy levels. **Corporate strategy** generally refers to the strategy of multi-business or multi-industry companies, where the problem for top management is how to select, manage, and allocate resources among a portfolio of diverse businesses. As far as is known, no Irish company practises corporate strategy in this sense, because even the largest do not operate in multi-industry contexts.

**Business strategy** focuses on how a particular business is run; it must state explicitly how the business will compete in its markets, how each functional area will contribute to the strategic objectives, and how resources will be obtained and allocated.

**Functional area-support strategies** flesh out the details of how the key business areas will contribute to the strategic plan and to the development — or maintenance — of competitive advantage. They provide the background for detailed **operating strategies** which specify precisely the action plan and policies of the lowest level of management as they conduct the day-to-day activities of the business. The actual activities performed are tactical actions, and cannot be completely specified in advance; but their context must be explicitly linked to a long-term perspective if the strategic benefit is to be obtained.

### 8.2.4 Strategy Formulation — Analytical Techniques
Figure 8.4 (opposite) gives a simplified summary of the major analytical processes and activities that must be carried out to formulate and realise strategy (this is distinct from the conceptual phases depicted in Figure 8.1).

### 8.2.5 Industry Structure Analysis
Michael Porter has derived a comprehensive theory of how industry structures change. He has identified a number of forces, which, singly or in combination, create pressures leading to industry evolution, either by creating incentives to change or by

imposing penalties on unchanging behaviour. These forces stem from all of the environments in which industry is embedded, and they exert varying influences from industry to industry and at different times within each industry.

**Figure 8.4: The Formulation of Strategy**

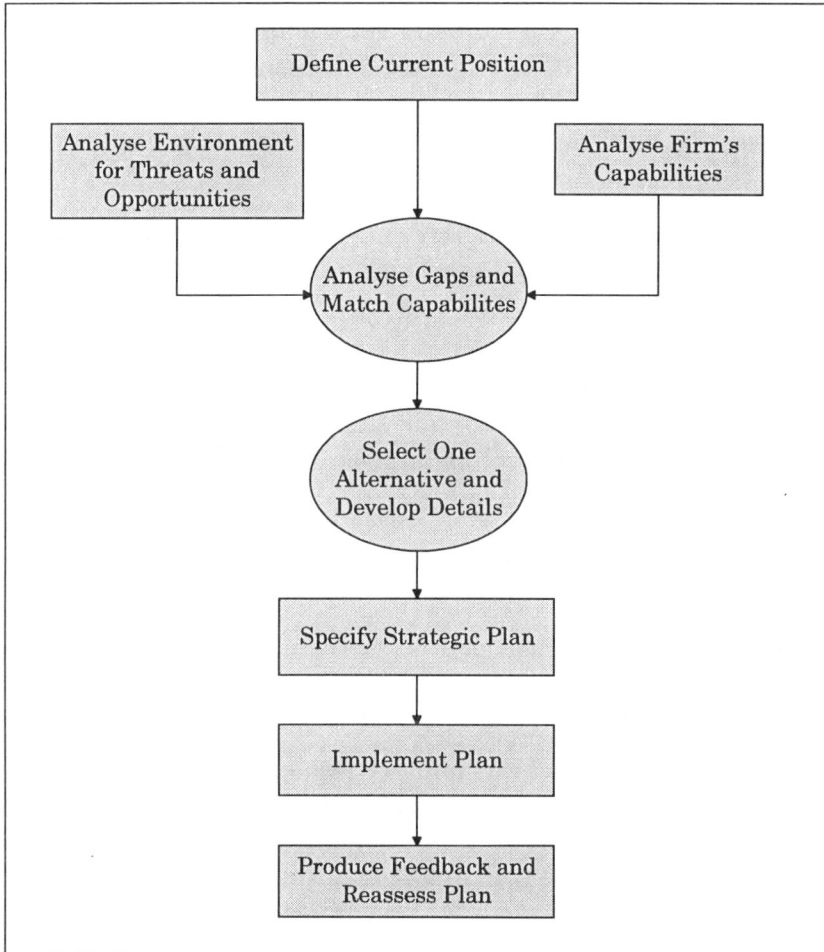

The structure of an industry is described in terms of sellers and their relative sizes, the structures of supply and distribution, the degree of backward and forward integration in the industry, the industry's size and geographical boundaries, and the barriers to entry and exit (this is summarised in Figure 8.5). When this current description is combined with an understanding of the forces driving industry change, it is possible to reach some sort of conclusion about generic industry type: whether or not it is dominated by technological progress. The purpose of industry structure analysis is to assess the attractiveness of the industry, in terms of likely growth, ease of entry, and the distribution of power among industry participants.

Conclusions about the industry generic type can then be used to help define the industry's strategic issues and problems, which of course have to be addressed and solved by the firm, in addition to its coping with immediate competitive activities. Some of the more important industry-specific issues are:

- The threat of competition from substitute products (outside the present industry definition), which could reduce industry attractiveness and increase competition

- The population-based factors that affect long-term market growth

- The possibility of abrupt or large-scale changes in the fundamental economics of the industry

- The effects of economic conditions, which might have unusual or special impact on the industry

- Changes in government policies or regulatory controls bearing on the industry.

The final decision of which industry issues are strategically important remains very much a question of judgment, but a formal industry analysis helps to ensure that consideration has been given to a wide range of factors and plausible scenarios.

### 8.2.6 Drivers of Change

In order to understand fully the environment of a particular industry, it is crucial to identify and analyse specific macro forces that give rise to change. In addition, it is necessary to track the rate at which change is occurring. These drivers ultimately affect the existence of sustainable competitive advantage within a particular industry, primarily because they affect industry attractiveness. Twelve key driving forces can be identified as follows:

- *Changes in long-term industry growth rate*: This affects the rate of entry or exit into an industry and affect the balance between industry supply and buyer demand.

- *Changes in who buys the product and how they use it, along with new ways to use the product*: For example, the computer industry was transformed by a movement away from mainframe towards personal and mini-computers.

- *Product innovations*: This can broaden the customer base, rejuvenate industry growth, increase product differentiation and ultimately sustain competitive advantage.

- *Process innovation*: Experience curve effects caused by technological advances affect manufacturing cost advantage.

- *Marketing innovation*: Creativity further down the chain can have similar effects.

- *Entry or exit of major firms*: The loss or gain of skills and resources affects the balance of competitive advantage within an industry.

- *Diffusion of proprietary knowledge*: As information about a particular product or process innovation diffuses through the marketplace, the competitive advantage created by the proprietary knowledge evaporates.

- *Changes in cost or efficiency*: Industries with swift learning-curve effects have to evolve to cater for such radical change.

- *Buyer preference for differentiation or standardisation*: The trend is primarily towards the former as consumer's needs become more selective or sophisticated. Firms may take a proactive or reactive stance to this change.

- *Regulatory influence of government policy changes*: This is a key driver, particularly in Europe as the EU and member states attempt to increase competitiveness, competition and standards.

- *Changing lifestyles and societal priorities*: Consumer concerns about health or the environment can force change in required industry practice.

- *Reductions or escalation in uncertainty and business risk*: A prime example of this was the oil crisis in the 1970s, which forced change in terms of fuel efficiency and alternative energy research.

All of these forces may be occurring at any given time within a particular industry and with varying influence. In order to develop a useful strategy it is important to focus on the major drivers or the ones that directly affect a firm's competitive advantage. This avoids a paralysis-by-analysis phenomenon creeping into strategy formulation.

Drivers of change can be revolutionary, such as the invention of steam energy or some other rapid technological advantage, or they may be much more evolutionary in nature, such as the development of competition legislation in Europe from the 1960s to the present day.

Several ideas can be usefully employed to interpret the industry structure once it has been described. One such idea is the identification of strategic groups within an industry. These are those groups of rival firms that follow similar approaches to the market, and they often resemble each other in any of several ways, including the fundamental competitive strategy pursued. If a firm can relate its own strategic position to those of existing strategic groups, it may be possible to infer viable and non-viable strategy options.

Similarly, the idea of Key Success Factors (KSFs), which embraces a number of different analytical techniques, can help to identify areas of strategy that must be addressed and incorporated if the strategic plan is to be successful.

### 8.2.7 Competitive Situation

In Porter's theory, the analyses of the industry structure and of competitors are closely interconnected. He has developed a five-element model, which provides considerable insight into the nature and intensity of competitive forces. It is not possible here to give detailed reasoning behind this theory, but the main elements are summarised in Figure 8.5 and Table 8.1 below.

## Figure 8.5: Elements of Industry Structure

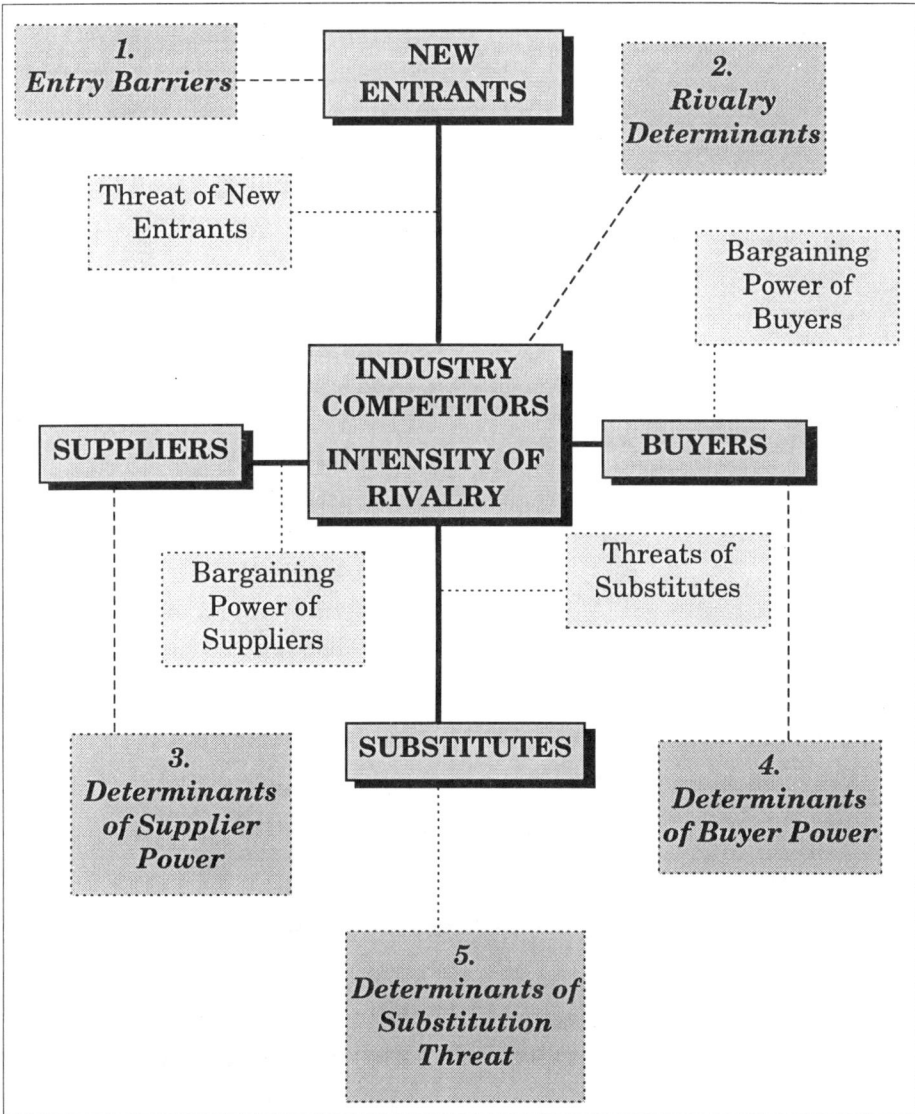

Source: Michael E. Porter, *Competitive Advantage,* 1985.

*Table 8.1: Factors Influencing Industry Structure*

| | |
|---|---|
| **1.  Entry Barriers**<br>• Economies of scale<br>• Proprietary product differences<br>• Brand identity<br>• Switching costs<br>• Capital requirements<br>• Access to distribution<br>• Absolute cost advantages<br>• Proprietary learning curve<br>• Access to necessary inputs<br>• Proprietary low-cost product design<br>• Government policy<br><br>**2.  Rivalry Determinants**<br>• Industry growth<br>• Fixed (or storage) cost/value-added<br>• Intermittent overcapacity<br>• Product differences<br>• Brand identity<br>• Switching costs<br>• Concentration and balance<br>• Informational complexity<br>• Diversity of competitors<br>• Corporate stakes<br>• Exit barriers<br><br>**3.  Determinants of Supplier Power**<br>• Differentiation of inputs<br>• Switching costs of suppliers and firms in the industry<br>• Presence of substitute inputs<br>• Supplier concentration | • Importance of volume to supplier<br>• Cost relative to total purchases in the industry<br>• Impact of inputs on cost or differentiation<br>• Threat of forward integration relative to threat of backward integration by firms in the industry<br><br>**4.  Determinants of Buyer Power**<br>*4.1  Bargaining Leverage*<br>• Buyer concentration versus firm concentration<br>• Buyer switching costs relative to firm switching costs<br>• Buyer information<br>• Ability to backward integrate<br>• Substitute products<br>• Pull-through<br><br>*4.2  Price Sensitivity*<br>• Price/total purchases<br>• Product differences<br>• Brand identity<br>• Impact on quality /performance<br>• Buyer Profits<br>• Decision-makers' incentives<br><br>**5.  Determinants of Substitution Threat**<br>• Relative price performance of substitutes<br>• Switching costs |

*Source*: Michael E Porter, *Competitive Advantage*, 1985, p.6.

The purpose of competitive analysis is two-fold: to obtain an understanding of the total range of dynamic forces operating in the competitive environment; and also to pinpoint the exact competitive positions held by the firm's major (existing and potential) rivals. This latter analysis is similar to how the firm must analyse its own operations, though of course much less information is available. This points to the necessity of maintaining a permanent and constantly updated bank of information on competitors. The important factors for each major competitor are:

- The relative cost position and competitive advantage

- The current strategy being pursued and its success

- Likely future strategy

- Likely retaliations to other competitors' strategies

- Capabilities — strengths and weaknesses.

Taken together, the analysis of environments is summarised in terms of strategic threats and strategic opportunities. Opportunities generally relate to the possibility of expanding sales or profit through the identification of new market segments, new customer needs that the firm can satisfy, a competitor's weakness that can be exploited, or an opportunity for either vertical or horizontal integration. Similarly, threats arise from a potential or actual limitation on sales growth or profitability. Firms competing in an industry devise strategies to cope with these threats and opportunities — anticipatory or reactive, appropriate or inappropriate, well-executed or not — and the interplay among strategies and between them and the environment leads to the evolution of the industry.

Industrial evolution generally consists of relatively long periods of incremental change, with shorter periods of more abrupt change occurring from time to time. The environment analysis provides a framework for understanding the mechanisms driving industry evolution, but it needs to be supplemented by a continuous scanning of the environment to see which threats and opportunities are being actualised, and what further threats and opportunities are developing. Thus, once strategic planning is formally initiated, it becomes a continuous process, and the strategy itself evolves in line with the dictates of the environment and the initiatives that the firm's management can formulate and implement. The final analytical element in formulating strategy relates to this last point, the assessment of the firm's ability to compete in its environment.

### 8.2.8 Analysis of the Firm's Situation and Competitive Advantage

The environmental analysis provides a background against which the firm's own position can be assessed. It is necessary to match the list of potential opportunities with the firm's actual and potential capacity to exploit them. Good strategies build on the things that a firm does well and avoid or compensate for weaknesses that increase the risk of failure. The identification and development of a firm's distinctive competence — the activities it performs particularly well by comparison with its competitive rivals — is the cornerstone for building a sustainable competitive advantage. Competitive advantage is what provides customers with better value, either through cheaper products or through superior product characteristics. This allows a firm to maintain its position in the marketplace. The main thrust of a firm's assessment of itself should be towards objective appraisal of what it does best and how this can be improved upon and focused on market needs to create a sustainable competitive advantage.

The assessment of a firm's strategic situation needs to cover four areas:

1. The **quality of present strategy**. This is easy to measure, but more difficult to explain. Good strategy leads to good positions along the main indicators of performance:

   - Market share growth

   - Profit margins compared to competitors

   - Net profits and returns to capital

   - Sales growth compared to market growth

   - Competitive position improvement.

If performance is not satisfactory, the reasons should be made as clear as possible. Are we addressing market needs correctly? Do we have the correct skills and resources for what we are attempting? Did competitors pre-empt us? Are problems a result of bad strategy or bad implementation? As answers to these questions emerge, a future orientation is added, feeding on the results of the environmental analysis: Is the present strategy compatible with the driving forces and future direction of the industry? Does it provide a defence against future competitive forces?

2. The firm's **strengths and weaknesses** determine its ability to act — to initiate moves, to react to competitors' strategies and to cope with environmental events as they occur. Figure 8.6 below gives a checklist of areas where significant strategic strengths and weaknesses might occur. (This checklist should also be applied to the most important competitors in the industry, as part of the competitive analysis).

3. The firm's **relative competitive position** has two broad elements: the overall market position in relation to competitors (e.g. dominant, major, follower, newcomer, or fringe positions); and the type of generic competitive strategy being carried out (if indeed there is a focused strategy at all). Porter, again, has contributed to theory by identifying three possible types of generic strategy:

a) Trying to become the lowest-cost producer in the industry (a cost leadership strategy);

b) Trying to differentiate your product in the eyes of customers who are then willing to pay a price premium for the extra value (a differentiation strategy); and

c) Concentrating on a narrow customer or product group within the industry (a focus strategy).

The firm's relative competitive position requires knowledge of competitors' positions. With this information, the strategic issues can then be addressed: Is the current position desirable? Tenable? Likely to improve or deteriorate? What better position could be reached?

4. The **firm's unique issues and problems**. A general analysis of strategy formulation cannot be carried down to the level of the individual firm, because ultimately each firm has to develop a strategy that is unique to itself and to its particular circumstances. In fact, part of the purpose of describing the general industry structures and competitive strategies is to help to devise a strategy that is unique and at the same time superior to rivals' strategies.

*Figure 8.6: Areas of Strengths and Weaknesses*

| 1. Marketing and Selling | 3. Staff and Organisation |
|---|---|
| • Customer base | • Appropriateness of structure to strategy |
| • Product Portfolio, standing in each market segment | • Quality and skills of management |
| • Use of distribution channels, relationships with distributors | • Leadership, strategic and motivational skills of CEO |
| • Company skills in various aspects of marketing | • Recruitment and development policies |
| • Product R & D; ability to develop new products, | • Flexibility of management and workforce |
| • Quality of salesforce and after-sales service | • Board membership and strategic links with other organisations. |
| • Company image Relative competitive position. | **4. Finance** |
| **2. Operations** | • Profitability and financial operating ratios |
| • Quality of facilities, equipment | • Overall cost structure |
| • Manufacturing cost structure | • Sources of new capital, debt and equity |
| • Flexibility of plant equipment | • Quality of financial management. |
| • Proprietary knowledge and R & D skills | **5. Other** |
| • Labour productivity | • Regulatory constraints |
| • Product quality standard | • Favourable access to government |
| • Suitability of location | • Industrial critical success factors |
| • Adequacy of raw materials and supplies arrangements | • Quality and extent of management technology |
| • Industrial relations climate | • Quality of strategic planning process. |
| • Degree of vertical integration | |
| • Possession of unique production skills. | |

*Source:* Michael Porter, *Competitive Advantage*, 1985.

### 8.2.9 Activity-Cost Chain Analysis (Value-Added)

Strategic cost analysis looks at the firm's competitive situation in terms of relative cost positions. The "Activity-Cost Chain" or "Value-added Chain" analyses the structure of costs from raw materials purchase to the end price paid by ultimate consumers. Value-added analysis is critical in manufacturing, as production at a competitive price level may be dependent on cost-factor back up the supplier chain or forward in distribution channels. Activity-cost chain analysis can be used to identify areas of value-added potential within the overall industry or, more specifically, to identify areas of competitive cost advantage *vis-à-vis* competitors. Technological change, process innovations or productivity gains can shift the centre of gravity of a chain. Figure 8.7 shows a simplified activity-cost chain for a conventional manufacturing firm. Three key cost areas exist: the suppliers' part of the chain, manufacturing-related activities and forward-channel activities. Establishing cost competitiveness may well occur outside manufacturing and may involve:

- Negotiating with suppliers and distributors on price
- Integrating backward or forward where feasible
- Using lower-priced inputs
- Searching for savings in shipping or logistics
- Changing to a more economical distribution strategy.

When the relative cost disadvantage is internal, options include:

- Cost-cutting retrenchment
- Investing in cost-saving technological improvement
- Innovating around troublesome cost components
- Redesigning the product
- Subcontracting activities where internal cost competitiveness cannot be achieved successfully.

The development of activity cost chains is useful not only in revealing much information on the cost competitiveness of a firm but also in tracking key drivers of change on a micro level. It is a key mechanism for framing an overall strategy for the firm.

Figure 8.7: *Generic Activity-Cost Chain for a Manufacturing Firm*

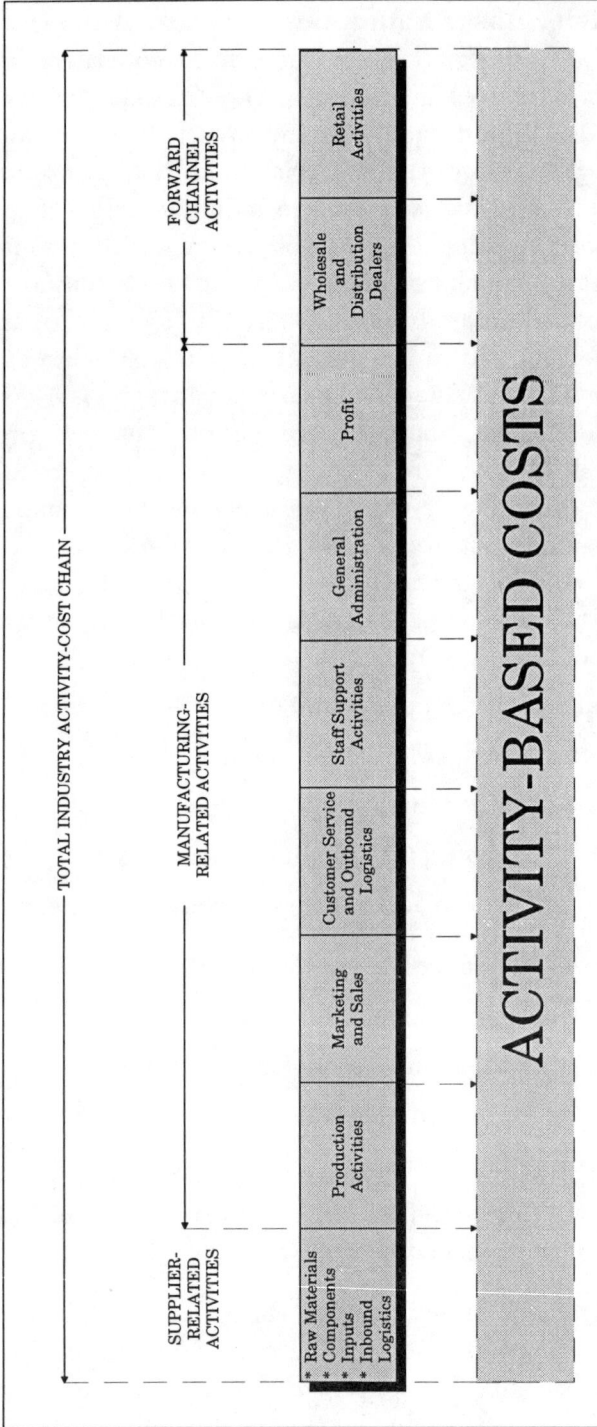

| | | | | | | |
|---|---|---|---|---|---|---|
| TOTAL INDUSTRY ACTIVITY-COST CHAIN | | | | | | |

| SUPPLIER-RELATED ACTIVITIES | MANUFACTURING-RELATED ACTIVITIES | | | | | FORWARD CHANNEL ACTIVITIES |

* Raw Materials
* Components
* Inputs
* Inbound Logistics

Production Activities

Marketing and Sales

Customer Service and Outbound Logistics

Staff Support Activities

General Administration

Profit

Wholesale and Distribution Dealers

Retail Activities

ACTIVITY-BASED COSTS

*Source:* Adapted from Thompson and Strickland, *Strategy Formulation and Implementation*, 1989.

## 8.2.10 Identifying Key Success Factors

For the managers of individual firms there is a necessity to pinpoint the firm's unique position in the industrial structure in order to formulate good strategies. The concept of Key Success Factors (KSFs) or Critical Success Factors provides a useful bridge between environment and internal strategy formulation. The idea is that there are several factors in each industry, which, if they can be identified and managed, lead to success. One comprehensive definition states that Critical Success Factors are:

> Those characteristics, conditions or variables that when properly sustained, maintained or managed can have a significant impact on the success of a firm competing in a particular industry. (Leidecker and Bruno, 1986).

Within each industry, the KSFs are derived from the interaction of the economic and technical characteristics of the industry with the competitive strategies adopted by firms. In industries with high labour content, for example, labour productivity would be a KSF, and that would lead to strategies concerning labour costs, labour inputs, and price premia for higher quality. Industries relying on high import content or on export sales might well find that foreign exchange management becomes a crucial factor. The PIMS (Profit Impact of Market Strategy) study undertaken by the Strategic Planning Institute in the US, which seeks to identify the relationship between market share and profitability, indicates that market share in low growth situations may be the most important competitive advantage, and strategies in such circumstances would be heavily focused on the marketing effort and on achieving high market share.

If the KSFs for a given industry can be identified, they will then become the main strands of the strategic structure, along with each firm's unique strategic position. If a good perspective is obtained, it may be possible to develop and apply "business" innovations, which would alter the structure in favour of the firm that has this strategic viewpoint. This is particularly important in Ireland, where markets are so small that in many cases they can be exhaustively described. In such circumstances it has often been possible for a single firm to innovate in such a way that the entire industry is compelled to follow suit, and arrives at a new equilibrium. An example is in the Dublin liquid milk market, where one company de-employed its delivery staff and made them into subcontractors, thereby reducing distribution costs. Other firms were quickly obliged to do the same.

While illustrative examples are easy to find, the problem remains of how to identify for each particular industry its particular KSFs. It is also necessary to obtain some idea of the relative importance of each. Leidecker and Bruno's review of KSFs suggests eight techniques, addressing different levels of focus, which together enable a picture of KSFs to be built up:

- **Environmental Analysis**: This is the subject of Chapter Two. Environment analysis is broad in scope, and it may be difficult to relate the results to a particular firm, or even industry. However, for those industries whose survival is dependent on forces outside the industry competitive environment, it is crucial to understand as much as possible about those forces in their wider environment. It is useful to know what a malign environment will not permit — general high interest rates, for example, will make competition based on long credit terms a very bad risk.

- **Analysis of Industry Structure**: Michael Porter of Harvard has developed the most advanced conception of how industries are structured, basing his work on the PIMS data. He provides a framework for defining industry, identifying the chief actors, and describing the critical inter-relationships between the actors in the industry.

- **Industry and Business Experts**: While not an objective analytical technique, purposeful consultation with industry experts can yield new, or confirm old, insights into what is critical in the industry. There are some structured techniques, such as "Delphi" forecasting, to gather this kind of information, and trade magazines can also be very useful.

- **Analysis and Competition**: Porter's framework narrows the focus onto the firms competing with each other in an industry where the broader industry analysis also includes buyers, suppliers, distributors and substitutes.

- **Analysis of Dominant Firm in Industry**: A useful way of determining industry KSFs since these are often set by the dominant firm, but the technique is limited to industries that have rather obvious dominant firms. Thorough understanding of what this firm does successfully is vital for forming one's own strategy, with the possibility of either emulating this, or, more innovatively, avoiding or neutralising KSFs dictated by the dominant firm.

- **Company Assessment**: This approach is specific to the firm carrying out the analysis. A variety of techniques, such as the Strengths/Weaknesses, Threats/Opportunities structure or comprehensive checklists, have been described to help pinpoint what the firm does well or badly, and to suggest what the firm may or must do in the future. (See Chapter 7 on services.)

- **Temporal Intuitive Factors**: These are firm-specific, but more informal than a company assessment, and somewhat wider in scope. Examples are the factors such as weather; underlying cyclical or random variations; the availability of key management talent; or an unexpected breakthrough, either by the firm or its competitors, which changes the industry cost structure.

- **PIMS Results**: By now, PIMS data have yielded a good deal of knowledge about the direction and magnitude of factors influencing profit. The most important of these are market share, relative market share and relative product quality, all of which have highly positive effects on profits; on the other hand, investment as a percentage of sales and as a percentage of value added have been identified as factors with strongly negative effects. The PIMS results have the advantage of being empirically-based, but are very general, and it is sometimes hard to define whether a result is applicable in a specific case.

Leidecker and Bruno suggest four approaches that are helpful in assessing the relative importance of the KSFs, once identified in a specific context.

The first involves determination of the importance of the different areas of functional management. In manufacturing firms, for example, superior management of say, inventories, purchasing or foreign currencies, could make the difference between profitability and failure, and thus become a KSF.

The second approach is to examine a firm's cost structure to identify where the largest amounts of money are being spent (80/20 rules or ABC analysis can be useful here). In labour-intensive firms, labour productivity will be a KSF. For firms producing branded consumer products, the marketing function accounts for a high proportion of costs and the effectiveness of promotion expenditure may be critical. If raw materials account for a good deal of cost, purchasing and inventory management policies could be a KSF.

A third approach is to assess the sensitivity of profit changes in certain activities. A small price change may have more impact than a doubling of advertising expenditure.

A final clue to assessing the importance of KSFs is given by analysis and monitoring of the firm's management information to see whether fundamental change is occurring in the cost or profitability structure. Sudden or significant change will often be linked eventually with a KSF.

The Leidecker and Bruno analysis omits what many economists would consider to be of critical importance, the concept of elasticity. In product/markets which are price elastic — where sales volumes are sensitive to purchaser income — environmental trends in real incomes are of obvious importance.

### 8.2.11 Strategy Types

Industry environments and competitive situations vary widely and each firm follows a unique strategy to fit its activities to its context. Despite this diversity, it seems that there are only three fundamental or generic types of business strategy.

### *Cost-Leadership Strategies*

Being the lowest cost producer in an industry gives a good deal of protection against competitive forces. However, only one firm in each industry can achieve cost leadership, and the competition to reach this position may be extremely costly to the losers. Cost leadership stems from the achievement of optimum economies of scale, of having a market share that can cope with this output, and of maintaining tight control of overhead costs. Low cost is measured relative to competitors' costs, and the quality features most desired by buyers must, at least, be matched by the low-cost producer. Cost-leadership strategies are particularly effective when:

- Demand is price elastic

- Products are standardised, or commodities

- Products are difficult to differentiate in buyers' eyes

- Buyers have similar requirements for the product

- There are few switching costs for buyers.

Cost leadership cannot long be maintained if there are low barriers to creating the cost advantage, when rivals can quickly catch up. It is generally based on high investment in production technology, which is vulnerable to technological breakthrough. Continuous investment must be made in state-of-the-art technology, and this brings further risk of becoming locked into technology that may become inappropriate as customer needs change.

### *Differentiation Strategies*
The intention here is to add value to a product in the customer's eyes by providing it with characteristics that competitors cannot easily match. The many different ways of differentiating products can be placed into four main categories:

1. Superior technical performance

2. Superior quality

3. Wider range of customer support services

4. Lower price.

Lower price in this instance is not the same as a low-cost producer strategy. In this case, a lower-value "bundle" of product attributes is offered for the lower price, for example, "no-frills" airlines. Differentiation strategies work best in situations where:

- The product lends itself to different kinds of differentiation

- Buyers' needs and uses for the product are diverse

- Switching costs are high for buyers

- Rival's products are not highly differentiated.

To be effective, a differentiation strategy must be sustainable, which requires that barriers must exist to prevent rivals from copying the strategy. This underlines the importance of building a strategy that is firmly rooted in the firm's distinctive competence and strengths. It is usually possible to succeed at only one type of differentiation, partly because a firm does not have distinctive competence in every area of operations, and partly because too many types of differentiation blur the product/market focus. At the same time, the extra costs of achieving a differentiated product must not exceed the extra contribution resulting from increased sales or from higher prices.

### *Focus or Specialisation Strategies*

Also known as niche strategies, these approaches focus narrowly on a portion of the product/market only; on needs of a particular customer group, on a geographical area or on only certain uses of the product. The competitive advantage of a focus strategy stems from differentiation by servicing target-market needs particularly well, or by servicing them at lower cost, or both. Focus strategies work best where:

- There are distinct buyer groups with different needs, different costs of servicing, or different uses for the product

- Competitors opt for broad-focus strategies

- Industry segments vary in attractiveness

- The firm has limited resources.

The threats to a focus strategy are that a broader-based competitor will be able to achieve focus on the firm's target market, or that other competitors will be able to split the target into smaller segments on which they focus, or that buyer preferences will shift so that the target segment becomes less differentiated from the market as a whole.

Irish firms are quite limited in the types of strategies they can apply, especially in terms of export markets. Lack of resources and small size (relative to competitors) mean that there are virtually no options except niche strategies, although a small number of firms in the modern sector have managed to achieve success with differentiation strategies. The logistics costs of procuring inputs and delivering products to foreign markets, the necessity of importing most industrial raw materials, and the inability to achieve economies of scale in the domestic market, all combine to make cost leadership an improbable strategy for Irish firms.

Corporate strategy options are different in nature from business strategies. Corporate strategy comes into play when a firm operates more than one Strategic Business Unit (SBU), each of which is effectively capable of standing alone. The corporate strategy is concerned with the selection of the portfolio of businesses and the allocation of resources among them to achieve corporate objectives. Within such a corporation, the SBUs have to formulate business strategy in the normal way, though they have to accept the constraints imposed by corporate objectives, and they may be able to access the greater resources of the corporation as a whole.

There is a variety of techniques for analysing and evaluating portfolios, but these techniques are only of theoretical interest to Irish managers. Some of the MNCs in Ireland would have SBU status, while many others would not be true stand-alone businesses. As far as is known, no Irish company utilises a corporate strategy in this sense of the word. The Jefferson Smurfit Group and CRH would be likely candidates in terms of size, but both have followed strategies of vertical integration and then geographical diversification, while remaining essentially single-line-of-business companies.

## 8.3 STRATEGY IMPLEMENTATION

When strategic planning — under several different names — began to come into widespread use in America in the 1960s and 1970s, many attempts floundered because the links between the formulators and the implementors were inadequate. Strategy development was often thought to be a specialist function, carried out by headquarters staff and imposed on the operating line managers. The more common view now is that senior line managers — those who will be responsible for seeing the plan into effect — bear the main responsibility for formulating strategy, with help as appropriate from specialist analysts and a scheduling/facilitating administration service. This section details some of the concerns and issues of implementation for the general manager: the contents of the strategic plan, implementation tools, the important "soft" human factors and the need for monitoring the reformulation.

### 8.3.1 Contents of Strategic Plan

As the analytical phases of the strategic planning process proceed, the strategic position becomes clearer. Gaps between present and desired future performance, between resource requirements and resource availability, between capability and opportunity are identified and analysed. Some strategic elements are determined or strongly suggested by external forces, but the act of devising successful strategies requires a good deal of creativity and decisions of judgment, and it cannot be reduced to analytical procedures alone. Luck also plays a part.

The strategic plan that emerges from the formulation process will contain five major elements:

1. A definition of the business mission and a listing of the strategic objectives that are to be achieved within the timescale of the plan.

2. A statement of the competitive advantage that will be developed or created to allow the objectives to be achieved. This would include the reasoning behind the selection of a cost leadership, differentiation or focus strategy, and the major strategic moves that will be taken to support the strategy.

3. A detailed specification of the products and markets that are to be targeted during the planning period, together with the logic behind this selection.

4. A detailed specification of resources required over the planning period, together with plans for acquiring those not currently available, and details of the timing of their development.

5. A series of detailed functional and operating strategies for each area of the business, which focus on the results to be achieved. It should be explicitly stated how each functional area's results will contribute to the overall strategy, and how they interact with each other.

Devising the strategic plan is basically an entrepreneurial task, because it sets the future direction of the firm. When the strategy has been decided upon, the managerial emphasis shifts from entrepreneurship to administration. The decision focus shifts from effectiveness issues (what should we be doing?) to efficiency issues (how can we do it best?) General management concentrates on putting programmes in place, on motivating the organisation to perform, and monitoring progress towards objectives.

### 8.3.2 Strategic Programmes and Strategic Budgets

Strategic programmes are among the major instruments by which strategies are put into place. They translate the strategic plan into the detailed tasks that have to be performed in order to achieve specified results. Programmes also act as co-ordinating mechanisms, because they specify all of the firm's functional activities that are required to achieve the programme objectives, which are formulated in terms of results. They could be viewed as a temporary structural layer placed over the firm's organisation structure until the programme objective is achieved. (Of course, bureaucratic forces will tend to incorporate "temporary" structures into the formal structure — a potential problem for the next generation of strategy.)

Strategic programmes are activated and also controlled by means of strategic budgets, which allocate financial resources to, and set detailed short-term targets for, the programmes. Analysis of budget variances is an important component of the feedback process, which provides a measure of the success of implementation. It is useful to distinguish between "baseline" funds programmes, which provide funds and budgets to maintain ongoing operations, and "strategic" funds programmes, which are directed at changing the strategy. When the strategic process is working well, strategic funds proposals will exceed the firm's resources, and there must then be a process for evaluating and choosing from among them.

A strategic funds proposal will address in detail three questions:

1. How much will it cost (tangible assets, working capital, extra current expenses for programme)? The answer to this question lists asset requirements, procurement details and payable schedules.

2. How much will it earn (revenue from operations, cash flow, return on investment, pay-back period)? The answer to this question contains sales volume and value targets, which form part of the budget.

3. How will it be funded (earnings and cash flow from programme, earnings and cash flow from other operations, borrowings, equity and grants)? A programme will not be initiated unless it is expected to be viable in the long run, but there is often a funding shortfall from in-house resources in the initial period, and the cost and availability of outside funds must be specified.

Without detailed realistic budgets, attempts at strategy implementation will be plagued by financial inconsistencies — some activities will be underfunded and some overfunded. This is not just a waste of scarce resources, but also hampers other functional activities. Although budgets need to be consistent (that is, linked to the strategy), they must also contain a degree of flexibility to allow for changes in plan. Furthermore, they should be expressed in such a way as to facilitate decision-making by the operations level of management.

The strategic budget will generally have four major components, which have to be closely integrated:

1. A capital budget dealing with all aspects of funding and returns

2. Sales budgets specifying sales volumes and values, penetration targets and product mix

3. Production or operations budgets for deploying resources and

ensuring that output matches sales volumes and cost targets

4. Overhead budgets for cost control and also for overhead investment such as R & D, new enabling technologies or staff development.

Strategic programmes and budgets are the "hard" part of the implementation phase, because they are quantified, or at least explicit. However, the "soft" part of the equation — the people side — is of at least equal importance. A good strategy can fail if the organisation culture does not support the needs of strategy, or if the right people are not in the right positions.

### 8.3.3 Organisation Structure and Strategy

Organisation structure can be thought of as the set of authority and responsibility relationships operating in a firm. There is no single best way to organise a firm, though a few themes are common: organisation by function, by geographical area, by customer group, or as a decentralised or strategic business unit. Less common are intermediate forms such as matrix structures, task forces and venture teams. The dynamics of human interactions within the organisation generally cause an imbalance between the formal structure and the actual relationships of authority and responsibility. To carry out a strategic plan successfully requires that the organisation be appropriately structured, and the strategic plan must therefore include a specification of any structural changes that will be necessary.

A general approach to deliberately designing an organisation structure to match strategy should:

- Be based on the strategy, identify the critical tasks that have to be accomplished, and derive the managerial functions that are needed to perform these

- Understand the relationships among these strategy-critical functions and tasks

- Group the functions and tasks into organisation units, focused on strategic results — this may demand that the old organisation units be reorganised

- Determine levels of authority needed to manage each unit — this gives them all relative positions on the formal organisation chart

- Provide mechanisms, and perhaps organisational units, to ensure that the units are properly co-ordinated and integrated.

Where rates of change within an industry or firm are slow, the organisational structure may persist unchanged for long periods. However, rates of change in general are accelerating and the evolution of organisation structures must keep pace in order to remain appropriate. On the other hand, changing the formal structure in response to strategic needs is not enough. The people in the organisation must be motivated if the structure is to be made effective.

### 8.3.4 Organisation Culture and Strategy

Broadly speaking, the culture of an organisation is the set of beliefs and expectations about the firm that are shared by its members. These lead to habitual patterns of behaviour, concerning the way that decisions are made, the kinds of reactions taken to threats and opportunities, the way members react with each other, and the quality of work done. The culture is rooted in the past successes and failures of the firm, and especially in policies of staff treatment. Culture can have an impact on strategy if there is a conflict between the requirements of the action plan and the beliefs of the individuals who have to carry it out. On the other hand, the strategic planners are themselves embedded in the culture, so an organisation will not often select strategies that conflict radically with its existing culture. However, radical change is sometimes necessary either in response to the external events, or because a new owner or a new chief executive has a different strategic vision.

Radical change of organisation structure and/or culture is complex, expensive and time-consuming, which is why most change is incremental. If a major change is required it must be carefully planned in advance, and carried out with a delicate understanding of the personal factors involved. The change should be closely monitored and adjusted if necessary. There must be:

- An explicit statement of strategy and of how the organisation change will help to achieve this

- Identification and clear understanding of the relevant culture and sub-cultures in the organisation

- Assessment of the risk of strategic failure as a result of cultural incompatibility and the critical aspects of culture isolated

- A planned process of change in these critical areas.

The change process itself must be managed carefully. Beginning at the top, all levels of management must be sold on the strategy and the changes needed to implement it. Recruitment of new staff, redeployment, and perhaps firing, of existing staff may be necessary. A most important means of motivation is to link the reward structure to actual performance in such a way that "doing a good job" becomes equivalent to "achieving agreed upon objectives". Finally, a programme of management training and development, tightly linked to strategic skills requirements, will ensure that appropriate skills will be available. Such programmes in themselves often result in added staff motivation and increased job satisfaction.

In certain kinds of firms, such as high-technology operations or businesses that have a very short life-cycle, the rate of change of the environment is so great that the organisation structure must undergo constant change. Temporary structures are assembled and disbanded as objectives are achieved or the focus changes. Depending on the business, there may be a relatively stable structure at the core of operations. In such cases, where there is a premium on adaptability, innovation and quick response to outside circumstances, the organisation culture must be highly supportive of an entrepreneurial climate. Systems and procedures must be set in place to identify and assess new ideas on an ongoing basis.

Successful organisation change stems from strong leadership, which must combine a true understanding of the kind of change called for by the environment, with the ability to motivate and inspire people with this mission. Communication is a vital ingredient in effective leadership. The strategies should be outlined and the logic behind them explained to the people who will carry them out. Individual contributions to objectives should be strongly and publicly supported, and higher management should be seen to lead by example. Particular attention should be paid to enlisting the support and enthusiasm of all line managers.

### 8.3.5 Monitoring Strategic Progress

The strategic plan is a blueprint for what the firm wishes to happen within the planning time horizon. The plan is a kind of "snapshot", based on information available at the time of formulation. As implementation proceeds, resources are committed to various projects, the firm's outputs (products, promotion, services, etc.) begin to change, and unconnected events, some of which impinge on the firm, occur in the environment. The strategic planning process must ensure that the plan takes account of circumstances as they unfold. Two questions must be posed continually: "Is this the right strategy?" and "Is it being implemented properly?" Answering these questions requires feedback, on two counts. Firstly, the firm needs to know how implementation is proceeding, and whether this is according to plan. Secondly, it needs to know how the environment is responding to strategic initiatives. The feedback and evaluation often leads to adjustment of operations and, less frequently, to changes in the strategic thrust.

Feedback comes from both formal and informal sources of information. The informal information network is maintained by management contacts with a wide range of industry participants. A philosophy of constant exchange of information leads to early feedback from the field, and helps to maintain a constant feel for the situation outside the firm. There is a large amount of literature on how formal systems can be designed to provide feedback information. For monitoring strategic progress the information flows should provide all — and only — strategically-relevant information, in a relatively simple form which interprets the strategic relevance. The information should be timely, quick and economical, and should be geared for taking corrective actions, if necessary. In the main, it should attempt to flag exceptions, rather than just to provide confirmation of progress for its records.

The most important quantitative factors that need constant monitoring include:

| Sales Growth | Output Growth | Asset Growth |
|---|---|---|
| • Market Share | • Net Profit | • Share Price |
| • E.P.S. | • Value-added | • Gross Margins |
| • Return on Equity | • Return on | • Return on Sales |
| • Sales/employee | Investment | • Production Costs |
| | • Profits/employee | and Efficiency |

Many firms will have qualitative results that are uniquely important for them to monitor. The results from operations are compared with strategic targets, with competitors' results, and with the firm's own historical performance.

## SUMMARY

This chapter introduces the concept of business strategy, which may be defined as the intended business relationship between the organisation and its environment, and the way in which this relationship is to be developed and implemented. There are a few fundamental steps involved in the strategic planning process, outlined as follows:

• Business definition and mission statement: management develops a definition of what its business mission is by using the Tri-Polar Model.

• Environment analysis: management constantly tracks environment influences and drivers of change (at both a macro and micro level) — in order to forecast the effect on the firm and industry and to diagnose whether the current mission should be reformed.

• Establish strategic objectives: strategic objectives quantify the mission statement in terms of specific measurable results that are to be reviewed within the time scale of the strategic plan, and are defined in more detail through functional and operating objectives.

• The industry structure can be analysed using Porter's model which looks at the influencing factors and the various centres of power.

- The firm's strengths and weaknesses are determined to understand the nature of competitive advantage and the firm's relative competitive position.

- Activity-Cost chain analysis can be used to distinguish further the firm's relative cost-competitiveness *vis-à-vis* other industry players. From this the key success factors which fuel competitive advantage can be identified.

- Once the strategic objectives are identified, the strategy type has to be chosen or modified. Three central strategy types have been identified:

    - Cost leadership (low-cost)

    - Differentiation (value-added)

    - Focus or specialisation (niche strategy).

- The strategic plan should outline the above-mentioned but should also detail specific action plans, programmes and required budgets in terms of the following: business mission, competitive advantage, strategic objectives and detailed product/market strategy.

- Specification of resources required in terms of capital, technology, personnel, etc.:

    - Detailed functional operating strategies

    - Detailed programmes and budgets, i.e. the strategic funds proposal.

- Other issues that should be addressed include the appropriate organisation structure, organisation culture, and monitoring/control issues.

## FURTHER READING

Hope, Charles W. and Dan Schendel, *Strategy Formulation: Analytical Concepts*, West Publishing Company, St Paul, MN, 1978.

Kotler, Philip, *Marketing Management: Analysis, Planning, Implementation and Control*, 7th Edition, Prentice Hall International, Englewood Cliffs, NJ, 1991.

Leidecker, L.K. and A.V. Bruno, "Identifying and Using Critical Success Factors", *Long-Range Planning*, Vol. 17, No. 1, 1986, pp. 23–32.

Murray, John A., *Marketing Management: An Introduction*, Gill and Macmillan, Dublin, 1984.

Porter, Michael, *Competitive Advantage*, The Free Press, New York, 1985.

Thompson, A.A. Jr. and A.J. Strickland, *Strategy Formulation and Implementation (Tasks of the General Manager)*, 4th Edition, Business Publications Inc., Plano, TX, 1989.

CHAPTER NINE

# MARKETING MANAGEMENT

## 9.1 INTRODUCTION

*T*his chapter, together with the three chapters which follow, is intended to explain the strategic inputs of each of the major functional areas. The chapter therefore covers four main marketing topics as follows:

- Strategic marketing

- Marketing tactics and the marketing mix

- Marketing systems and activities

- Contemporary issues and applications in marketing management.

Firstly, the purpose, need for and functions of marketing are examined, together with the changing marketing environment and the three levels of marketing:

- Strategic

- Tactical

- Activities and contemporary issues.

In considering strategic marketing, emphasis is placed on the marketing inputs, particularly the selection of products/markets and competitive positioning. Also examined is the concept of product portfolio analysis, marketing innovation and international marketing. Tactical marketing and the development of the marketing mix are considered in relation to the strategic marketing issues. Issues such as the product and service mix, branding and product life cycle, together with pricing strategy, communications and selling, distribution and logistics, are all considered. In the section which analyses marketing systems and activities, consideration is given to the activities required to implement marketing strategy effectively. The new product development process and direct marketing systems are also analysed. Finally, contemporary issues in marketing are briefly considered, including business-to-business marketing, industrial, services and environmental marketing.

### 9.1.1 Purpose of Marketing

The economic justification for a business — sustained long-term profit levels above the cost of capital — stems entirely from the satisfaction of customer needs at a cost that allows adequate profitability. Companies that are not strongly focused on the identification — or creation — of customer needs, which do not provide customer satisfaction, or which cannot provide satisfaction profitably, will ultimately succumb to the activities of competitors. Marketing is one of the four major managerial functions, and it concerns itself with the customer aspects of the company's overall activities. That is, the management of the relationship of the firm with its customers and the management of the firm's position relative to its competitors. Unlike the other major functions (finance, operations, and human resource management) marketing is uniquely and entirely outward-focused. Because of its concern with customers and with the marketplace, marketing is also the function best placed to understand the firm's environment. Therefore, successful marketing management must be driven by two imperatives: satisfying customer needs and doing it better than the competition — and one constraint — doing it profitably.

### 9.1.2 The Changing Marketing Environment

This view of the marketing function is in contrast with the traditional perspective, which equated marketing with sales activities alone, or which saw the firm as essentially a production organisation which just delivered goods to waiting markets. The changed and broadened approach is a result of fundamental changes that have taken place in the general business environment. The first important change concerns the customer. The continued development of industrialised society has resulted in demands for increased variety, greater discernment and general fickleness of customer tastes. At the same time, continued technological developments have caused continual evolution of industrial and commercial needs. These evolutionary processes have resulted in great diversity of products/markets. This variety has in turn placed a major strategic emphasis on the correct selection of the market segments the company can serve and the products being offered.

The second major change in the general business environment which has broadened the concept of marketing is the changing nature of competition. Free-trade policies (e.g. WTO/GATT Uruguay Round, EU and NAFTA), the advance of production technologies, and the application of strategic management principles and methods have resulted in a general level of competition that is much more intense than that which prevailed pre-1966, when Ireland was just contemplating removal of tariff barriers. Today the only way to compete successfully in the modern world is through devising and implementing superior strategies. These strategies are vital in the perpetual war with competitors, where the battlefield is the marketplace, and the chief tactical weapons are the elements of the marketing mix.

The third major change area is rooted in the nature of the economy itself, in addition to the manner in which the structure of the global economic environment has developed. After a period of stagnation in the early 1980s, Ireland has experienced sustained growth which is forecast to continue into the next century. Ireland is now a very open economy, highly influenced by European Union and World Trade Organisation policy, and highly susceptible to multinational companies' strategies. Despite the openness of the economy and its commensurate competition, many Irish firms have competed successfully on the export and domestic markets. There is, however, still an inadequacy of indigenous marketing skills, and while companies like Guinness, Waterford Glass, Bailey's Irish Cream and Kerrygold Butter have been successful, overall the level and sophistication of marketing management techniques compared to US, Japanese and European multinationals is low. The fundamental weaknesses in Irish marketing performance in the 1980s and 1990s have been concentrated in strategic rather than operational areas. Specific strategic weaknesses are reflected in inadequate market information for the purpose of defining the most appropriate markets, inadequate new product development and innovation, together with a defensive approach to new market development among many Irish firms.

Areas where Irish firms have underperformed in the past are as follows:

- There is insufficient awareness of the need for strategic marketing, with marketing activities being dominated by tactical perspectives.

- The small size and openness of the Irish economy forces many companies into exporting at an earlier stage of their development than their overseas competitors.

- Past industrial policy has tended to encourage production-oriented companies with inadequate marketing skills. However, the creation of An Bord Bia, which consolidates the activities of many food marketing agencies, is an example of how the traditional focus is changing.

- The marketing function, generally, is not held in high regard by Irish firms.

- The firms do not appreciate the vital need to develop new products, relying too much on mature and traditional products.

It is interesting here to note that three of these five points are concerned with attitudes held by managers (the other two points involve the focus and integration of state support services). It is also interesting to note that many of these problems have not been fully addressed by industry and are key areas for development in the National Development Plan.

### 9.1.3 The Different Levels of Marketing Activity
A large number of different kinds of activities are carried out

under the aegis of the marketing function, and these can usefully be broken down into three major types:

- Strategic Marketing

- Tactical Marketing

- Marketing Activities.

The key areas within the three types are depicted in Figure 9.1.

It should be noted that, from the viewpoint of the strategist, each of the three levels contributes to a different strategic task. The first kind of activity is at the strategic level, i.e. the strategic marketing function. The activity is concerned essentially with the selection of the competitive battleground, that is, who will be competed against and with what weapons. It is also concerned with the selection of strategic approaches. This is the marketing input into the strategy formulation process, which is at heart the matching of market potentials with the company's capability to carry out operations to compete.

Tactical marketing is essentially operational. This is nearer to the core of earlier thinking on what marketing is, and this probably still represents a consensus viewpoint for many Irish firms. Marketing operations are concerned with implementing strategy by means of day-to-day tactical activities — persuading customers to buy, delivering the product/service for consumption, monitoring customer and competitor responses. This kind of activity gets the lion's share of marketing management attention, often to the detriment of strategic marketing. On the other hand, it is vital that marketing operations be carried out effectively and efficiently, or even the best of strategies will not succeed.

The third type of marketing activities is a little harder to define, but it embraces the ideas of integration and ideology. To ensure long-term success it requires that the firm be truly responsive to its customers' needs. The marketing function is the logical place for the "customer advocates" to reside. Someone has to ensure: (a) that the whole firm adopts a customer orientation, and (b) that the firm's operations actually result in getting the product/service bundle, in a satisfactory form, to the customer.

*Figure 9.1: The Levels of Marketing Strategy*

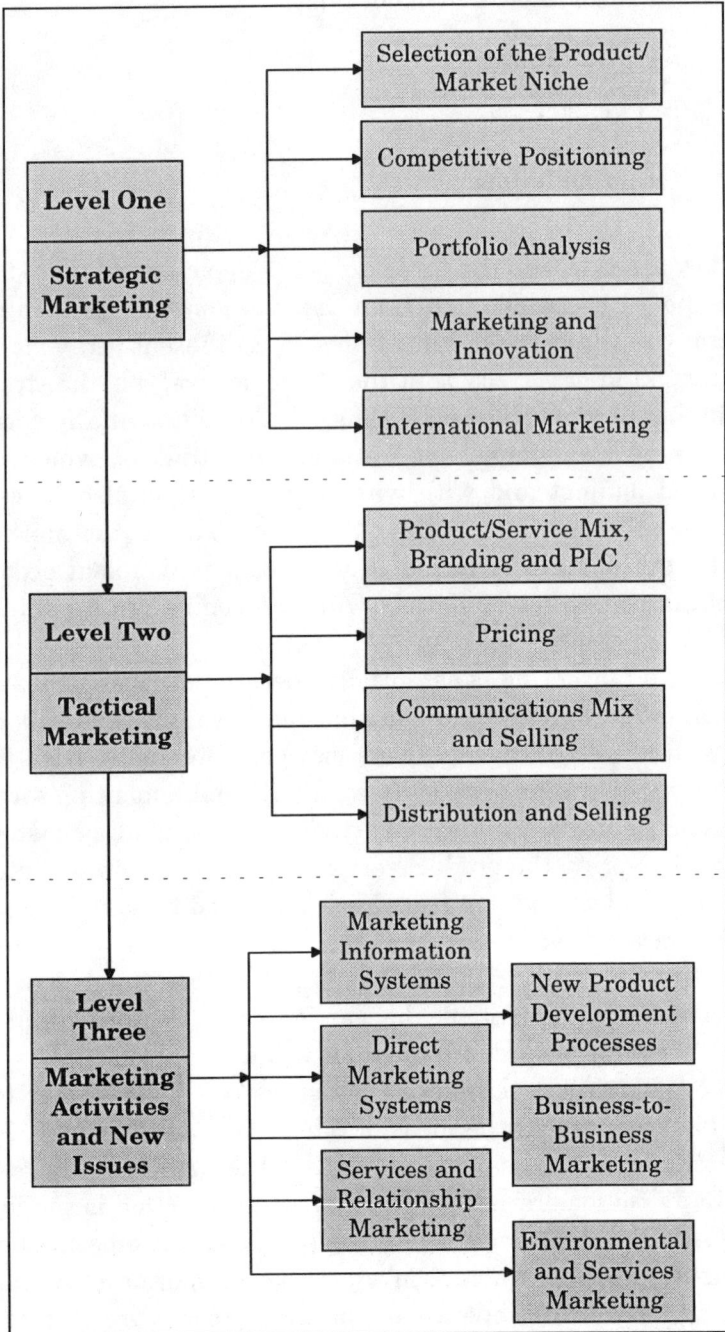

## 9.2 STRATEGIC MARKETING

Marketing has a major input into strategy formulation, chiefly in the way that it helps to define precisely the firm's business and basic approach to the market. This section looks at the strategic marketing elements of positioning, portfolio analysis and international marketing.

### 9.2.1 Selection of the Product/Market Niche

A most important strategic concern of marketing management is the selection of the company's competitive arena. This involves the choice of: (a) customer group(s) to be served, and (b) the choice of the product "bundles" that will be offered to them.

By implication, the choice selects the competitors that are active in these product/market niches. An example here is the development of the major commercial banks in recent years. Today their product bundles consist of insurance, house mortgages and commercial finance, in addition to their normal banking services. For most companies, and especially for small ones, selection of competitive area will commit the firm to a particular direction for a long time. Once operations have commenced, it is difficult to change this fundamental thrust quickly. The selection of product/market niches, or competitive arena, is only slightly less wide in scope than the statement of the firm's business mission. The latter tries to see various actual or potential niches as being related in a way that is meaningful for the firm as a whole.

### 9.2.2 Competitive Market Positioning

When a company has selected its product/market niche, the products then must be positioned with respect to competing products. Product positioning is carried out for each product and for each market segment. Correct product positioning requires a good deal of information about customers and their needs. The general approach is:

- Identify customer purchasing criteria, that is, the aspects of the product that are important to the customer. These may be grouped into three types: (a) price- or cost-related criteria (e.g. purchase price, consumable usage, discounts, financing, operating costs); (b) functional- or performance-related criteria (e.g. ease of use, maintenance, precision); and (c) psycho-social criteria (e.g. acceptability to others of one's purchase, fit with self concept). These criteria are best identified through formal market research, but personal questioning of buyers and previous managerial experience of selling in this field can also be very productive.

• Identify the value that customers place on each of these criteria. The simplest form of this is a ranking of customer priorities (see Figure 9.2), which can be elaborated into more detailed "performance maps" which attempt to display ideal customer preferences for various positions on each purchase criterion.

### Figure 9.2: Rank Order of Importance of Customer-Evaluation Criteria

|   | Electrical Retailers | Paint Retailers | Cigarette Retailers |
|---|----------------------|-----------------|---------------------|
| 1. | After-sales service | Quality of goods received | Quality of goods received |
| 2. | Quality of goods received | Discounts offered | Delivery reliability |
| 3. | Guarantees | Inventory reliability | Inventory reliability |
| 4. | Contactability | Guarantees | Guarantees |
| 5. | Delivery reliability | After-sales service | Sales representation |

Source: Murray, J.A. and S.A. McEntee, "Measuring the Effect of Customer Service Levels", *Journal of Irish Business and Administrative Research*, Vol. 1, No. 1, 1979.

• Identify customer perceptions of competing products for each purchasing criterion. This information can be overlaid onto the ideal customer preference maps, and the result yields suggestions for where the firm might position its own product.

When this information has been obtained, the marketing manager can then take the positioning decision. Three alternative positioning strategies are available:

1. Introduce new products or product attributes to fill gaps in the market (which are expressed on performance maps as unfulfilled "ideal" customer preferences), e.g. Low-fat dairy spreads targeted at people who want a lower-fat butter.

2. Alter the position of existing products to bring them closer to buyers ideals or to differentiate them further from competing products.

3. Alter buyers' perceptions of purchasing criteria, either by introducing new criteria, or by changing the importance buyers attribute to existing criteria.

### 9.2.3 Product Portfolio Analysis

One of the most important methods of strategic market planning is portfolio analysis, which compares a company's product range to the shares in an investor's portfolio. Portfolio analysis is a useful technique for diversified companies or companies with large product ranges. To demonstrate the portfolio concept, the Boston Consulting Group (BCG) developed a graph that plots a company's relative market share versus market growth. Divided into four quadrants, the portfolio graph (see Figure 9.3) has important ramifications for a company's cash flow.

Figure 9.3 displays four categories in matrix form and the arrows between each quadrant show the direction in which cash available for investment moves from one to another. The circles represent the various businesses within the firm and their relative sizes. The vertical axis indicates annual growth rates, while the horizontal axis represents relative market share *vis-à-vis* the market leader. In this manner, it will be possible to visualise a number of products supporting each other as they progress around the matrix from one to three, and preferably avoiding quadrant four.

## Figure 9.3: BCG Product Portfolio Classification

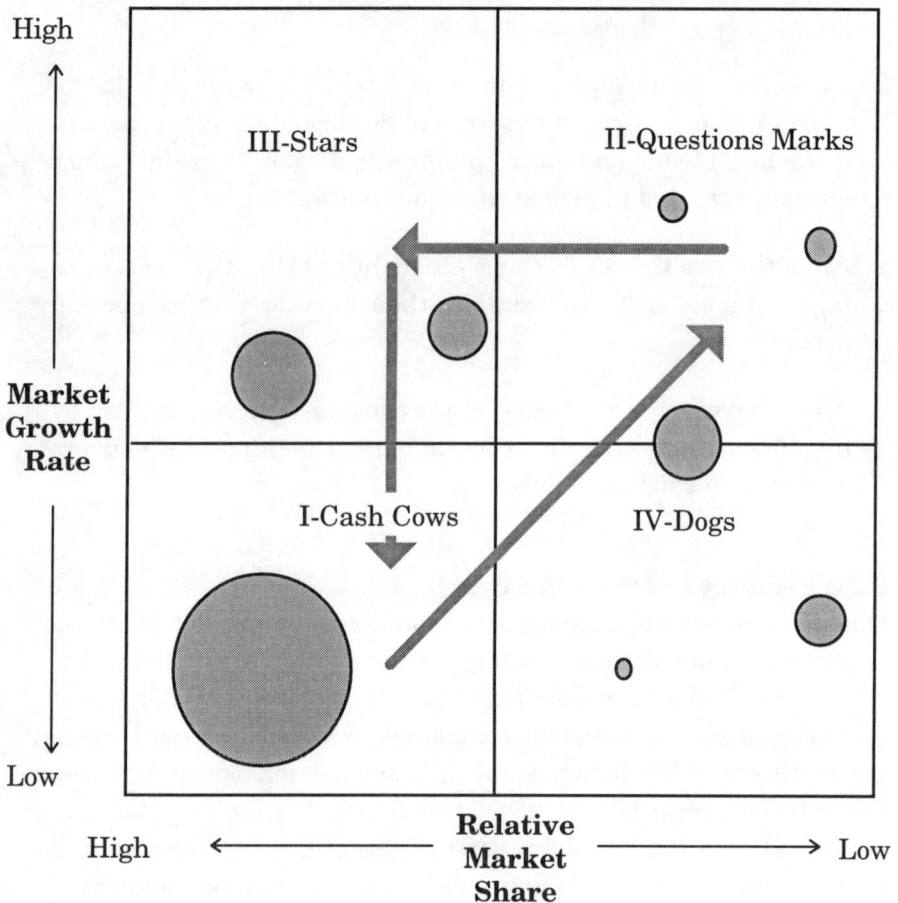

*Source*: Heldey, B., "Strategy and the Business Portfolio", *Long-Range Planning*, February 1977.

The launch of any new product contains all kinds of uncertainties and no guarantee of success can be assured. This product is identified with a question mark (II). It uses a lot more cash than it generates (negative cash flow). When a product really appeals to the marketplace, growth follows and is designated a star (III). It has a high profit potential but needs a lot of cash to finance growth (sometimes positive but more often a negative cash flow).

While the product is approaching, and then remains in, the maturity stage it provides cash surpluses, which can be milked to support other products and is called a "cash cow" (generates more cash than needed to maintain its high market share) (I). Finally, the product ceases to contribute cash surpluses and is deemed to be a "dog", which is the loser in the portfolio (functions at a cost disadvantage, has few opportunities to expand market share and has a negative or poor cash flow) (IV).Additionally, these four categories can be viewed as progressing along the product life cycle (see Figure 9.5). One certainty is that any investment in a product (outflows) must over the course of time be more than recovered by inflows for any real success to be claimed. It is in the early stages of the product life cycle then that these outflows are usually made and, consequently, they should be regularly monitored and tightly controlled. In theory, cash cows should be fuelling question marks in order that the latter become stars.

A major shortcoming of the BCG matrix approach is that using only two variables (relative market share and market growth) may oversimplify what is an extremely complex process. To overcome this problem, General Electric (GE) introduced a multi-factor portfolio matrix, which encompasses overall market size, relative market share and competitiveness. The last two dimensions are most important in rating a business. Competitive position and market attractiveness can be further broken down by underlying factors affecting them, for example, a market will be more attractive if the annual market growth rate is high, historical profit margins are also high and competitive intensity is low. The GE matrix is divided into nine cells rather than four, which in turn fall into three zones:

- Invest/grow

- Selectivity/earnings

- Harvest/invest.

Figure 9.4 portrays an example of the GE matrix for a diversified firm with seven Strategic Business Units (SBUs).

**Figure 9.4: The GE Market Attractiveness-Competitive Position Portfolio Classification and Strategies**

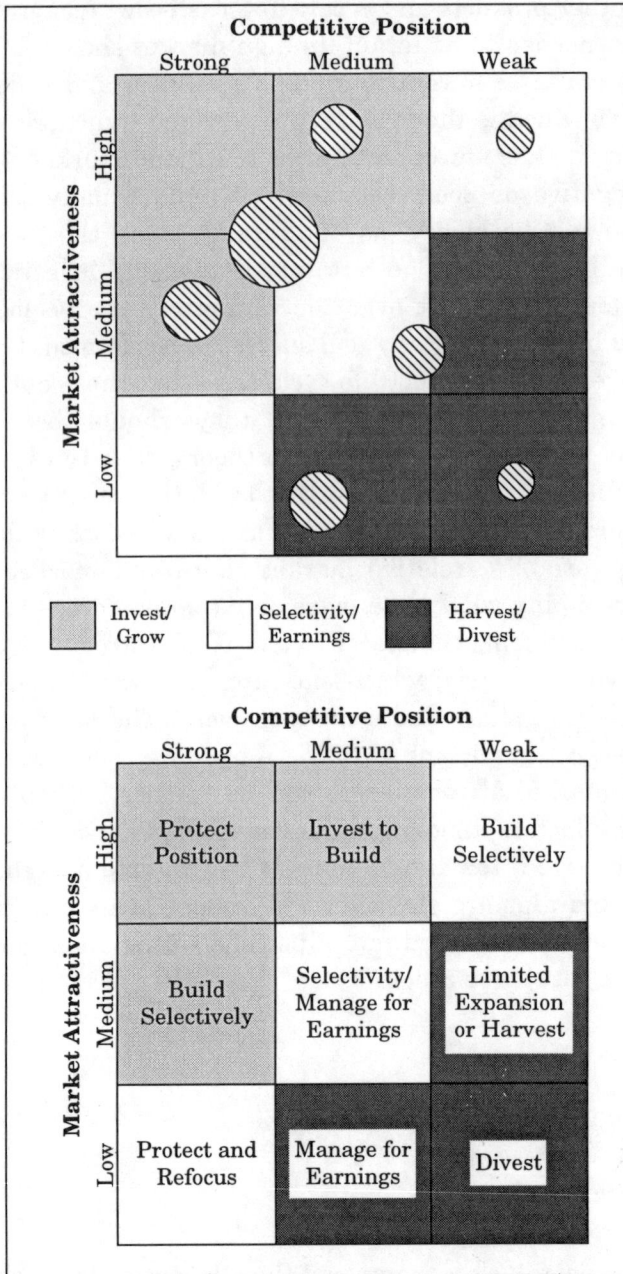

Source: Adapted from Kotler, P., *Marketing Management: Analysis, Planning, Implementation and Control*, Seventh Edition, 1991.

### 9.2.4 Ongoing Review and Evaluation

A further aspect of strategic marketing consists of the adjustment of strategy in the light of unfolding operations and market events. As has been mentioned in the previous chapter, the strategy-formulation process should not be looked upon as a once-a-year only event. The strategic plan represents the best assessment of the situation, and an intention that certain things will occur in the future. However, nothing stands still: the original information could be incomplete or incorrect, operating decisions could be flawed, or the competitive, industrial or economic environments could have changed in unforeseen ways. Since marketing is the major outward-looking function in the firm, it carries the responsibility for monitoring these environmental changes and comparing achievements with original targets. Sometimes adjustments will be made to operating strategies, sometimes the requirements are for changes in the basic strategy, and the marketing manager is at the fulcrum of these decisions.

### 9.2.5 Marketing and Innovation

The marketing function may be a source of "business" innovation, which is a fundamental change in the way business is done in the industry. This could consist of, for example, the discovery of a new distribution channel, a new promotional medium e.g. Estée Lauder in-store promotions, or discovery of a new use for the product, such as Kaliber non-alcoholic beer. Though successful innovations of this kind are usually copied by competitors, it may be possible to create barriers, and there are usually first-mover advantages. There is unfortunately no systematic procedure for this kind of innovation. It requires a high order of managerial creativity.

### 9.2.6 International Marketing

As outlined in Chapters One and Six, foreign market development has become vital for over 60 per cent of firms operating in Ireland. This manifests itself in balance-of-trade figures since the early 1980s. Therefore, in deciding whether to go abroad — the first major decision in international marketing which is taken for granted in most industry areas — the next steps are as follows:

- **The Markets/Regions/Countries to Enter**: As in the domestic market this decision rests on market attractiveness in terms of current and figure market potential, familiarity with the marketplace, transferability of competitive advantage etc.

- **The Mode of Entry into the Market**: International market development ranges from direct exporting, to licensing, joint venturing with foreign firms and finally to full-blown direct investment.

- **Marketing Operations**: The programme to be undertaken in terms of product and branding, pricing, channels, logistics and selling, and communications strategy.

- **Marketing Organisation**: Foreign market development can be managed from home via an export department or from an international division which controls country or region.

Irish companies such as CRH and the Smurfit Group are in developed stages of internationalisation and have become global companies. The key decisions to be made at this stage of the process are whether the product/service mix strategy should be modified for each significant market or standardised worldwide, for example, Coca-Cola. In addition, a decision has to be made on the level of independence to be given to each market or region. This is a question of centralisation versus decentralisation.

## 9.3 MARKETING TACTICS AND THE MARKETING MIX

Once the strategy has been decided upon, marketing activities are the cutting edge of implementing it. Together they "tailor" the product so that customers will buy and, in most cases, buy again. Marketing operations are concerned essentially with the selection and implementation of the marketing mix. The marketing mix, sometimes known as the "four Ps" — Product, Price, Promotion and Place — is the combination of factors under the control of the firm with which the segmentation and positioning decisions are implemented. While the four Ps are a useful mnemonic, a more accurate description of these vital ingredients would replace product with product/service mix, promotion with selling, and communication and place with distribution, and would include systems and processes such as market research, new product development and direct marketing.

### 9.3.1 Product and Service Mix

From the marketing point of view, a product (or service) is a bundle, or collection, of physical, service and psychological benefits designed to satisfy customer needs at a profit. "Physical" attributes of the product include the functional characteristics that provide the expected performance, the structural characteristics that deliver the functional performance in different ways (e.g. size, colours, materials, etc.) and aesthetic characteristics, if these are relevant to the particular products. "Service" attributes of the product bundle are often crucial in buyers' eyes, especially for industrial and consumer durable products, which may otherwise be difficult to differentiate functionally. Service characteristics could include such things as guarantees, training, maintenance, spare parts replacement, and technical advice. Understanding — and satisfying — customers' service needs is often the key to a superior competitive position. An example of the emphasis on service is the computer company, IBM. "Psychological" attributes of the product, while intangible, are especially important in mass-market consumer goods, where the "image" that is purchased with the product is the major differentiating factor. An example would be the marketing of cosmetics like Max Factor, Helena Rubenstein and Estée Lauder. However, psychological benefits are also sought by industrial customers, and here they relate more to the image that the firm has in the market in terms of technical reputation, reliability and advice like Mercedes (Germany), Brown Boveri (Switzerland), Siemens (Germany) and IKEA (Sweden).

### 9.3.2 Branding

Differentiating a product by branding can be a very effective strategy, especially in consumer products/markets. The brand name conveys a concise image of the product bundle to the consumer and makes it easier for consumers to recognise and choose the branded product. A branded product can usually obtain higher sales for the manufacturer, and consumer loyalty can

greatly increase the manufacturer's power *vis-à-vis* the distribution channels, because the consumers demand that the branded
product be stocked, e.g. Cadbury's chocolate. (This phenomenon is
sometimes described as the "pull-through" effect). Although product branding normally adds more value to the product (a higher
price can be obtained), a successful brand launch tends to be
expensive and takes a long time to develop, and so is beyond the
resources of many small firms. In industrial and durables markets, the company name itself may perform many of the functions
of a product brand name, being associated with an image for
quality or reliability that is valued by customers, e.g. Philips
(Holland), Sony and Honda (Japan), Mercedes (Germany) and
Chivas Regal (Scotland).

### 9.3.3 Product Life-Cycle

A final product-related feature that requires marketing management attention is the product life-cycle. This looks at the product
over the entire time-period of its existence, from conception of the
ides, through developments and introduction to the market,
through periods of sales growth, stagnation, and finally declining
sales. This concept can be used in analysing product categories
product forms or brands. Many products do go through this cycle,
but there are often great difficulties in deciding where a particular product lies in the cycle, and how the remainder of the cycle
will behave in terms of growth (or decline) rates.

The product life-cycle can be measured in either sales or profits. When sales and profits are charted on the same graph (Figure
9.5), the relationship between them can be measured for every
stage of the product's cycle. Typically, profits are non-existent in
the introductory stage because of heavy promotional and other
start-up costs. During the growth stage, both sales and profits
improve substantially. Profits usually peak later in the growth
stage, whereas sales reach a high point during the maturity
stage. A decline follows for both sales and profits, continuing until
the end of the cycle as newer versions and more competitive products enter the market arena.

For some industries, product-groups, and products, this cycle is
well-known, e.g. colour TVs; for others, it is irrelevant or

imperceptible, as products are undergoing continual development. Despite these problems, it is very worthwhile to attempt to understand the product's life-cycle position. There are important strategic implications and financial considerations, and different kinds of managerial attitudes are appropriate to the various stages.

The introduction of a new product is the riskiest stage of the life cycle. Cash-flows are usually negative, as working capital needs grow faster than sales revenues. Figure 9.5 below shows a typical pattern for this relationship.

### *Figure 9.5: The Product Life-Cycle*

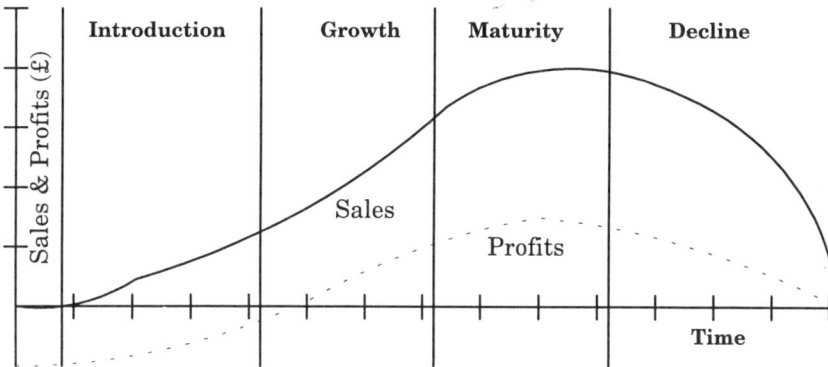

Great attention must be devoted to securing initial sales to key customers, to making early repeat sales (for consumable products) and to very close and frequent monitoring of actual sales against targets. In the growth stage of the life cycle, the emphasis shifts towards ensuring the adequacy of supplies, and to anticipating and thwarting the growing competitive pressures. Market share position and product improvement become critical.

The maturity phase is reached when sales growth slows to about the rate of general economic growth. Marketing management attention shifts towards achieving maximum profitability to recoup initial investment and using the cash to provide funds for the development of new products. Strategies centre on defending market share and attempting to prolong the mature phase of the life cycle through product improvements and penetration of new segments. The decline stage of the cycle also needs careful

management, to curtail investment, to harvest what profits are
still available, and finally to cease production and sales together
in an orderly manner. As firms expand beyond single-product
companies, it is necessary to align the overlapping life cycles of
different products to reduce risks and balance total cash-flows.

Apart from the conventional s-shaped curve of a product life
cycle, many other shapes have been identified according to the
nature of the market, environmental factors driving change and
the effectiveness of the marketing management strategy. Two
examples are an organic or tapered growth pattern and the
cycle/recycle pattern.

*Figure 9.5a: Alternative Life-Cycle Patterns*

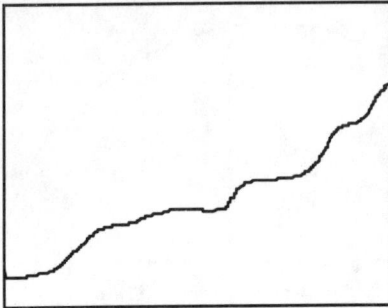

Organic Growth Pattern          Cycle/Recycle Pattern

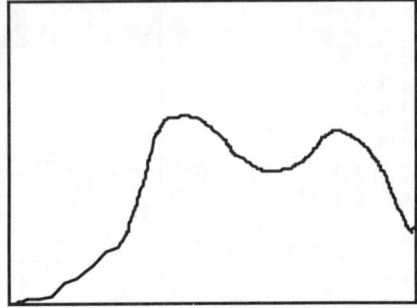

In addition, special cycles exist, such as fashion cycles for items
which may come in and out of style and fad items which show
very fast growth and very fast decline.

*Figure 9.5b: Alternative Life-Cycle Patterns*

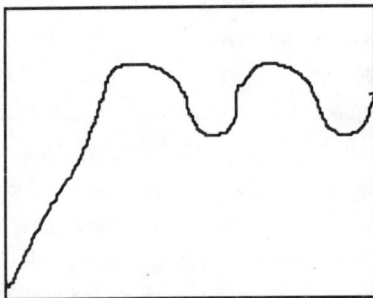

Style and Fashion                      Fad

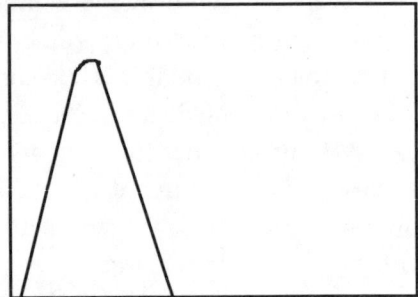

### 9.3.4 Pricing Strategy

A product's price affects its image (e.g. Mercedes cars), its market share position, and most important, the firm's profitability. The theory of how to set price correctly has to make so many simplifying assumptions that it is of limited use in practice. Probably most pricing decisions are based on production cost plus some margin of profit contribution, together with some influences, such as competitors' prices, or price-lining from the market.

There are four major areas which impact on the pricing decision, and these are integrated into an actual price by management judgments. These four areas are:

1. The product's cost function and the product's position in the company's overall product range

2. The demand function for the product, that is, how buyers change their volume of purchases with changes in price

3. The profit objectives of the company

4. Competitors' pricing policies and market practices.

The basic objective of pricing is to maximise price, subject to all relevant considerations. Price increases (with no change in the cost structure) translate directly into profits, and setting the price level is worthy of great care and attention.

### *Cost Function Approach and Pricing*

This function requires accurate information about the relationship between costs, production volumes and profits. Many small companies do not have cost-accounting systems that will yield this information in usable form. Where the information is available, using this approach alone still has two serious flaws: when the desired profit margin is added, the price may be too high to achieve enough sales; or the cost-plus price may be lower than what the customers are prepared to pay. If the product forms part of an integrated range of products, then the price may have to conform to its position within this range, e.g. pricing strategies employed by car manufacturers.

### *Demand Function Approach and Pricing*

This approach focuses on what the market will bear. Some people state that an example of this approach is the pricing policy of energy in Ireland. The gas, electricity and solid-fuel industries compete for business and the price reflects this competition, but overall price levels are set to what the market can bear. However, the demand approach can be very difficult to identify exactly, even with the most sophisticated use of market research. In consumer markets, buyers' perceptions about value for money can be explored by means of conjoint analysis, which treats price as one of the attributes of the product, and determines the trade-off in consumers' eyes between price and other attributes. Price sensitivity for industrial products varies from extreme to slight, and is related to product differentiation, competition and overall cost.

### Profit Objectives and Pricing

The cost approach sets a lower limit to what the price can be. The demand approach should set an upper limit, but measuring elasticity is costly and difficult. What many Irish companies do is add a gross percentage to primary direct costs, which is intended to cover all other costs and profit. This procedure places a risk on achieving a desired bottom line because manufacturing costs may absorb more than is intended. Better is a net profit objective added to total costs. Setting the actual level of desired net profits hinges on many factors, and is in the end a subjective decision. It should at least exceed the return to equity holders of alternative investments. Setting this level, and applying it to costs, gives another threshold to price (and another test of mobility). Once this level has been decided upon, the intention should be to explore how much further the price can be raised, subject to the constraints dictated by market acceptance and competing prices.

### Competitors and Pricing

Pricing is also a tactical weapon in relation to competitors. It is a major component of product positioning. For instance, Mitsubishi (Electric) Ireland has become the market leader of colour TVs in Ireland, despite having entered the market only in 1981. In the initial stages of its rise, it used pricing policy as a weapon *vis-à-vis* its competitors. However, more factors are involved than purchase price alone — credit terms, discounts, coupons may all play a part. Price-skimming tactics involve setting a high price at first, then reducing it progressively to draw in more customers as the higher price segments dry up. Such a policy prevailed in Ireland on the introduction of colour TVs and VCRs. Penetration pricing introduces products at low prices in anticipation of future cost declines caused by large volumes.

### 9.3.5 Communications and Selling

While other elements of the marketing mix are determined largely outside the marketing function, the selection and implementation of communications and selling strategy occur almost entirely within it. The essence of marketing operations is the performance of communications activities which affect the behaviour of people so that they purchase the firm's products or services. An example of this would be the use of above- and below-the-line communications activities by Bailey's Irish Cream.

*Figure 9.6: Communication Strategy: The Decision Process*

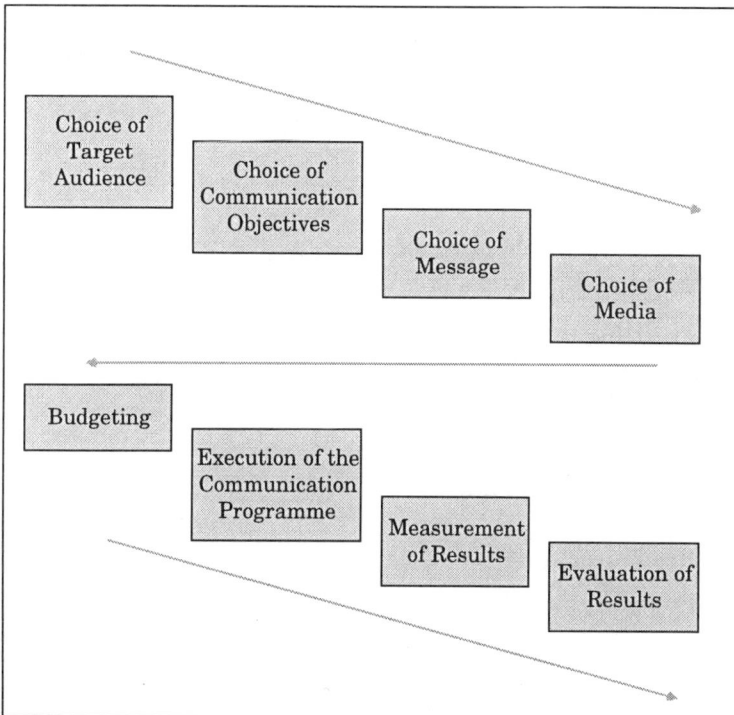

*Source*: John A., Murray, *Marketing Management*, 1984.

In developing a communications strategy, there is a logical sequence of steps, outlined in Figure 9.6 above. There are many different, and often difficult, decisions to be taken within each of these phases. These decisions require good information, good analysis, and the "feeling" for the correct choice that comes from experience in marketing management.

### 9.3.6 Distribution and Logistics

The distribution element of the marketing mix is concerned with how the goods get from the factory door to the point of consumer purchase (or for some kind of products, to the point of consumption). There are two main areas to be managed — the first concerns the intermediaries that lie between the manufacturer and final consumer (the channel of distribution); the second concerns the arrangements for the physical delivery of the product to the consumer (physical distribution). The products should ideally be delivered where and when most suitable for the purchaser; however, for most firms this would require infinite resources, and so a compromise is reached on the level of service that will be provided and the extent to which the firm itself, rather than the channels, will perform the distribution tasks.

### *Distribution Cost*

There are many kinds of costs associated with the distribution of goods, the most important of which are:

- Stockholding
- Transportation
- Import/Export
- Collection of Payments
- Cash-flow
- Credit and finance
- Information collection
- Communications
- Legal

- After-sales

- Repairs and maintenance.

Each of these cost areas has a different cost structure, and economies of scale occur at different levels of operational scale. The channel members are employed because they achieve greater economies of scale than the manufacturer, by specialising in limited aspects of the process. The manufacturer must negotiate or agree with channel members how these costs will be distributed and how the total value-added will be shared.

### *Strategy and Selection of Distribution System*
Distribution decisions are strategic in two senses — they are the main means by which marketing objectives are achieved; and they cannot be quickly or easily changed. One long-term strategy is to share these costs with either suppliers or customers, or both. For industrial goods, it may be possible to align customers' and suppliers' transport networks. For consumer products, it may be possible to share assembly costs, for example in the case of packaged furniture or model kits, e.g. IKEA of Sweden.

### 9.4 LEVEL THREE — MARKETING SYSTEMS AND ACTIVITIES
To allow strategic marketing to occur, and to assist in the implementation of the marketing mix, certain systems and processes must be in place. The key systems in question are marketing information systems, new product development processes and direct marketing systems.

### 9.4.1 Marketing Information Systems
In order that decisions can be made on strategy and operations, and in order that information be disseminated to customers, publics, channels etc., an effective marketing information system is necessary. Figure 9.7 describes a general marketing information system which assesses and disseminates timely information both internally and externally.

An overall Marketing Information System may be divided into four main subsegments or subsystems:

1. **Internal Records System**: Companies can utilise internal records in the decision-making process. For example, retailers are now using electronic point of sale (EPOS) information to analyse sales and trends, reorganise inventory management etc. Internal records provide results-based data.

2. **Marketing Intelligence**: This is data sourced primarily outside the firm, which offers information on the business environment and trends. Common sources would be trade journals, magazines and newspapers.

3. **Marketing Research**: This relates to the collection and analysis of information for specific needs or situations such as advertising research, product research and sales or market research.

4. **Decision Support Systems**: These are statistical and computer-based tools and models available to managers for analysing data and assisting in making more effective strategy-related decisions.

*Figure 9.7: A Generic Marketing Information System*

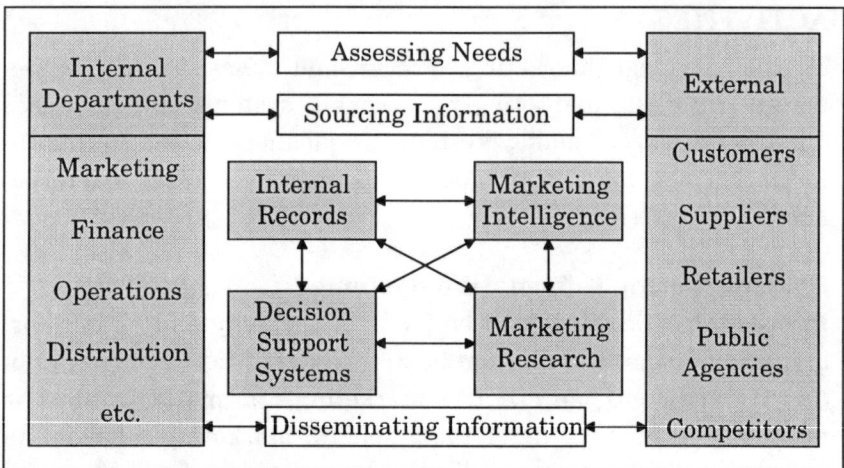

Source: Kotler, P. *Marketing Management: Analysis, Planning, Implementation and Control*, 1991.

### 9.4.2 New Product Development Process

A vital aspect of the dynamic marketing process is the addition of new product/service mixes according to developing consumer needs and developing technological capability. In 1994, there were 20,076 new consumer goods on the shelves of US super-markets and drug stores. This was an increase of 14 per cent over 1993 and compares with only 1,300 new product launches in 1970. It could be argued that the vast majority of new products are variants of others (e.g. different flavours). Such "line extensions" are seen as less risky. However, it is estimated that only 10 per cent are successful enough to continue marketing after two years, and only 1 per cent of new products introduced into fast-food restaurants succeed. Recognising the risks involved, a firm can minimise its risk outlay either by acquiring other firms or brands, patents, etc., or by simply initiating a new product-development process. New products could take the form of inventions, product-line extensions or improvements, repositioning or some other form of innovation.

The New Product Development process goes through five key stages in bringing a product to the market:

1. Idea generation and screenings

2. Business analysis

3. Product development

4. Market testing

5. Real-time commercialisation.

This is a complex process, but necessary in order to minimise the threat of market failure for new products and to ensure a long-term view from the firm on market needs. Close co-ordination is required among many functions including R & D, manufacturing, marketing and market research and finance. The commitment of resources to new product development is a cornerstone in most successful innovative companies, in particular Japanese and "Dragon economy" firms.

### 9.4.3 Direct Marketing Systems

Traditionally, firms have concentrated on advertising, sales promotion and personal selling to move products. A phenomenon of the 1980s and 1990s is the growth in usage of direct marketing, which combines the three elements into one activity, which is targeted at a specific and defined audience. An example would be American Express sales of cheap airline tickets to small groups of cardholders according to their spending patterns. Direct marketing is also closely related to direct-mail campaigns, e.g. Nestlé promotion of pasta via the Casa Buitoni Club; telemarketing, e.g. Dell Computers; and "below-the-line" sales campaigns, which create and utilise a targeted marketing database of attentive rather than apathetic consumers. The trend towards direct marketing and integrated marketing has been fuelled by reductions in overall marketing budgets and the need for closer pound-for-pound accountability.

The criteria for selection of distribution channels and physical distribution systems are also factors that need monitoring after the distribution system has been set up. They are:

- The fit with customer behaviour and preferences

- The fit with overall marketing strategy

- Economic performance of system

- Control influenced by manufacturer over channels

- Flexibility of channel to changes in market, competitors and customers.

The choice of target audience is determined during overall strategy formulation, as is the choice of communications objectives, expressed usually in terms of sales targets. Marketing management has the direct task of formulating the messages and selecting the media by which they will be transmitted. The messages contain descriptions of the product characteristics of presumed interest to purchasers. A great deal of skill is required to develop really effective messages.

The choice of media alternatives and the balance between them — usually known as the communications mix — varies greatly between industries and to a lesser extent among companies within an industry. The basic nature of the product and market have a great deal of influence on type of media used. Specialist industrial markets, e.g. large industrial boilers, electrical generating equipment and building materials, would be serviced by technical salespeople, with attendance at industry trade fairs and exhibitions, together with highly selective advertising in trade journals, e.g. *Irish Electrical Review* and *Heating & Ventilating News*. Consumer markets tend to rely on mass advertising, with a personal sales force servicing major distribution outlets, e.g. motor cars. (In some cases the same product is promoted by two different messages in two different media, and to two different audiences — the housewife does not buy soap powder for the same reason as the supermarket purchasing manager does. Of course, they are not buying the same product at all.) Figure 9.8 below shows the most important media, and also some examples of products with different communications mixes.

## *Figure 9.8: The Communications Mix — Alternative Media*

|  | Photo-copiers | Tissues | Aeroplanes | Books |
|---|---|---|---|---|
| Personal Selling | x |  | x | x |
| Trade Fairs | x |  | x | x |
| Exhibitions |  |  | x | x |
| Sales Promotions | x |  |  | x |
| Merchandising |  | x |  | x |
| Advertising | x | x |  | x |
| Public Relations |  | x | x |  |
| Publicity |  |  | x |  |

Most firms employ most of the mix elements, but the share of marketing resources devoted to each is probably unique to each firm, e.g. Mercedes cars versus Hyundai cars. Two areas tend to predominate in terms of cost and difficulty in management:

1. **Advertising** — itself composed of many different media — can be very costly because of the number of potential targets addressed. It is often difficult to assess the cost-effectiveness of advertising expenditures.

2. **Personal selling** is the most effective form of communication because of the amount of attention devoted to each target, but it is also the most costly, and there is a high proportion of fixed costs. Managing a salesforce is a complex task demanding a high level of both analytical and interpersonal skills.

## 9.5 CONTEMPORARY ISSUES AND APPLICATIONS IN MARKETING MANAGEMENT

As already mentioned, most Irish firms have to consider the development of international markets as a necessary aspect of a firm's growth strategy. This section briefly analyses some other contemporary issues and applications in the marketing environment, which are impacting on the marketing and company strategy among Irish firms including:

- Business-to-Business and Relationship Marketing

- Services and Internal Marketing

- Environmental and Societal Marketing

- Micromarketing.

### 9.5.1 Business-to-Business and Relationship Marketing:
Conventional marketing assumes that markets are consumer-based, i.e. there are many end-consumers purchasing through traditional channels. However, much of the marketing undertaken in Ireland would not necessarily be consumer marketing, rather *business-to-business* or *industrial marketing* where the market would consist of a few large buyers who are geographically concentrated, where demand is relatively inelastic and where the purchasing process is initially high involvement. The same concepts are used in business-to-business marketing and reseller marketing, i.e. selling to multiples and marketing to government departments and agencies. In general, there are three types of buying situation.

1. **New Task**: Where the purchaser is buying a product or service for the first time. This calls for a high-involvement decision

process, involving many people in the decision-making unit. Examples of these could range from the purchase of computer and office machinery or the supply of primary agri-food for secondary processing to the supply of own-branded products to the multiples. The selling process is generally prolonged and technical in nature.

2. **Straight Re-Buy**: This occurs when the customer re-orders on a routine basis, for example, re-ordering office supplies. In contrast to "new task" purchasing, the decision process is low in involvement, as the customer relies on past satisfaction and the word of the supplier. Multiples may negotiate Long-Term Agreements (LTAs) with their major suppliers where the product mix and volume may not alter, only the price agreement.

3. **Modified Re-Buy**: This occurs when the buyer modifies the terms of the agreement in relation to product specifications, price, delivery, etc. The supplier may use this situation to add on products and services in the overall agreement.

A key development related to industrial marketing in particular has been the introduction of Japanese management and manufacturing techniques, which includes a trend toward just-in-time (JIT) production, which is discussed in more detail in Chapter 10 on Operations Management. A key strategic skill in JIT management is the concept of relationship marketing, which contrasts with conventional transaction marketing. In essence, relationship marketing refers to the partnership between suppliers and buyers which goes beyond the normal trading relationship and maximises profit over the entire relationship. For example, suppliers may be involved in manufacturers' R & D or product-design processes, or manufacturers may advise retailers on merchandising, etc. Trust between firms increases while switching costs grow and barriers to entry develop.

A key example of re-seller relationship marketing in practice would be the relationship being forged between Irish agri-food processors such as the dairy PLCs and mushroom producers and the UK retail multiples.

### 9.5.2 Services and Internal Marketing

The importance of services marketing cannot be underestimated in an economy where 60 per cent of the workforce is directly employed in services (see Chapter One) and where most firms rely on their service component to add value or create competitive advantage. Service companies can be people-based or equipment-based using unskilled, skilled or professional people. Services can meet personal needs or business needs, can be profit or non-profit making and can be publicly or privately owned.

In contrast to traditional marketing where the product is fairly standardised, services marketing generally revolves around a selling "experience" such as in catering or hotel management. The services firm has to focus its marketing activity on this "moment of truth" in terms of competitive differentiation, service quality and productivity. This is sometimes referred to as "Interactive Marketing", i.e. managing the marketing relationship between the employee and the customer.

One key area related to services marketing is the concept of "Internal Marketing", which can be defined as the work done by the firm in training and motivating its internal customers — primarily the customer-contact employees and supporting service personnel — to work as a team to provide customer satisfaction or assume a customer orientation. This is especially important in larger firms such as Telecom Éireann, where the core mission and objectives may not be highly transparent or communicable to thousands of employees.

### 9.5.3 Environmental Marketing and Societal Marketing

As the global business world enters the twenty-first century, a trend is developing in business and marketing strategy which is environmentally-centred, and considers the long-term welfare of society at large, in short and medium-term strategic planning, while still ensuring profit considerations. A number of push-and-pull factors are bringing about this change, some of which are examined as follows:

- **Compliance of Regulation**: Increased legislation in the USA and Europe, for example, in the area of waste-reduction management, recycling and "clean" industry, is forcing industry to address the environmental issue. For example, global chemical companies are being forced by legislation to erase production of Chlorofluorocarbons (CFCs) because of their detrimental effect on the earth's ozone layer.

- **Consumerism and Public Interest Pressure Groups**: Similar to compliance factors, consumer desire for environmentally safe products and services has created a growing segment of genuine non-apathetic consumers to whom firms are responding positively. For example, in Scandinavia and in Germany (the *Grüne Punkt* label), producers are reducing packaging and the "frills" of modern marketing, while customers are being encouraged not to force such wastage.

- **Necessity**: The oil crisis of the early 1970s revolutionised the automotive industry away from high-level consumption and high-pollution emissions. Another example of necessity forcing strategy is "Negative Marketing", where lower, rather than greater, usage of a product is promoted, in order to satisfy strategic requirements. An example of this in practice would be energy suppliers using non-renewable energy sources, such as the ESB and Bord Gáis Éireann encouraging efficient use of their product.

- **World Class Business and Total Quality Management**: Part and parcel of the focus on quality management and higher standards is the need to reduce wastage and increase efficiency. Ethical and environmental standards are at the root of Total Quality Management (TQM) and Relationship marketing. As the incidence of ISO standardisation increases, firms are searching for new forms of differentiation and competitive advantage. An example would be Waterford Foods and Carbery Milk Products which demand high standards of waste and quality management standards from their suppliers, and use this as a promotion message to multiples and other retailers.

Environmental and societal marketing in all its forms is refocusing marketing strategy and management by providing a real source of competitive advantage in the eyes of the public intermediaries, customers and consumers.

### 9.5.4 Micromarketing

The failure rate of new products, the continual cost of advertising and its questioned effectiveness as media outlets proliferate and their audience fragments has attracted consumer-product companies to "micromarketing" or database marketing. In addition, these companies recognise that retail point-of-sale scanning technology and own-label goods have given the pole position to retailers in terms of market information. To overcome this problem, powerful data-crunching computers hold out new visions for marketing, in that, instead of advertising their products indiscriminately to the entire (and maybe inappropriate) population, they can make contact directly with individuals. Such a situation will alter the marketing organisation of many consumer and industrial goods companies. Proctor and Gamble, the company which invented "Brand Managers", is now re-engineering the marketing staff with cross-functional teams consisting of marketing, financial and operations personnel. These teams are responsible for managing all the firm's relations with its big retail customers.

Today, database marketing is more applicable to higher price, repeat purchase products. In addition, it has proven better at helping firms to keep existing customers than at winning new ones, e.g. airlines with their "Frequent Flier" programmes. While the retention of customers is central to any marketing strategy, database marketing can win new customers, and give instant access to detailed information about individuals, and increase cost-effectiveness.

### SUMMARY

This chapter analyses the importance of the marketing function in relation to strategy formulation and general operations. Firms which are not strongly focused in terms of marketing orientation will normally not be able to create long-term sustainable competitive advantage. Unlike other functions such as finance, production and human resources, which are inherently inward-looking, marketing forces the firm to focus outwards towards economic reality. The key issues which this chapter analyses are:

- Irish firms have traditionally been production-oriented and have thus lost competitiveness in export markets. This orientation is gradually changing.

- Marketing works on three levels: on a strategic level guiding long-term market oriented strategy formulation; on an operational level implementing strategy through day-to-day activities; and finally, on an aspirational level, motivating employees of the firm to hold a marketing orientation.

- Key aspects of strategic marketing include Product Life Cycle analysis and Competitor analysis.

- Marketing operations implement the thrust of marketing strategy. The key elements of marketing operations are product/service factors; communications factors including selling and promotion activities; distribution and logistics activities; marketing research, direct marketing and new product development.

- From an Irish business viewpoint, there are four contemporary issues which are of particular interest, namely:

  1. Industrial marketing or business-to-business, which focuses on the need for close partnership and/or alliances between suppliers, manufacturers and channels, i.e. "relationship marketing".

  2. Services marketing which focuses on person-to-person marketing relationships, in full-blown service firms or manufacturing firms requiring a service element. Internal marketing is the concept of training and motivating employees towards an efficient marketing orientation.

  3. Environmental marketing considers the long-term welfare of society apart from conventional marketing aspects, and has come about primarily because of consumer pressure, compliance factors and the need for continued differentiation among firms.

  4. Micromarketing or Database marketing has become increasingly important for both consumer and industrial goods firms, which are losing media power to the retailers and multiples. Micromarketing is most useful for higher-priced, repeat-purchase products.

In conclusion, when considering marketing opportunities, the four elements that constitute the marketing mix must be complementary and co-ordinated. Together, they form the firm's interface with its market and with its competitors. Since these change over time, quickly or slowly as may be, the marketing mix must be either incrementally or comprehensively adjusted so that the total interchange between the firm and its environment furthers the firm's ultimate strategic mission, namely, survival and growth.

---

**FURTHER READING**

Bradley, M.F., *International Marketing*, Prentice Hall, Second Edition, 1995.

George, Michael, Anthony Freeling and David Court, "Re-inventing the Marketing Organisation", *The McKinsey Quarterly*, No. 4, 1994.

Heldey, B., "Strategy and the Business Portfolio", *Long Range Planning*, February 1977.

Kotler, Philip, *Marketing Management: Analysis, Planning, Implementation and Control*, Seventh Edition. Prentice Hall International, Englewood Cliffs, NJ, 1991.

Lynch, John J., *Legal Aspects of Marketing*, Marketing Institute of Ireland, 1988.

McIver, Colin, *The Marketing Mirage: How to Make it a Reality*, Heinemann, London, 1987.

Murray, John A., *Marketing Management: An Introduction*, Gill and Macmillan, Dublin, 1984.

Murray, J.A. and S.A. McEntee, "Measuring the Effect of Customer Service Levels", *Journal of Irish Business and Administrative Research*, Vol. 1, No. 1, 1979.

## CHAPTER TEN

# OPERATIONS MANAGEMENT

## 10.1 INTRODUCTION

*F*ollowing on from the previous chapter, which examined the firm and its marketing management, this chapter turns to the equally important issue of operations management and manufacturing, and the strategic role it plays in linking the formulation of the firm's strategy to implementation within the firm. The chapter initially examines the evolution of the operations management function and the philosophy of World Class Business. It explains operations and manufacturing in Ireland, and continues by identifying the levels at which operations strategy impacts on the firm, namely:

- The strategic level

- The tactical level, and

- The implementation or operational level.

Following this introduction, the chapter analyses operations strategy and its role at the strategic level in terms of the following:

- The relationship between operations strategy and business strategy

- The strategic importance of operations and manufacturing

- The link between operations strategy and World Class Manufacturing (WCM)

- Operations strategy and its role in overall competitiveness

- The concepts of World Class Business and Business Process Re-engineering

- The need for innovation in operations strategy and its role in the "coupling" process.

The chapter then examines the tactical level of operations management, particularly the concepts of:

- World Class Manufacturing (WCM), which covers,
    - Total Quality Management (TQM)
    - Just in Time Manufacturing (JIT), and
    - Employee involvement
- Service Quality.

Finally, key elements of operations implementation are considered under the headings of:

- Scale of Operation

- Process Technology

- Production Control

- Materials Handling

- Purchases

- Research and Development.


### 10.1.1 The Evolution of the Operations Function

The operations and manufacturing function has evolved over time, and has become one of the most challenging areas of business, involving the bulk of the human and financial resources of the organisation. Its evolution can be broadly classified into the following stages:

- Repetition

- Automation

- Scientific Management, and

- The Modern Era.

The concept of repetition was a move towards increased efficiency in the manufacturing process. The master craftsmen of times past only allowed certain people to become skilled in a particular job. This problem was overcome by the standardisation of products and parts. With standardisation came repetition in manufacture and consequently greater efficiency, e.g. gunsmithing in the US. Parts were made to a standard size and shape, as opposed to being individually crafted to suit each other.

The next step in the evolutionary process was automation. Automation built on the repetition and standardisation of parts and job specification. It was a substitute of labour by capital, so, in essence, machines replaced craftsmen and semi-skilled workers. This development, which began with the industrial revolution and its power-driven machinery, together with the shifting of work from the home to factories, started a process that is still with us today. However, with the changing requirements of the market, the idea of mass craftsmanship embodied within World Class Manufacturing offers an alternative to the concept of mass production in the automation principle.

The early 1900s saw the study of production systems called Scientific Management, which measured and broke down work into smaller elements, so improving any operation. It was a valuable tool for the manufacturing firm in its time.

The modern era is assumed to have started in 1925 with the study of behaviour, progressing to linear programming, statistical models and simulation. The advent of the computer has assisted these developments. Manufacturing today focuses on technology, its implementation and speed, together with the emergence of global markets. It is these global markets, and the ensuing need for global competitiveness, that have been responsible for the widespread use of the World Class Business philosophy.

### 10.1.2 The World Class Business Philosophy

The World Class Business philosophy embraces a wide range of management tools. The perspective held by firms is that low cost, high quality and customer responsiveness are the keys to market growth, that the firm with the biggest market share is usually the lowest-cost producer, and that investment in equipment is not sufficient to ensure survival and growth into the next century. Companies using the World Class Business philosophy are investing in their people, their systems and their plants to prepare for the future. The World Class Business philosophy attempts to harness the minds of employees to address and apply new management technologies to the old problems, and to achieve not only manufacturing excellence, but overall business excellence. Management must co-ordinate and link the production function with other managerial functions to ensure that cross-functional development is established. Building an organisation capable of delivering constant improvements in productivity and quality is a difficult task and may well require fundamental change in the structures of authority and responsibility.

The implementation of these kinds of strategies among World Class Japanese firms like Fujitsu, Canon and Mitsubishi have fuelled many of the concept changes related to the World Class Business philosophy. The World Class company focuses on waste identification and eradication. Its production systems are designed and operated for what they are, systems. Any sub-optimisation of any section of the system needs to be avoided and an overall holistic synthesis view should be taken. World Class Business offers a medium for this holistic approach, incorporating a wide range of tools, including Just-in-Time Manufacturing, Total Quality Management and Employee Involvement.

Lowest-cost-producer strategies are generally unsuitable for small to medium enterprises in Ireland. However, there are still many lessons to be learnt about product cost reduction and quality improvement in the production process.

### 10.1.3 Operations and Manufacturing in Ireland

The effectiveness of Irish firms in their usage of the operations function has been quite varied. Obviously, the larger multinational firms in their quest for low-cost leadership and economies of scale have been at the forefront of innovation and process improvement in the past. Many of the improvements have occurred in countries where automotive industries are strong, such as Germany and Japan with firms like Volkswagen, Mercedes Benz, BMW, Nissan and Toyota. This is not the case in

Ireland, and Irish SMEs have not been as successful in accomplishing improvements in this area in general. Apart from the low level of R & D activity (see Chapter Two) and the lack of focus on production of high value-added materials (see Chapter Five) other major weaknesses of Irish SMEs in the area of operations management and innovation include the following:

- Overemphasis on production at the lowest cost and not on quality, service and design characteristics

- Limited attainment of World Class Manufacturing (WCM) standards, although there has been significant growth in Irish companies achieving ISO and BS certification

- Limited use of information technology applications in production, e.g. computer-aided design (CAD), computer-aided manufacturing (CAM) and computerised numerical control (CNC)

- Insufficient investment/reinvestment in equipment.

All these weaknesses have led to a problem of competitiveness in many areas of Irish industry, particularly in traditional manufacturing. In practice, many manufacturing-based firms are set up initially with a focus on production operations, and the associated marketing effort consists of trying to sell at a profit what the factory can produce. There are many examples in Irish manufacturing industry of firms that failed, despite having good products, because they did not adequately take account of market needs and requirements (for example, Glen Abbey's knitwear products, while acknowledged to be of high quality, seemed to lack the designs that appealed to export-market tastes). On the other hand, there are also many examples of failure caused by overmarketing the product — overselling either the performance characteristics or the volumes that the production system is able to provide, e.g. Sportsfield, a company which marketed a product called "Waterhog" for clearing water from golf courses, oversold its performance ability at the early stages of marketing, which subsequently resulted in marketing problems at a later stage. Therefore, it is vital that the marketing and operations functions work in close harmony with each other, united by their complementary roles in the strategic plan.

### 10.1.4 The Levels of Operations Management Strategy

As with the marketing function discussed in the previous chapter, overall business strategy is translated into operations strategy implementation on three levels within the firm the strategic level, the tactical level and the operations activities level. The aspects of these levels are summarised in Figure 10.1, opposite.

### 10.2 OPERATIONS STRATEGY OVERVIEW

This section reviews the important role that the operations-management function plays in the implementation of overall strategy. It begins by looking at the key relationship between operations strategy and business strategy. It then addresses the strategic importance of both operations and manufacturing strategy and goes on to analyse the importance of World Class Manufacturing principles in the overall operations strategy.

### 10.2.1 The Relationship between Operations Strategy and Business Strategy

The linking of both business and operations strategy is a central building block of the modern firm. Decisions made when designing and running the production system need to be consistent with the overall strategy of the firm. It is important to realise that policies, plans and implementation activities within the operations area must be mutually supportive of the broad business strategy and in harmony with other functional strategies (i.e. Marketing, Human Resources and Finance) if the organisational objectives are to be achieved. If the decisions are independent or inconsistent they will affect productivity. In addition, it must be remembered that strategic decisions are usually made by senior management, but it is up to the staff to implement them effectively. The entire company must be aware of and understand the objectives of the company. The doers and the thinkers need to be linked, hence the importance of cross-functional teams.

A firm whose operations strategy is based on the World Class Business philosophy needs to position it relative to the firm's business strategy. The commercial *raison d'être* for both manufacturing and service firms in an economy is to satisfy consumer

*Figure 10.1: The Levels of Operations Management Strategy*

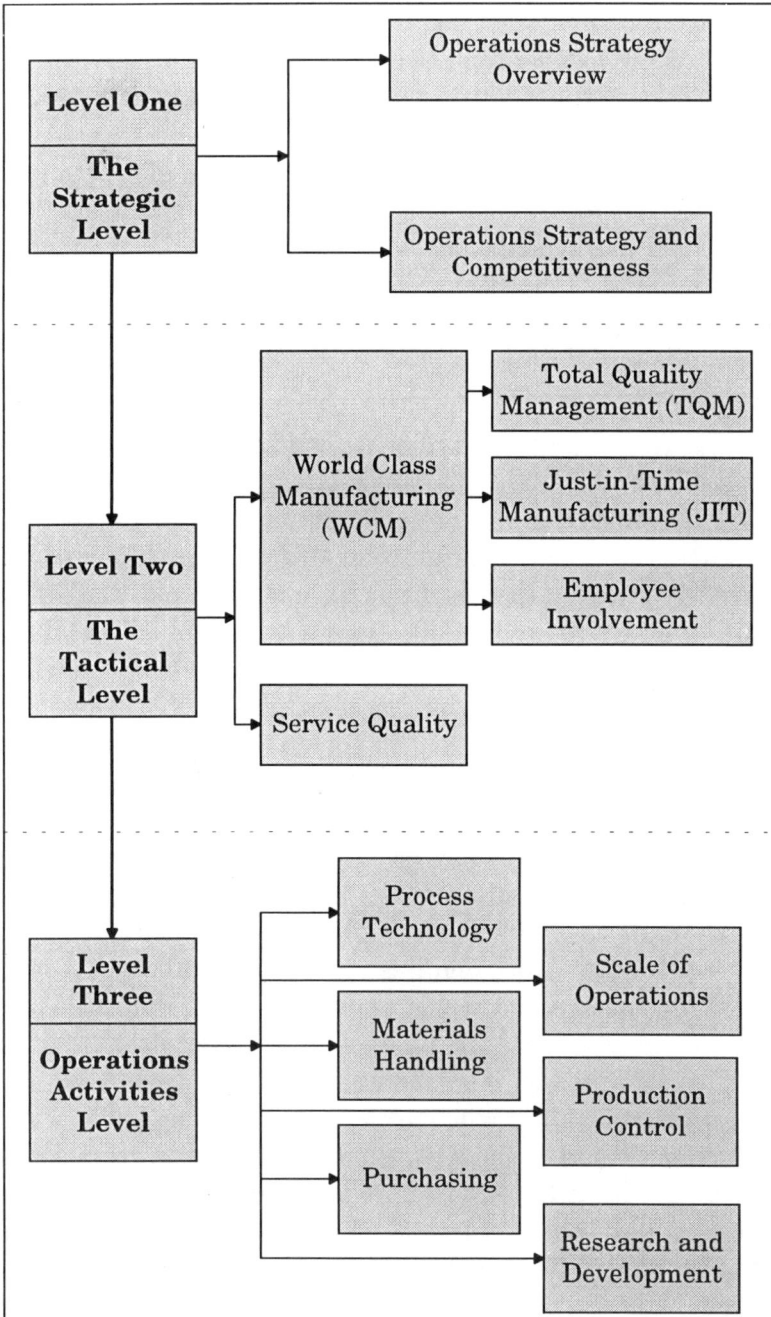

needs at a profit. Therefore, these firms need to be market-orientated in order actually to determine which customer needs to address. Successful implementation of a strategy depends ultimately on the ability of the productive system, whether it be product- or services-centred, to deliver the goods or services — at the right cost, at the right time, in the right quantities and with a specified quality.

Linked to this is the continuing process of identifying and eliminating waste in the business-transformation process. Three key concepts are synonymous with strategic operations management: Coupling, Innovation and Competence Building, all of which are integral parts of a World Class Business approach to the business-transformation process.

### 10.2.2 Strategic Importance of Operations

It is clear that Japanese companies have taken lead positions in many of the world markets. The operations function of these companies has become a major source of strategic direction and competitive advantage. Japanese firms have been able to achieve and sustain productivity and quality improvements in excess of their global competitors. They have translated the resulting lowering of costs of production into lower prices to the market. These price reductions have been sufficient in some cases to ensure not only market penetration, but market dominance. (Consider consumer electronics companies like Sony, Sanyo, Pioneer, Panasonic and Hitachi, which were all unknown outside Japan in the 1970s.) This came as a surprise to many Western companies, as quality levels of Japanese products rose while prices dropped.

Further market expansion has allowed continued price reduction and increased economies of scale, while the product life-cycle has been reduced. As each product approaches decline, a new more advanced product is introduced to balance cash-flows, capital requirements and production capacity. Consider colour TV. On introduction, it had 8 channels, then 50 channels, progressing to 50 channels with remote control, to 50 channels with remote control and a flat screen, then 50 channels, remote control, flat screen and stereo sound and currently moving to High Definition Television (HDTV). So, the shortening of the product life-cycle and the product line-extension allowed Japanese firms not only to introduce up-to-the-minute features to their products, but to incorporate improvements in production methods and to make quality improvements based on customer feedback. This approach to using operations and manufacturing as a competitive weapon has been taken on board by many American, European and Irish-based firms (e.g. Bausch & Lomb and Microsoft) who have recognised that operations strategy is a source of competitive advantage, and in certain cases is necessary for survival.

### 10.2.3 Operations Strategy and World Class Manufacturing

As stated earlier, operations strategy needs to be positioned relative to a firm's overall business strategy. World Class Manufacturing (WCM) is a phrase coined by Dr Richard Schonberger in the mid-1980s to define what was occurring among Japanese firms at that time. World Class Manufacturing is a significant element of any operations strategy and must have as its objectives specific product, price, quality and delivery targets to identified customers.

As noted earlier, a perspective held by many firms that employ World Class Manufacturing concepts in their operations strategy is that low cost, high quality and customer responsiveness are the keys to market growth, that the firm with the largest market share is usually the lowest-cost producer, e.g. Intel in microchip technology. It is also accepted that lowest-cost producer strategies are generally unsuitable for small to medium-sized enterprises in high-labour-cost countries, e.g. Waterford Glass, with its middle-price-range "Marquis" brand produced in low-labour-cost countries, while its hand-cut higher-price glass is still produced in Waterford. However, there are still lessons to be learnt about product cost reduction and quality improvement in the production process.

A significant part of the answer lies in attitudes to the problem, and another part in the application of management techniques. In truth, the World Class Manufacturing concept considers all these issues. It harnesses the minds of people to address and apply new management techniques to traditional problems.

The application of these concepts allows the continual reduction of total costs associated with production using the talents of all staff while striving to achieve manufacturing excellence. The firm integrates its different elements into a World Class philosophy and strives to achieve a level of excellence in not only the manufacturing area of the company, but throughout all the other functions. Marketing, Finance and Human Resources. Management must encourage staff to work in designing the production system and its supportive communications and information systems so that the efficiencies can be achieved. Management must also co-ordinate and link the manufacturing function with other managerial functions, to ensure cross-functional development.

The three core WCM concepts of Total Quality Management (TQM), Just-in-Time (JIT) and Employee Involvement (EI) are intrinsically linked to the Product Market cycle which every firm experiences. As described in Figure 10.2 opposite, the product market cycle begins with the need for new or rejuvenated products because of internal or external forces, which in turn places demands to reduce costs through increased productivity, and therefore reduce price, which invariably increases market share, while World Class manufacturing fuels this cycle process.

It should be noted that to implement a World Class Manufacturing system successfully requires building an organisation capable of delivering constant improvements in productivity and quality, a difficult task that may well require fundamental change in the structures of authority and responsibility. The problem is exacerbated in a small to medium-sized firm with its limited resources of time, money and personnel.

## 10.3  OPERATIONS STRATEGY AND COMPETITIVENESS

This section continues the discussion on the integral link between the product market cycle and operations strategy and addresses the areas of competitive advantage that can be created via the operations function. It begins by discussing the use of manufacturing as a competitive weapon, and continues with a discussion of World Class Business and Business Process Re-engineering. It ends by addressing the importance of innovation and the "coupling" process in operations strategy.

## *Figure 10.2: The Product Market Cycle*

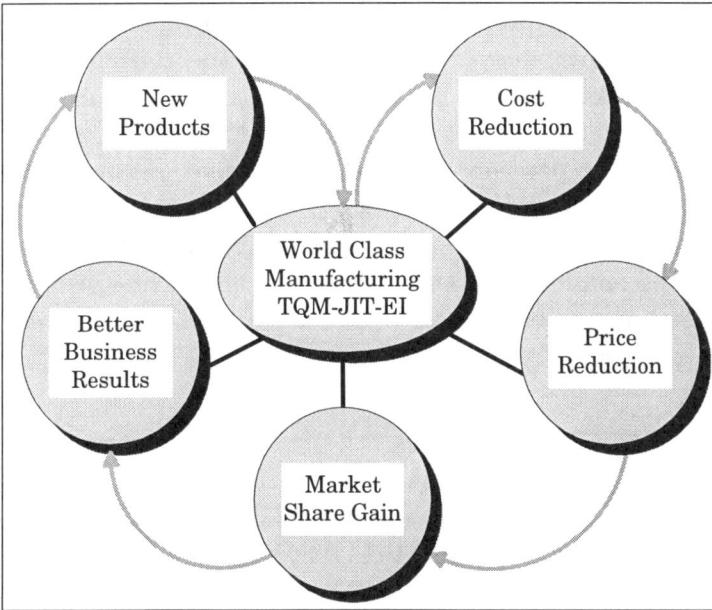

### 10.3.1 Manufacturing as a Competitive Weapon

The use of operations as a competitive weapon is now an accepted norm in firms that have embraced the World Class Business philosophy, e.g. IBM, Ford, ICI and Guinness. A production system can be either a support to the strategic goals of a firm or a dead weight, holding it back from meeting its targets. In the traditional firm, top management has often abdicated responsibility for large portions of business strategy to operations management, so creating significant problems (the Leyland Motor Group decline is often cited as an example). As a result, many firms are encumbered with an inappropriate resource mix to achieve the targets required of them. Once acquired, these resources can be very difficult to replace with the right ones, assets can quickly become liabilities.

In the World Class firm, operations and manufacturing now have a strategic importance. The new approaches developed by Japanese firms with their long-term outlook on investment and high-quality production are guiding firms into the twenty-first century. It is clear that operations management is faced with a new challenge. Firms must be able to produce products quicker, better and cheaper. To do this, they must move away from a mass-production concept and towards a concept of mass customisation or craftsmanship; they need to embrace the concepts of World Class Manufacturing to achieve these goals. This ensures that the firm can offer superior products and services at the same lower price as the competition. (The Psion Organiser retail price is virtually the same as when launched in 1984, yet it has more power, features and is more adaptable). Thus, the manufacturing function can be employed as a strategic and competitive weapon, and does not have to be restricted to multinational companies with large resources.

### 10.3.2 World Class Business

As discussed earlier, the concept of World Class Business (WCB) is relatively new to Ireland and has its origins in many different schools of thought and practice worldwide, particularly in the World Class Manufacturing (WCM) concept. The concept has been discussed by McIver Consulting in the FÁS sectoral studies on the printing, textile and clothing sectors of Irish business, as mentioned in Chapter Four. World Class Business (WCB) combines a number of related traditional and modern approaches to improving the competitiveness of both manufacturing and service operations, including TQM, JIT and EI. The primary objective of WCB is to make a company capable of competing at the top level in its industry. One element of this is to benchmark the operations of the firm against best practice in the industry on an international level. It is primarily concerned with:

- Reducing manufacturing or process lead time

- Improving set-up and changeover times

- Eliminating work in progress inventories in manufacturing

- Reducing the level of indirect labour where appropriate

- Designing product or service quality.

There are some other concepts which can be considered components of WCB, or equivalent in meaning, depending on the industry and production process. They are:

- Total Quality Management
- Just-in-Time (JIT) Manufacture
- Time-Based Competition
- Lean Manufacturing
- KANBAN (Demand Control System)
- Kaizen (Continuous improvement).

As already mentioned, WCB is a key operations and process methodology which will impact on many sectors of Irish industry in the mid- to late 1990s and beyond. WCB relates to the overall organisation and operation of manufacturing and service processes in a way that is equal to best practice on a global level. This means reforming or creating manufacturing operations using principles that are becoming well established throughout the industrialised world.

WCB is about reducing waste and improving quality, through designing manufacturing and work processes well, and through harnessing the intellectual capabilities of all workers. The elimination of wasted time (set-up time, time in inventory, time in transit etc.) has a particularly important competitive impact in the manufacturing firm. WCB gives the firm an opportunity to create a sustainable competitive advantage in terms of quality, productivity, cost efficiencies and customer service. WCB in general is more suitable for medium, and particularly for larger, firms as smaller firms often do not attract such business-process complications. WCB implementation is a difficult and time-consuming process for management and supervisors, and requires a willingness by all involved to accept change. In summarising the fundamentals of World Class Business, McIver Consulting identify 10 key aspects, described as follows:

1. **Simplicity**: Simple systems tend to be more flexible, more efficient and easier to improve than complex ones.

2. **Continuous Improvement**: Continually seeking (ideas from employees) and implementing improvements in the manufacturing process

3. **Teamworking**: Organising work around teams (inter- and intra-functional) which manage much of the production process, and play a key role in identifying opportunities for improvement, and then implementing them.

4. **Devolution of Power**: Decision-making and responsibility are delegated to those directly involved in the production process.

5. **Design for Perfect Quality**: Products and processes should be designed in such a way that it is difficult not to produce perfect quality. Acceptable Levels of Quality (ALQ) is now an outdated concept.

6. **Statistical Process Control**: A method of statistically tracking the quality of output.

7. **Benchmarking**: Identifying best practice in any industry for each manufacturing or business process carried out by the firm.

8. **Programmed Preventative Maintenance**: Preventing operation shutting down and stopping deterioration in the quality of output.

9. **Multi-skilling and Flexibility**: Maximising production-process adaptability

10. **Training**: Key to successful implementation.

For WCB to be successful on both the strategic and operational levels, two key human factors have been found to be essential. First, the company's senior management must be committed to WCB as a central part of business strategy in order that change can occur. This *leadership* element is critical in helping supervisory management and middle management in particular to take responsibility in times of uncertainty. Second, *trust* is crucial in WCB. When properly implemented, WCB benefits the workforce by safeguarding the future, and trust between management and workers is crucial in order to allow this to happen. This can be difficult when the change involved in WCB can lead to job losses, more work hours and removal of demarcation. In a sense, WCB implementation has as much to do with human resource management as operations management.

### 10.3.3 Business Process Re-Engineering

A key concept underlying WCB or WCM is that of organic or continuous improvement in the overall business transformation process. However, certain business situations require a more fundamental and radical approach in thinking and in the redesign of systems. An example of this would be domestic carriers of post in Europe, such as An Post in Ireland, or Royal Mail in the UK, attempting to compete against global carriers such as DHL, TNT and UPS, in addition to competing against technologies that are emerging in telecommunications, such as facsimile, Internet and EDI. In cases such as this, Business Process Re-Engineering (BPR) is being employed. The term "re-engineering" was introduced into common business usage in 1990 by Michael Hammer in a *Harvard Business Review* article titled "Re-engineering Work: Don't Automate, Obliterate". Hammer went on to develop the concept further in his book *Re-engineering the Corporation*, written with James Champy. Hammer and Champy defined re-engineering as:

> . . . the fundamental rethinking and redesign of business processes to achieve dramatic improvements in critical, contemporary measures of performance, such as cost, quality, service, and speed.

According to Hammer and Champy, the central focus in the design and management of business activity should be on processes rather than the functions of manufacturing, finance, sales and distribution. As already mentioned, firms exist to create and deliver goods and services to their customers, and the rationale behind re-engineering is that most firms are not designed to support the processes required to meet this primary objective. While customers are interested in the end-to-end or horizontal process, many firms focus inwardly and on the vertical chains of command through which they manage their departments, which does not easily cater for cross-functional business flows. Similar to World Class Business, re-engineering seeks to address lack of trust and limited training. A key challenge in re-engineering is empowerment, which implies giving employees:

- Training to perform a variety of roles within a process, thereby improving flexibility

- Areas of responsibility to make decisions on behalf of the organisation without seeking management approval

- Authority to fulfil those responsibilities, and a supportive environment to allow them to learn from mistakes.

Firms have interpreted re-engineering in different ways, from
basic process improvement through to process re-engineering, on
to business re-engineering. Real re-engineering, however, relates
to fundamental business transformation or "reinventing the business". Firms that interpret re-engineering start by asking why
they exist and what they are trying to achieve. Hence the need for
fundamental rethinking on a business-wide level, which involves
much risk for the firm and its employees.

Defined as such, re-engineering appears simple and attractive.
However, many firms which have tried to apply it have not been
entirely successful, as they have not understood the complexity of
defining new ways of thinking and working. Sustainable performance gains through re-engineering cannot be achieved simply by
redesigning processes and telling employees that they are empowered. It requires a transformation in the mind-set, attitudes
and behaviour underlying the functional approach to business
activity.

In summary, effective re-engineering needs to be based on six
fundamental breakthroughs of thought and activity:

1. **Process-Based**: Traditional hierarchical and inward-looking
   management philosophy has to be replaced by an obsessive
   commitment to adding value for customers. The firm has to
   look at the business from the "outside in" and concentrate on
   the end-to-end management of the processes which serve their
   customers.

2. **Fundamental Rethink**: Redesign of key processes must focus
   on the extent to which current structures detract from adding
   value by introducing complexity and delays, the retarding
   effect that the structure can have on an attempt to introduce
   change, and the cross-functional conflicts and tensions that
   create internal friction, diverting energy away from serving the
   customer.

3. **Radical Improvement**: The emphasis in re-engineering should be on achieving sustainable leaps in performance. Re-engineering should not be used if more effective gains can be achieved using an alternative approach, such as continuous-improvement-based process change.

4. **Integrated Change**: A cross-functional approach that best serves the customer is vital. Initiatives can often be based around a functional focus, or clouded by personal ambition, which can divert attention or cause confusion. A well-balanced and holistic solution is required, for which the relevant systems, people and training have been put in place.

5. **People-Centred**: Old-style management, risk avoidance and fear will destroy the re-engineering process. In addition, those in newly empowered cultures may not understand the business goals and the knowledge of its processes adequately to be able to make decisions and take risks on behalf of the firm.

6. **Mindset Change**: The firm must lose the intellectual baggage and conditioning that binds it and its employees to the past. This requires the development and communication of a shared understanding of the firm's future, and the creation of an environment and infrastructure that actively promote learning and allow imagination, and not conditioning, to guide the business transformation process.

In general, three key phases exist in the re-engineering process: initiation, implementation and exploitation.

### *Programme Initiation*
This involves building an awareness and understanding of business processes and re-engineering, and their benefits; defining the strategic scope, scale and direction of the firm; and planning the overall change programme.

### *Design and Implementation*
This involves analysing current operations in order to capture performance measures that highlight the need for change; generating a range of options for redesigning the process that will

deliver significant performance improvement; testing and selecting the options against key measures such as customer requirements, cost and quality objectives; and developing, enhancing and refining the redesigned processes into the live business environment.

### *Exploitation of the Re-engineered Business*

This involves providing ongoing support to re-engineered operations; helping managers and staff to adjust to new roles, responsibilities and methods of working; and monitoring performance and initiating ongoing refinements.

### 10.3.4 Operations Strategy and Innovation

As already mentioned, the production and operations function has become a major source of strategic direction and competitive advantage in its own right. These competitive advantages have been created through coupling market needs with competencies, primarily in the area of operations management, through a commitment to quality. The key competitive weapons are:

- Efficiency in the overall productive system

- Quality and quality control

- Dependability (JIT) and reliability

- Technological innovation (product and process).

There are certain factors that must be addressed for innovation to be successful. Figure 10.3. analyses the main drivers for successful innovation in the coupling process. Essentially, the firm must be capable of coupling or matching market requirements with internal competencies, and this requires giving genuine status to innovation, allowing for consciousness of the coupling process in research, and creating structures to support the process internally.

The overall concern of the Operations function is to interrelate these decision levels so that the required output is in fact produced.

*Figure 10.3: The Coupling Process in Innovation*

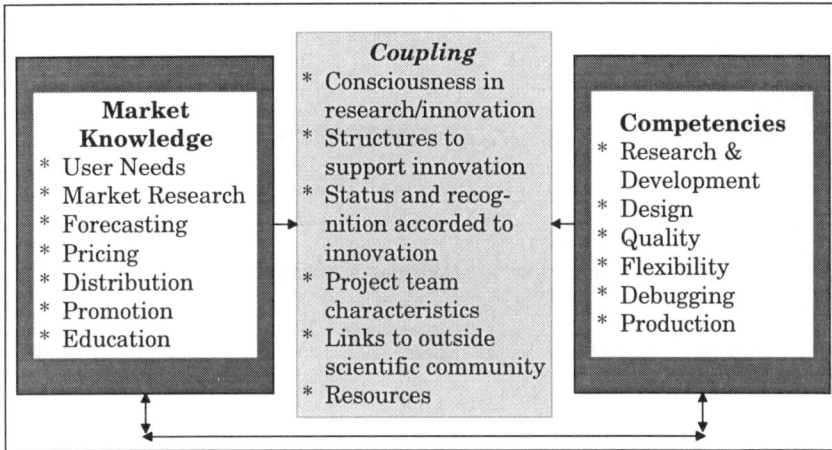

| Market Knowledge | Coupling | Competencies |
|---|---|---|
| * User Needs<br>* Market Research<br>* Forecasting<br>* Pricing<br>* Distribution<br>* Promotion<br>* Education | * Consciousness in research/innovation<br>* Structures to support innovation<br>* Status and recognition accorded to innovation<br>* Project team characteristics<br>* Links to outside scientific community<br>* Resources | * Research & Development<br>* Design<br>* Quality<br>* Flexibility<br>* Debugging<br>* Production |

## 10.4 LEVEL TWO — TACTICAL LEVEL OPERATIONS

As operations strategy moves closer to production activities, the operations tactics employed in translating the firm's strategy into output results become more important. This section analyses the key operations tactics utilised by firms in this area in the 1990s, most of which are brought together under the World Class Manufacturing concept. This concept has developed since the 1980s in an environment of increased economic turbulence and competition and changing technology. As described in Figure 10.4, the three key concepts under WCM are Total Quality Management (TQM), Just-in-Time (JIT) Manufacturing and Employee Involvement (EI). This section also analyses Service Quality and reviews the ServQual model.

### 10.4.1 Total Quality Management and Strategy

This section analyses the specific area of TQM as a strategic and competitive weapon and looks at the core concepts and processes relating to quality management. The key to gaining competitiveness in the marketplace for any firm is gaining a reputation for quality, reliability, price and delivery, and once a bad reputation is acquired it becomes very difficult to lose it. Total Quality Management (TQM) has been defined by Feigenbaum as:

The total composite product and service characteristics of Marketing, Engineering, Manufacturing and Maintenance through which the product and service in use will meet the expectation of the customer.

## Figure 10.4: Key Concepts within World Class Manufacturing

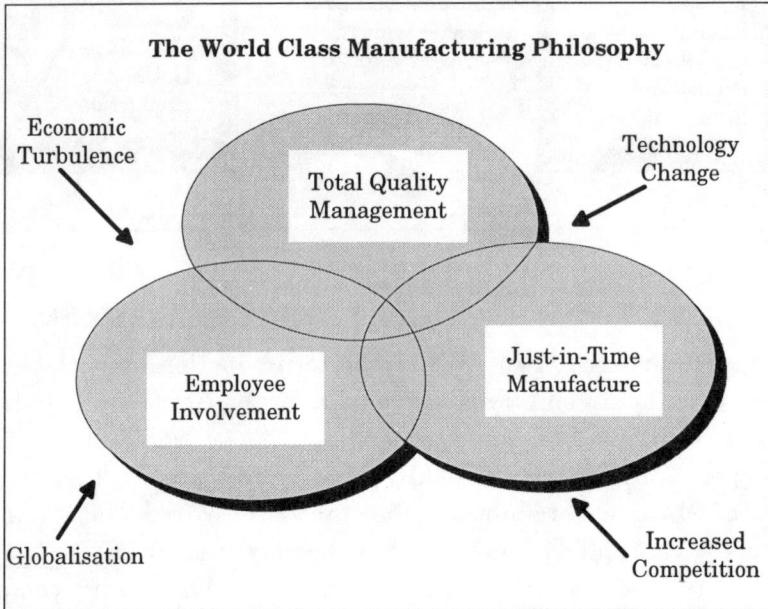

**The World Class Manufacturing Philosophy**

Economic Turbulence

Total Quality Management

Technology Change

Employee Involvement

Just-in-Time Manufacture

Globalisation

Increased Competition

Total Quality Management calls for continuous rather than radical improvement on the overall business-transformation process, that is, coupling the skills and inputs of the firm to create outputs that satisfy customer needs and wants in a progressively more effective manner. The key factors in Total Quality Management are outlined in Figure 10.5 and relate primarily to international quality standardisation, quality assurance, waste identification and elimination, and product and process development.

### International Quality Standards

Quality standards increased in importance in Ireland in the 1980s and 1990s. The International Standards Organisation introduced a set of quality standards in the 1980s which are

generically known as ISO 9000. The British standards organisation introduced an equivalent standard, known as BS5750.
The standards relate to a number of core clauses which deal with
the key elements of a basic quality system. The introductory standard is ISO 9000-1 progressing to ISO 9001, which relates to companies designing, building, supplying and servicing products, and
through to ISO 9004-1 for companies servicing products. The key
to ISO 9000 is the removal of ambiguity and uncertainty, combined with an additional emphasis on Preventative Action,
Preservation (of products in storage), Servicing and the use of
statistical techniques.

*Figure 10.5: Key Factors in Total Quality Management*

The acceptance of the ISO system has been widespread in
Ireland. In relative terms, the percentage of firms acquiring ISO
certification is one of the highest in Europe. Firms have taken on
board the original system and have at least examined their operations as they wrote the procedures and put quality systems in
place. However, it should be noted that putting a quality system
in place does not always ensure quality products and services.
Some quality systems can often merely proceduralise existing

inefficient activities if a holistic fundamental and strategic approach to the firm's business is not taken.

### Quality Control and Assurance

Quality Control relates to the activities and techniques employed by the firm to achieve and maintain the quality of a product, process or service. It is essentially a monitoring activity, but it is also concerned with finding and eliminating causes of quality problems. Quality Assurance relates to the prevention of quality problems through planned and systematic activities, including the establishment of a good quality management system and the assessment of its adequacy, the audit of the operation of the system, and the review of the system itself.

### Waste Identification and Elimination

Identifying and eliminating waste is a key concept within World Class Manufacturing, and is closely related to Just-in-Time Manufacturing which is discussed in more detail later in this chapter. Key tools for identifying waste in the business transformation process include pre-production quality records, in-process quality records, sample analysis reports, flow charts, fault records, Pareto analysis, etc.

### Product and Process Development

The WCM principle is based on the idea of product and process development, and the original ISO standards were criticised for not doing enough actively to improve products, processes and services, i.e. ISO could be applied equally well to a good or bad product. The new standards are attempting to address this shortcoming. The quality system records, the maintenance system records, employee involvement (discussed later) in development teams and the overall management commitment to improvement are all essential ingredients in product and process improvement at a world class level.

There are many approaches to Total Quality Management. The most famous and widely used frameworks are the Malcolm Baldridge National Quality Award in the USA, The Deming Prize in Japan and the European Quality Award (EQA) in Europe. The criteria used for measuring quality in these concepts form the basis for points scoring in the quality and safety assurance systems ISO 9000 and BS 5750. In Europe, the technique of quality self-appraisal has been promoted by the European Foundation for Quality Management (EFQM) through its European Quality Award. EQA recognises that processes are the means by which a firm harnesses and releases the talents of its people to produce results.

The concept of TQM had been taken on by many, if not most, firms, in particular in Japan, and its basic principles surround the Japanese approach to business management. Although the Japanese business context is very different from Ireland's, and indeed, from that of the rest of the world, Japan's implementation of these kinds of strategies has led to many changes in the concepts associated with production operations. Material flow control has dominated the thinking within manufacturing management in recent years. Production systems need to be designed and operated for what they are — systems. Clearly, sub-optimisation of any section of the system should be avoided and an overall holistic systems-synthesis view should be taken. To this end, Material Requirements Planning (MRP), Manufacturing Resource Planning (MRP II), Just-in-Time Manufacturing (JIT), and Optimised Production Technology (OPT), are techniques developed to assist in the processing of systems synthesis. In another sense, these are all manufacturing philosophies within the disciplines of which the day-to-day operations are undertaken. Naturally, each of these techniques and/or philosophies has its advocates and detractors. Indeed, it is possible to design production systems incorporating two or more of these philosophies. It should be noted, however, that there are considerable training costs involved in the installation of any of these approaches.

### 10.4.2 Just-in-Time Manufacturing

The Just-in-Time (JIT) Manufacturing principle was created in the main by firms attempting to deal with the extremely high logistics, storage and inventory costs related to manufacturing and changing market requirements. JIT manufacturing focuses on waste identification and its elimination or minimisation, and is a critical part of any WCM programme and in the overall product market cycle. Waste in this sense is defined as any cost added to a product or service that does not add any value, and includes machine breakdown, absenteeism and quality problems. Toyota, the pioneers in the area of JIT, define waste as "anything other than the minimum amount of equipment, materials, parts, space and workers' time, which are absolutely essential to add value to the product". One of the most popular JIT tools is the KANBAN system, which is a demand control system developed by Toyota. Toyota identified seven possible sources of waste in its automotive production system, as follows:

- Waste from overproduction

- Waste from waiting time

- Transportation waste

- Processing waste

- Inventory waste

- Waste of motion

- Waste from product defects.

The key areas in JIT are shown in Figure 10.6, and include Process and Physical Flow Analysis, Cellular Manufacturing, Inventory Management and Total Productive Maintenance.

### Process and Physical Flow

Process flow is an integral part of any quality system and relates to an analysis of the specific stages within the business transformation process. As already mentioned, Business Process Reengineering has become an important concept in the overall World Class Business philosophy. Apart from the material flow in the production process, the information flow through the organisation can be critical in ensuring efficiency.

### Cellular Manufacture

A key concept related to Process Flow Analysis is Cellular Manufacturing, which groups "product families" of similar parts, size and processing requirements, and not just on product range. Analysis is carried out on the process flow and requirements of the family, rather than the single products. The main benefit of cellular manufacturing is that lead times are reduced, which in turn reduces waste considerably.

## *Figure 10.6: Key Tactics in JIT Manufacturing*

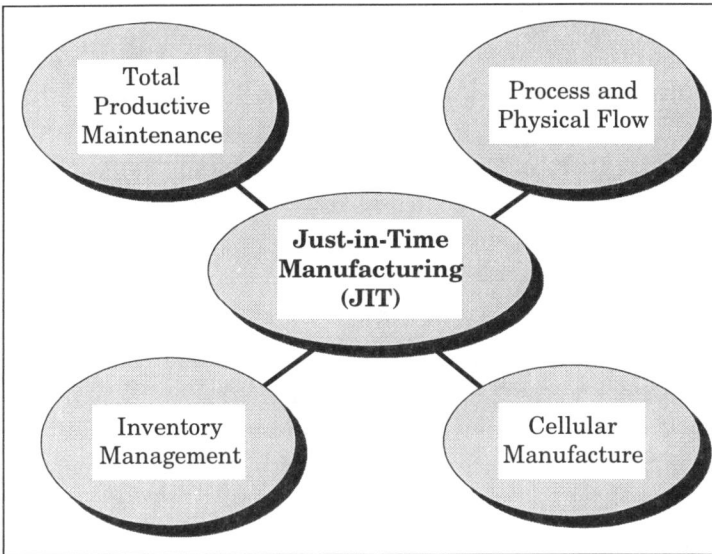

### *Inventory Management*
This is another key aspect of WCM. The approach endeavours to remove as much of the cost of inventory control as possible. As lead times are reduced, large amounts of work in progress material are eliminated. Effectively, parts are used when they arrive at the factory. Again the focus is on simplicity and adding value to the product.

### *Total Productive Maintenance*
One of the basic requirements of a WCM programme is that machines are available to work when they are wanted and that they will work at the output required of them. Therefore, the maintenance programme employed by the firm is crucial and depends on the type of plant and the type of equipment involved in the process. The various types of maintenance activities include

fixed-time maintenance, condition-based maintenance, opportunity maintenance and design-out maintenance.

To allow a JIT manufacturing programme to be implemented effectively, close and participatory relationships must be developed with suppliers and customers. For example, Munekata (Ireland), a supplier to the electronics industry, places great emphasis on working closely with its main customers in all aspects of its business. Supplier development and network production are intrinsically linked to WCM in relation to JIT. One reason why this approach has been so effective in Japan has been its traditional network structure of business associations and relationships, and can be traced back to the success of the Mitsui family in business and trading

### 10.4.3 Employee Involvement

A key element of a firm's operations and manufacturing strategy is its interface with the human resource strategy. The ability of a company to address the changing demands of a market is completely dependent on the ability of its employees in coping with the change. Without this inherent ability to deal with change, it is practically impossible for a firm to support strategic initiatives. A firm's people make the strategies work, they carry out the plans and provide the results. It is the harnessing of the abilities of employees in problem solving that allows competitiveness and improvements to be achieved.

Within an environment of changing technology and economic turbulence with short product life-cycles, many firms worldwide have turned to the concept of Employee Involvement (EI) as a key part of their overall business strategy to improve quality, productivity or employee motivation, or to allow the firm to adapt to environmental change more easily in the future (Lawler et al., 1992). The concept of Employee Involvement is not new and has existed in some form with varying degrees of effectiveness for many years. The Employee Involvement concept revolves around four core activity areas related to the sharing of Information, Knowledge, Power and Rewards:

- **Information-Sharing Practices**: company's operating results, unit operating results, fellow employees' pay, new technologies, business plans and goals, competitor's performance.

- **Knowledge-Sharing Practices**: decision-making/problem-solving, leadership skills, understanding the business, quality skills, team-building skills, job skills.

- **Power-Sharing Practices**: quality circles, participation groups (Non-QC), union-management committees, mini-enterprise units, self-managing work teams.

- **Profit and Reward Sharing**: knowledge skill-based pay, profit-sharing, gain-sharing, individual incentives, workgroup/ team incentives, non-monetary awards, employee stock ownership plan, flexible benefits.

The impact of Employee Involvement programmes on organisational effectiveness can be twofold. It can change/improve internal operating processes and it can change/improve operating results. In general, the key areas of improvement seen through the use of EI programmes are in the areas of improved product and service quality, worker satisfaction and quality of work-life and, most importantly, in productivity. However, it should be noted that EI programmes can be problematic if the employees do not understand the reason for the programme, or do not have a genuine or useful input to make in the process. Employee Involvement programmes work best when integrated into an overall company development programme such as WCM or BPR.

### 10.4.4 Service Quality as a Strategic Tactic

Service quality has been defined by Lewis and Booms (1983) as "the measure of how well the service level delivered matches consumers' expectations. Delivering quality service means conforming to customer expectations on a consistent basis." Service quality relates to technical quality, which involves what the customer is actually receiving from the service, and functional quality, which involves the manner in which the service is delivered. It is also a key aspect of overall business for both services companies and manufacturers. For most companies it is an integrated part of overall business strategy, impacting on both marketing and operations strategy. Cara Computers is an Irish firm which concentrates on providing a high level of after-sales service and computer maintenance and has a primary focus on service quality.

Parasuraman, Zeithmal and Berry (1985) have developed a general service quality model. In general, five discrepancies or gaps can exist between expectations and delivery.

1. **Consumer Expectation/Management Perception Gap**: Service firm executives may not always understand in advance what features represent high quality to consumers, what features a service must have in order to meet consumer needs and what levels of performance on those features are needed to deliver high-quality service. If this gap is significant, then management is basing its design of service on the wrong premises.

2. **Management Perception/Service Quality Specs. Gap**: A variety of factors — resource constraints, market conditions and/or management indifference — may result in a discrepancy between management perceptions of consumer expectations and the actual specifications established for a service. Failure to design the service specifications correctly results in employees basing their delivery of service quality on a model which incorrectly specifies how this should be done.

3. **Service Quality Specs/Service Delivery Gap**: A service firm's employees exert a strong influence over the quality of a service delivered. If employees fail to perform according to service specifications, the service quality may suffer. Furthermore, it may not be possible to standardise some aspects of the service — in such a case, the quality of the service delivered will be purely in the hands of the employees.

4. **Service Delivery/External Communications Gap**: The external communications carried out by an organisation regarding the service can affect consumer perceptions of the quality of the service in two ways: If the organisation overpromises, expectations will be inflated and the perceived service quality will suffer. If management specifies aspects of the delivery of a service that are not apparent on consumption of the service, it

may be possible to enhance consumer perceptions of the service by educating consumers as to the level of quality that is being delivered.

5. **Expected Service/Perceived Service Gap**: Ultimately the quality of the service delivered will be dictated by the perceived gap between the expected service and the service as perceived by the customer. Both the magnitude (size) and the direction (i.e. positive or negative) will determine the perceived quality of the service delivered.

According to Parasuraman et al., customers will evaluate service on 10 service dimensions, which they use to measure service quality in the ServQual model. They are:

1. **Reliability**: consistency of performance and dependability

2. **Responsiveness**: willingness or readiness of employees to provide the service

3. **Tangibles**: physical evidence of the service

4. **Access**: approachability and ease of contact

5. **Courtesy**: politeness, respect, consideration and friendliness of contact personnel

6. **Communication**: keeping the customer informed and listening

7. **Credibility**: trustworthiness, believability and honesty

8. **Security**: freedom from danger, risk or doubt

9. **Understanding/Knowing the Customer**

10. **Competence**: the necessary skills and knowledge.

When measuring service quality, performance should be measured against customers' expectations and comparisons to competitors, rather than pre-set internal expectations. In addition, the relative importance of the various service dimensions and attributes should be performed by means of both qualitative and quantitative research, and research on the level of service quality attained should be ongoing and continuous.

## 10.5 LEVEL THREE — OPERATIONAL LEVEL MANAGEMENT

Once the strategic and tactical issues have been addressed, the day-to-day management of the productive system has to be organised, and an outline of these activities is given below. In general, the operations function oversees, co-ordinates and integrates the work of a number of different functional areas. Departmentalisation of these sub-functions depends on the complexity and scale of operations, and in very small firms there may be only one manager to oversee them all. The most important operations functions are given below.

### 10.5.1 Choice of Production/Process System

The starting point for production or process systems design is often the market requirements projections. The marketing function and the strategic plan spell out details of target quantities, target costs and target quality requirements, as well as the expected life of production of the product. It is necessary to consider at the initial design phase what kind of flexibility should be built into the system to allow for product improvements, expansion and differentiation. To a great extent, these parameters suggest the combination of product system, production technology and manpower that would be most appropriate. In practice, availability of finance may be an important consideration as limiting the range of production systems that could be considered.

The choice hinges around the production volumes going through the system and the degree to which output units differ from each other. The trade-off between throughput and differentiation allows a range of different combinations to be operated successfully within the same industry. Custom tailoring takes longer and is more costly, but standardisation appeals to more customers and yields greater sales volumes. Both are viable strategies in many industries.

Advances in production technologies, such as computer-aided design and manufacturing (CAD/CAM) and flexible manufacturing systems can facilitate the occurrence of economic differentiation at lower output volumes for each different type. Generally, firms following a lowest-cost strategy must continually invest in state-of-the-art production systems (of course, the point at which further investment ceases as a product reaches its decline phase is of great importance in maintaining lowest-cost status). The choice of production system and technology has a major impact on the firm's overall cost structure. High-level investment can preclude a lowest-cost strategy because of high repayment costs, difficulties in assimilating new techniques, slightly reduced volumes, etc. Similarly, the relative cost-structure position of competitors can be assessed from their choice of a throughput/differentiation system. There is a strong tendency for many products to increase in standardisation as they move through their life-cycles. Because of this, there are many examples of mature products shifting towards continuous-flow production systems.

### 10.5.2 Location Decisions
When the type of production process has been decided upon, the important decision must be made as to where it will be located. Some of the more general selection criteria include:

- Minimise input logistics costs (e.g. locate near suppliers of raw materials)

- Minimise output logistics costs (e.g. locate near to market)

- Minimise acquisition costs of site and factory buildings (including maintenance and disposal)

- Maximise access to infrastructural support (transport networks, research facilities, labour pool, etc.)

- Maximise employee benefits of location (climate, tax régime, etc.)

- Proximity to relevant third parties (e.g. government, industry concentrations).

It is, of course, not possible to fulfil all of these criteria simultaneously, and trade-offs are made by general management based on how important they judge the individual factors to be. In Ireland, location may be greatly influenced by the grant situation, and by the fact that there are advance factories available in many areas of the country. Astute combinations of transport and distributors can make most markets in Ireland accessible, regardless of location — there is a company (Mack's Bakeries Ltd.) selling fresh bread in the Dublin market from Kiltimagh, Co. Mayo. For many manufacturers, being located in Ireland is more of a problem than being located in a particular part of the country.

### 10.5.3 Process Decisions

The fundamental production processes required by the nature of a given type of product — extractive, analytical, conversion or assembly — when combined with the volume and differentiation requirements, indicate the choice of process technology and the scale of operations (or plant capacity). These then have to be actualised in the plant, involving decisions as to plant layout, line balancing, the selection of machinery, the definition of individual job content and work methods, and so on. These decisions may be very complex, involving difficult trade-offs between, for example, machine capital and running costs, or between capital and labour. (This latter debate became very public in Waterford Glass plc. recently.) The final choice of detailed plant and process design will determine the firm's operating cost structure for a long time. In Ireland, the state incentive schemes and the labour-cost environment have resulted in a tendency to substitute capital equipment for labour, where possible.

Overinvestment in capital equipment, which is sometimes generated by state funding policies, may expose a company to two kinds of risk. The first is that the cost structure will run against the grain of optimum industry requirements — for example, a high-capital cost element usually requires higher production volumes to justify — and there may be overcapacity (as in the bakery industry) and a tendency towards marginal pricing. The second area of risk is that of the capital intensity trap, mentioned in Chapter Four, where the cost of the capital investment is higher than the value of the gains achieved as a result of the investment.

### 10.5.4 Purchasing

Purchasing activities are often the single biggest expenditure within a company, since purchased inputs often account for over 50 per cent of the total cost of a product. It can be a very difficult task to carry out, since there are financial implications other than input cost alone — reorder cost, stock holdings and input quality all have financial implications. Just-In-Time systems try to reduce stock levels to zero, by arranging for suppliers and internal departments to deliver only when needed. Also, improving input quality may reduce downstream production costs. Both of these types of response require the sharing of logistics costs with the suppliers of inputs, and this is being given increased attention nowadays.

### 10.5.5 Production Control
This involves the scheduling and co-ordination of activities carried out on the factory floor. The basic tasks are planning (of machine usage, input deliveries, labour and output rates), routing the work through the factory, scheduling resource usage, controlling that work is being performed in accordance with plans, and dispatching the finished goods either to inventory or to customers.

### 10.5.6 Inventory Control
Inventory arises to balance out the different rates of inputs, production processes and sub-processes and customer demand. Another type of inventory — work-in-progress — has traditionally been thought of as necessary to keep production processes in operation. There are other types of inventory and all are a cost burden on the firm. This must be minimised, subject to certain requirements. There are many sophisticated procedures for handling inventory problems, but it is not always easy to develop a good model in specific cases. Other aspects of inventory control are storage procedures, which minimise deterioration, pilferage, and breakage and maximise "fundability" of stock items. Adequate record keeping is also important. When inventory is viewed through a WCM programme, strenuous efforts are made to reduce it in all its manifestations, thereby simplifying control procedures and storage requirements at the same time.

### 10.5.7 Materials Handling
Materials handling can seriously affect speed of throughput and costs, especially where unit product value is low and volume is

high. The materials handling system should be designed at the time of initial plant layout. In a WCM environment, materials handling is seen as a waste and every effort is made to reduce or eliminate it where possible, through careful focused design of the process layout.

### 10.5.8 Research and Development
In Irish firms, R & D is usually included in the production function. When these activities become extensive enough, a separate department may be set up. Industrial research and development generally concentrates on practical applications of theory and on how to solve production problems. The Japanese have led the field in the area of product development. They have effectively reduced product life-cycles by at least a half. In the car industry, GM used to work to a model life of 8 to 10 years, Honda work to 30 months. New design concepts such as Design for Manufacture, Concurrent Engineering, Lean Production and Value Engineering are some of the tools which have facilitated this dramatic shortening of design time for new products.

### SUMMARY
This chapter reviews the key role that operations management plays in translating overall business strategy into action and the cross functional role it plays in ensuring innovation and coupling with market requirements. Without a doubt, in terms of quality management and process improvement, operations management has become the key source of competitive advantage for firms competing in the global business environment. As competition increases, many firms, be they small or large, are embracing the core concepts of the World Class Business philosophy, which are Total Quality Management (TQM), Just-in-Time Manufacturing (JIT) and Employee Involvement (EI). The key points covered in this chapter are as follows:

- Business strategy is translated into operations strategy on three distinct levels: The Strategic level where decisions specify what to do, the Tactical level where decisions specify how and where to do it, and the Operational level where decisions are converted into action.

- Irish firms in the past have overemphasised production at lowest cost, rather than competition on quality, service and design. Information technology utilisation has been limited and there has been a lack of investment and reinvestment in equipment and people.

- Competitive advantage in this instance can be found in three distinct areas: quality, innovation and cost-minimisation. These three areas form the basis for the concepts associated with World Class Business (WCB) and Business Process Re-Engineering (BPR), where firms benchmark their standards against international rather than domestic standards, something that is very important for a small open economy such as Ireland.

- On a tactical level, Total Quality Management (TQM), ISO and BS certification are key tools for implementing strategy. In addition, the firm must address its service quality levels as part of the product/service mix to customers, and decisions have to be made in terms of the production system, where appropriate, and location and process issues.

- On the third level, business strategy is implemented on a daily basis in terms of activities such as purchasing, production control, quality control, inventory control, and research and development.

- One of the most crucial aspects of WCB is human resource planning. The resulting improvement in efficiency could make many activities and employees redundant. In addition, continuous improvement and flexibility creates an environment of change and insecurity for the workforce, and this has to be managed carefully in order that WCB can be implemented at all. The increase in competition can allow companies to develop further market share and increase the level of work available to a firm.

- As quality and quality management in all its forms become the norm for industry worldwide, innovative firms will create new forms or levels of differentiation, an example being competition on environmental standards and criteria.

## FURTHER READING

Coulson-Tomas, Colin et al., *Business Process Re-engineering: Myth and Reality*, Kogan Page, London, 1994.

Fynes, Brian and Sean Ennis, "Beyond World Class Manufacturing: Microsoft Ireland", *Irish Marketing Review*, No. 1, 1994.

Hammer, Michael, and James Champy, *Re-engineering the Corporation*, The Free Press, Macmillan, New York, 1994.

Lawler, Edward E. III., et al., *Employee Involvement and Total Quality Management, Practices and Results in Fortune 1000 Companies*, Jossey-Bass Publishers, San Francisco, CA, 1992.

Lewis, Robert C. and Bernard H. Booms, " The Marketing Aspects of Service Duality" in Berry, Shostack and Upah (eds.), *Emerging Perspectives on Services Marketing*, American Marketing Association, Chicago, IL, 1983, pp. 99–107.

Oakland, John S., *Total Quality Management: The Route to Improving Performance*, second edition, Butterworth-Heinemann, London, 1993.

Parasuraman, A., Leonard L. Berry and Valarie A. Zeithaml, "SERVQUAL: A Multiple Item Scale for Measuring Customer Perceptions of Service Quality", *Journal of Retailing*, Vol. 64, No. 1, 1988.

Parasuraman, A., Leonard L. Berry and Valarie A. Zeithaml, "Reassessment of Expectations as a Comparison Standard in Measuring Service Quality: Implications for Further Research", *Journal of Marketing*, Vol. 58, No. 1, 1994.

Schonberger, Richard J., *World Class Manufacturing: The Lessons of Simplicity Applied*, The Free Press, Macmillan, New York, 1986.

Suzaki, Kiyoshi, *The New Manufacturing Challenge: Techniques for Continuous Improvement*, The Free Press, Macmillan, New York, 1987.

Tunks, Roger, *Fast Track to Quality: A Twelve-Month Program for Small to Mid-sized Businesses*, McGraw-Hill, New York, 1992.

CHAPTER ELEVEN

# FINANCIAL MANAGEMENT

*T*he finance operations of successful enterprises are increasingly being used to gain strategic leverage as a source of competitive advantage. Smart businesses are building competencies in the area of financial management, and exploiting these skills resources. This chapter examines how finance and financial management play an important role in business strategy formulation and implementation. There is an extensive literature on the various aspects of financial management, and the intention in this chapter is not to summarise this literature, but rather to analyse some of the strategic implications of financial management.

Following this introduction is an overview of the objectives and role of financial management, the equity market in Ireland and the levels at which financial management strategy impacts on the firm. The role of financial management and the levels of financial management are reviewed. The three levels (strategic, tactical and operational) are then analysed in more detail. Finally, the equity and finance needs of Irish firms are identified in light of the preceding review of financial management.

## 11.1 OVERVIEW OF FINANCIAL MANAGEMENT

This section begins by examining the objectives and the role of finance and financial management, with a view to highlighting the importance of the finance function in strategic planning. It then reviews the current capital structure of business in Ireland and outlines the various levels at which business strategy relates to financial management.

### 11.1.1 The Objectives of Finance and Financial Management

The theory of finance is based on the key assumption that the main objective of the company is maximising the value of the company wealth for the ordinary shareholders, which can be valued in a variety of ways, such as market value or the value of assets on break-up. Money is the medium of measurement in economic activity, and is also the medium of exchange between the firm and its business environment. Successful company operations lead to a surplus of money over the long term, e.g. General Electric (GE) in the UK has in excess of £1 billion sterling in cash on its balance sheet. Usually in the case of money surplus, some of the surplus — called dividends — is distributed to shareholders for consumption, and the remainder is retained by the firm to fund future activities. The latter use of the surplus created by the firm's operations — called earnings capitalisation or capital development — shows up a further function of money, i.e. its role as one of the fundamental factors of production, together with raw materials, technological transformation processes, and human labour plus enterprise.

There are thus two major aspects of money dealings, usually known as financial management. The first concerns the acquisition and eventual deployment of funds. The second concerns the measurement and management of money as it flows into, around, and out of the firm in the course of its operations. Each of the two major functional aspects of finance — money as a resource and surplus on the one hand and as a flow on the other — are strategically significant, in different ways. Adequate financing, from the right funds sources, can provide a competitive cost advantage over firms whose funding is either inadequate or poorly structured. On the other hand, adequate initial and subsequent rounds of financing must be accompanied by rigorous financial management and appropriate financial information systems to make its use as efficient and effective as possible.

In addition to meeting the pure financial objectives of the firm, management must understand its wider obligations to society. The simple theory of finance is, in practice, far too simplistic to cater for these obligations, and in recent years there has been much debate as to the adequacy of the wealth maximisation objective in defining the firm's role in society. The modern firm's mission and business strategy is being met through the setting of multiple financial targets and a variety of non-financial objectives and criteria, including:

- The welfare of employees

- The welfare of management

- The welfare of society

- The upkeep of the environment

- The fulfilment of responsibility toward stakeholders, customers, suppliers, the public etc.

### 11.1.2 The Role of Financial Management

Financial management, therefore, relates to acquisition, management and spending of funds following certain internal and external criteria. In addition, there are four key roles or activities within the financial management function which impact on the overall business strategy of the firm. They relate to the financing of current operations, deciding on long-term financing strategy and making investment decisions on mergers and acquisitions:

1. **Identifying Short-Term Funds Requirements**: This relates to cash budgeting and bank financing in terms of identifying the seasonal and cyclical needs of the current operations and marketing activities (i.e. the working capital requirements) within the firm and how they affect the cash-flow requirements on a daily/weekly/monthly basis.

2. **Managing Short-Term Assets and Liabilities**: This relates to the financing of current operations and how the cash flow of the firm is affected by trade credit and trade debit policy.

3. **Long-Term Financing**: The firm needs to identify the longer-term financial requirements which flow from the strategic, operational and marketing strategies and outline a feasible financing strategy. This relates in general to the mix of financing tactics between debt funding and equity funding and hybrid forms of both.

4. **Strategic and Investment Decisions**: Over and above the short- and long-term financial requirements of the operations of the firm, the firm must analyse the financial implications of investment and diversification strategies of the firm, whether they be in related or unrelated business areas. The key areas of activity here would be the determining of the cost of capital, measuring the cost of capital versus risk, analysing industries and competitors, developing capital budgeting systems and investigating merger and acquisition proposals.

A fifth activity, which applies to larger firms, is the corporate treasury management function, which relates to the optimal management of the financial assets of the corporation. Consider the treasury management functions of ESB, i.e. Financial Treasury International (FTI), and Telecom Éireann, i.e. Irish Treasury International (ITI), which manage the large cash flows that these organisations accumulate on a daily to weekly basis.

As already mentioned, financial strategy is implemented via the acquisition, management and deployment of funds, all three of which are crucial in realising the firm's overall business strategy (see Figure 11.1).

*Figure 11.1: The Role of Strategy in Financial Management*

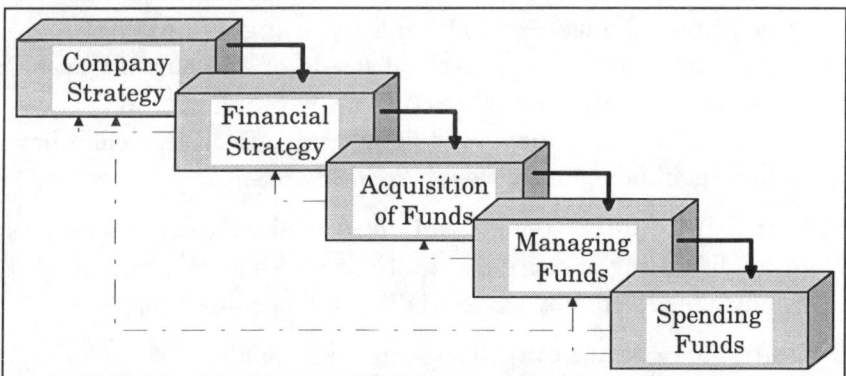

### 11.1.3 The Venture Capital and Equity Market in Ireland

As mentioned in Chapter One, there are only about a dozen indigenous firms that can be classified as large by international standards, and indigenous companies have seen a decline in investment over the last decade. This has implications in terms of the financial and equity strategies employed by Irish firms, and the capital structures related to them.

The Department of Enterprise and Employment analysed the equity and capital structure of Irish business in the early 1990s. Table 11.1 shows the capital structure of Irish Industry. It seems that the share-capital structure of Irish industry is quite strong, with 75 per cent of the long-term funding being share capital and reserves, with 16 per cent accounted for by long-term debt and grants at 7 per cent. Large firms (100+ employees) have a lower level of share capital because of higher levels of long-term debt and grant-aid available to them. Average gearing is 21 per cent, but for larger firms such as Cement Roadstone Holdings (CRH) or the Jefferson Smurfit Group, gearing would be in the mid- to higher thirties, which is nearly double that for very small firms (3–9 employees).

*Table 11.1: Capital Structure of Irish Industry, 1992 (%)*

| | Number of Employees | | | | | |
|---|---|---|---|---|---|---|
| | 3–9 | 10–19 | 20–50 | 51–99 | 100+ | Total |
| **Share Capital and Reserves** | 75 | 77 | 74 | 78 | 65 | 75 |
| **Borrowing due after 1 year** | 14 | 16 | 17 | 12 | 24 | 16 |
| **Grants** | 7 | 7 | 6 | 8 | 10 | 7 |
| **Other** | 4 | — | 3 | 2 | 1 | 2 |
| **Gearing (Debt/Equity)** | 100 (19) | 100 (21) | 100 (23) | 100 (15) | 100 (37) | 100 (21) |

*Source*: Enterprise and Employment, 1992.

The report outlined some other aspects of the financial structure of Irish industry:

• An estimated £40 million to £50 million of equity was supplied annually to the Irish market by venture capitalists, state agencies, BES Investors, etc.

- Venture-capitalist companies have vacated certain segments of the market, notably investments under £0.25 million, and are reluctant to supply some sectors, in particular start-ups.

- While the state's equity policy has been driven by a desire to achieve some measure of repayability by substituting equity for grants, rather than by filling these equity gaps per se, it has, nevertheless, become an important equity supplier of small investments to indigenous manufacturing industry and international services.

The information on start-ups is a cause for concern. In Ireland about half the start-ups are closed within a period of 10 years. However, US experience suggests that venture-capital-backed projects show a significantly lower failure rate at 18 per cent. It is assumed that this is partly caused by the selection process of venture-capital firms, and partly caused by the management input provided by professional venture-capital firms.

In 1994, the Chambers of Commerce of Ireland (CCI) analysed the financial and equity structure of Irish business with a view to focusing attention on the financial needs of small firms. The main findings were as follows:

- **Venture Capital**: Venture capitalists are tending to focus on a small number of potential investments, usually in the fast-growth traded sector. There is an almost complete absence of seed capital (pre-start-up and start-up capital) in Ireland. Therefore, there is a need to increase the supply of venture capital to non-fast-growth small firms which represent less exciting investments. Development capitalists tend to lend amounts which are in excess of the requirements of most small firms. There exists a need to provide equity investment for amounts between £30,000 and £200,000, i.e. the amount up to which firms are able to access bank funds with relative ease, and the minimum amount under which venture capitalists tend to invest.

- **Loan Finance**: Although many loan instruments are available to small firms, they do not adequately meet financial needs. Small firms in particular have difficulty accessing loans of £30,000–£50,000 and for time periods in excess of five years. One of the main reasons for this, according to the CCI, is the high collateral levels required by the banks to secure lending. The CCI found that the cost of funds (collateral, interest rates and bank charges/fees) is of greater concern to small firms than availability of funds. The introduction of the £100 million Government-subsidised loan scheme administered by ICC is a welcome step in the right direction.

- **State Finance**: State-aid concentrates on the traded sector and, therefore, precludes most small firms from accessing funds. The focus of public policy is based on concerns over dead-weight and displacement, the net result being that the importance of small business is not reflected in public policy and/or the availability of public funds. However, the County Enterprise Boards are not limited to funding the traded sector or firms with more than 10 employees.

- **Management Skills**: Many of the problems mentioned above can be explained by the fact that lenders and other analysts believe that many of the management skills, and in particular strategic management skills, are underdeveloped among small firms, and often a business plan does not exist. This adversely affects banks' and investors' perceptions of the small-firm sector and impacts on their willingness to lend to, or invest in, the sector.

Therefore, it could be said that a number of internal and external issues constrain the development of Irish firms, and all these issues relate to strategic financial management in Irish business, whether it be on a macroeconomic or microeconomic level, and have implications for firms and state agencies alike.

In order to understand the venture-capital market in Ireland, venture capital should first be defined. According to Walsh and Murray (1993), the key elements of a venture type investment are that it:

- Has an equity capital in orientation
- Is long-term in nature
- Is aimed at companies with rapid growth potential

- Offers higher expected returns to compensate for the higher risk in new projects

- Is aimed at unquoted companies

- Emphasises capital gain.

The sectoral distribution of venture-capital investment is very different between the United States, Europe and Ireland, as can be seen in Table 11.2. Compared to the US and European experience, venture-capital funding in Ireland is heavily concentrated in consumer-related products, and virtually non-existent in the relatively riskier areas of Telephony and Data Communications or Biotechnology.

**Table 11.2: Comparison of Venture-Capital Investment — USA, Europe and Ireland, 1993**

|  | Percentage Funds Invested (%) | | |
|---|---|---|---|
|  | **USA** | **Europe** | **Ireland** |
| Software and Services | 27.1 | 3.9 | 19.6 |
| Medical and Healthcare | 17.4 | 4.0 | 3.2 |
| Telephone and Data Communications | 14.4 | 3.9 | 1.3 |
| Biotechnology | 10.3 | 1.3 | — |
| Consumer-rated | 7.7 | 19.4 | 39.9 |
| Other | 23.1 | 67.5 | 36.0 |
| **Total** | **100** | **100** | **100** |

*Source*: Walsh and Murray, "Pension Fund Investment", 1993.

The Irish venture-capital market changed significantly in the late 1980s and early 1990s and has experienced contraction rather than growth. In the early 1980s, Allied Combined Trust (ACT), Development Capital Corporation (DCC), Investors in Industry (3I) and the Industrial Credit Corporation (ICC) were all active in the market. In addition, the Government-promoted National Enterprise Agency — subsequently the National Development

Corporation (NADCORP) — was active. The structure changed considerably in the 1990s. 3I withdrew from the Irish market, the size of ACT was greatly reduced, DCC moved away from venture capital towards an industrial-holding strategy and the Government closed the NADCORP.

The Smurfit Enterprise fund was set up in 1993 to supply funding of between £100,000 and £500,000 to individual projects. The County Enterprise Boards have approximately £18 million per annum available for local industry, and a software development fund has been created. AIB is promoting a £30 million venture fund with ACT. However, the problem still remains that the projects most likely to find a limited supply of funding are those which are too large for many of the Irish sources, too small for many of the UK venture funds, and are in non-traditional sectors of industry. Such projects are likely to require funding in the range of £300,000 to £4 million. Walsh and Murray recommend in their study of Pension Funds in Ireland that pension-fund investment should target this gap in the venture-capital structure in Ireland. Indeed, the government budget now requires that 0.08 per cent of Pension Funds goes to venture capital in Ireland.

### 11.1.4 The Three Levels of Financial Management

As in manufacturing and in operations, the strategic management of finance may be divided into three levels on which strategy is implemented:

- **The Strategic Level**, which filters business strategy into financial requirements (i.e. where decisions specify what to do)

- **The Tactical Level**, which determines the cost structure and sources of finance (where decisions specify how and where to do it)

- **The Operational Level**, which manages strategy on a day-by-day basis in terms of budgets, controls and working capital management (i.e. where decisions are converted into action).

The overall concern of the finance function is to interrelate these decision levels in order that the desired strategic output materialises. Figure 11.2 graphically describes the flow of financial decision-making activities down through the business hierarchy.

## Figure 11.2: The Levels of Financial Strategy

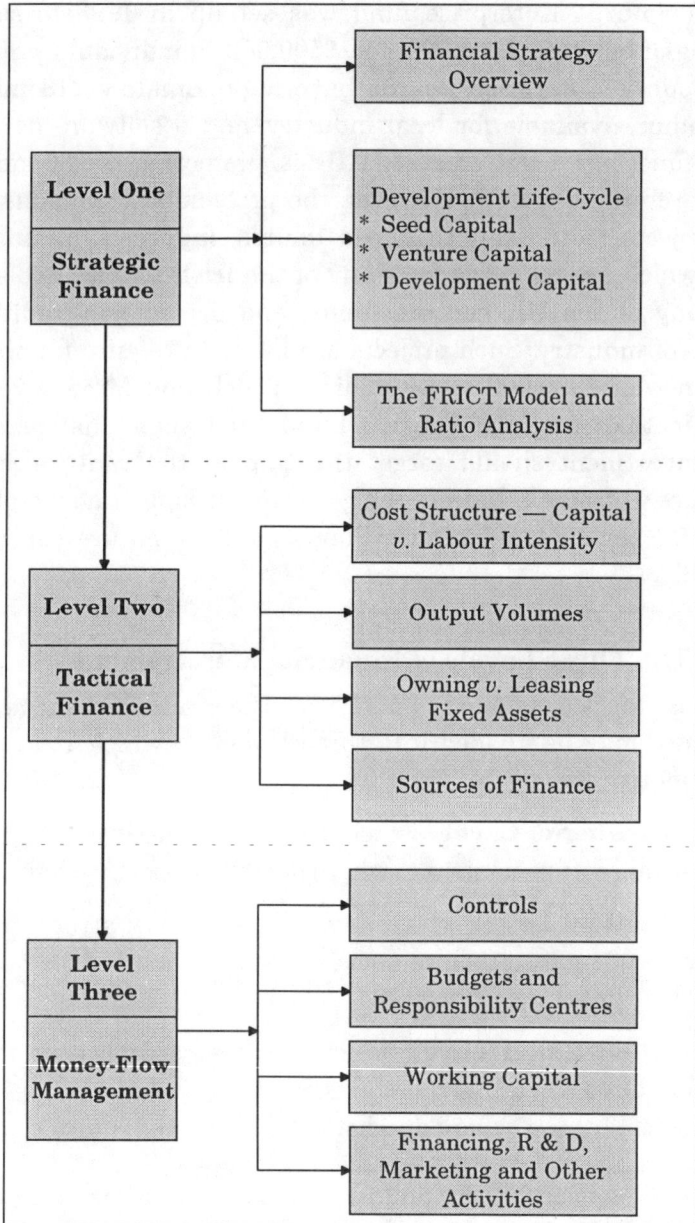

In practice, the three levels overlap to a very high degree. Indeed, it could be said that one cannot separate tactical and operational activities. For example, the cost structure of the organisation analysed at the tactical level is difficult to separate from working-capital management and budgeting. These activities are discussed in the following sections.

## 11.2 LEVEL ONE — STRATEGIC FINANCE

In the past, the use of finance as a strategic tool has, in general, been confined to corporate financial departments or treasury management arms of large multinationals. However, growing firms worldwide are realising that they can use finance as a strategic rather than an operational tool. Irish firms should understand the potential advantages that strategic financial leverage can accrue. In addition, the firm must realise that its financial needs evolve as the firm develops and grows. This section analyses the various stages of business growth and the resulting financial requirements.

### 11.2.1 The Development Life-Cycle

Perhaps the most important factor determining funding requirements is the life-cycle stage in which the firm is positioned. There are four major stages in the business life-cycle — development, growth, maturity, and saturation stages — and each has very different financial requirements. All firms in the start-up stage need capital until revenues come in, and the operations are brought up to net positive cash flow. Finally, if the firm is wound-up there may be a residual capital distribution. The same principles apply to new product developments within firms as to totally new enterprises, although existing firms usually have access to a wider range of capital sources. The various phases of capital funding are:

- Seed Capital Phase

- Venture Capital Phase

- Development Capital Phase.

### Seed Capital

Seed Capital is finance provided to research, develop and assess an initial concept before a business idea has reached the start-up stage. In Ireland, start-up capital is also included under the seed-capital banner. This is finance provided for companies for product development and initial marketing. Companies may be in the process of being set-up or have been in business for a short time, but have not sold their product commercially.

The seed-capital phase is a most critical phase of new business development. During this phase the new idea is explored and developed to the point of market entry (or the decision not to proceed). Funds are required for product and process research, for market research and for feasibility. The failure rate in this phase is very high (over 90 per cent) and there is a long lead time, typically over two years, before even the likely prospects can reach the commercialisation stage. Because of the very high risks, the most appropriate type of finance is equity (or equity-like finance, such as grants). The usual source is the promoter, the promoter's family and friends, and sometimes the local community. The Business Expansion Scheme (BES) does try to encourage seed-capital investment, but there are other distortions in the Irish tax system which discourage this kind of investment. There is a shortage of genuine seed-capital sources in Ireland, and perhaps the main source is Forbairt with Feasibility Grants and R & D Grants.

A survey by Kinsella, in 1991, of the fast-growth sector demonstrates that a high proportion of start-up capital comes from personal savings (50 per cent) and grants (20 per cent). Venture capital in the form of seed-capital investment was found to be an insignificant source of funding for start-up businesses, as the risk/reward structure is not conducive to encouraging potential capital investors, who consider a good track record to be important when evaluating a potential investment (the absence of a track record effectively precluding enterprises from accessing equity capital investment). In addition, the minimum amount invested by venture-capital companies is typically between £200,000 and £250,000, which exceeds the maximum requirement of most companies in the start-up stage, and the administrative and monitoring costs associated with investing in a new business are high relative to the level of funds involved, which acts as a deterrent to potential investors.

Because of these factors, there has been a marked reduction in the number of venture-capital companies providing seed capital in the Irish Market. Table 11.3 identifies this changing focus. Most state capital agencies now concentrate on the provision of development capital to established firms, although the efforts of the County Enterprise Boards is a step in the right direction in terms of seed capital.

*Table 11.3: The Focus of Ireland's Venture-Capital Industry, 1986–92*

|  | 1986 | 1987 | 1988 | 1989 | 1990 | 1991 | 1992 |
|---|---|---|---|---|---|---|---|
| Total Port-folio (£m) | 43.6 | 69.2 | 101.0 | 125.0 | 134.0 | N/A | N/A |
| New Invest-ments (£m) | 15.5 | 28.8 | 27.0 | 29.0 | 26.0 | N/A | N/A |
| of which: | % | % | % | % | % | % | % |
| Seed/ Start-Up | 35.1 | 29.2 | 32.4 | 1.6 | 3.0 | 13.0* | 5.2* |
| Development | 42.4 | 56.8 | 40.5 | 43.9 | 94.9 | 83* | 87.7* |
| Buy-out | 14.3 | 12.3 | 27.1 | 54.5 | 2.1 | 4.1* | 7.1* |

*Source*: Department of Enterprise and Employment, 1992.
\* Estimates

### Venture Capital

The Venture-Capital phase proper moves the project from the feasibility stage into commercial production and past the knothole stage. Capital funds are needed to set up the production system, to fund market development, and to provide for initial working capital. The failure rate is lower than in the seed-capital stage, but still high. In terms of greenfield projects, between 1978 and 1990, 61 per cent of all failures occurred in the first three years. In addition, 34 per cent of 1987 start-ups failed within three years. Typically, annual cash-flows for successful ventures become positive after two to four years, and cumulative cash-flows between three and five years after start-up. Funding for this stage should be primarily equity-based, not only because of the high-risk level, but also because interest payments on debt can add more costs than the project can bear. According to research undertaken on firms involved in Forbairt's Enterprise Development Programme (EDP) between 1987 and 1990, there is a strong statistical relationship between level of equity at start up and subsequent success or failure.

The venture-capital structure of Irish industry has already been discussed. Since the 1980s, the availability of venture capital in Ireland has been helped through the setting up of a number of specialist venture-capital firms such as the Industrial Credit Corporation (ICC), which administers the Government-subsidised loan scheme, and AIB Venture Capital. Companies receiving venture capital from the EDP included Poldys, which began producing own-label Pizzas for Quinnsworth, and Rye Valley Foods. Other companies that received venture capital include Monaghan Mushrooms, Buckley's (Builders Providers), Flogas (LPG and bottled gas distributors), Barlo Group plc (Radiator Manufacturers) and Lake Electronics (Telephone Switching Products and Electronic Components).

### Development Capital

Development Capital is the finance required to exploit the growth potential of a firm or business idea with a good record and prospects. Usually, new ventures will have reached at least the stage of annual positive cash-flows. Higher debt ratios can be reasonably contemplated during this stage since the business risk has decreased, but, ironically, specialist venture-capital funding is now much more readily available for the right projects, and the problem is lack of good projects rather than lack of funds. There are currently sufficient sources and instruments for provision of development capital. As already mentioned, the major providers of development capital are Development Capital Corporation (DCC) and Allied Combined Trust (ACT), Ulster Investment Bank (UIB), National City Brokers (NCB), and the Business Expansion Scheme — through various funds. Examples of the successful provision of development capital include Fruit Importers of Ireland (FII), Printech plc, and Irish Ferries.

**Table 11.4: Sources of Past Equity Finance (%)**

|  | Number of Employees | | | | | |
|---|---|---|---|---|---|---|
|  | 3–9 | 10–19 | 20–50 | 51–99 | 100+ | Total |
| Private Sourcing | 59 | 55 | 38 | 40 | 75 | 49 |
| BES | 19 | 25 | 32 | 40 | 25 | 27 |
| Venture Capital | 9 | 10 | 18 | 13 | — | 12 |
| Other | 13 | 10 | 12 | 7 | — | 12 |
| Total | 100 | 100 | 100 | 100 | 100 | 100 |
| Number of Equity Share Issues | 32 | 40 | 34 | 15 | 8 | 129 |
| As % of Total | 25 | 31 | 26 | 12 | 6 | 100 |

*Source*: Department of Enterprise and Employment, 1992.

### 11.2.2 The FRICT Model and Ratio Analysis

The strategic financial requirements cannot be defined solely by understanding the stage of development of the firm. Naturally, the output volumes and the capital/labour-cost structure will influence the decision and these issues are discussed in a later section. A number of other factors permeate financial management decision-making, and these influence the strategic financial balance. In summary, they are enveloped in the FRICT model as follows:

- *Flexibility*: The strategic financial package should allow some level of flexibility in order that business strategy can be modified if necessary. A very strict and rigid financial plan can constrain the development of the firm, for example, if it locks it into heavy repayment schedules in the start-up phase.

- *Risk*: The cost of capital increases as the level of risk involved increases, and many firms tend to underestimate the level of risk involved when formulating the financial plan. The form of financing will also depend on the level of risk involved, e.g. equity funding is more effective in the start-up phase.

- *Income*: The financial plan should account for the necessary income-flow requirements of the owners, workers, shareholders, venture-capitalists etc. This is just as important as the plan, allowing for day-to-day cash outflow requirements.

- *Control*: The amount of control that the firm or the owner wants to hold on to will affect the financial package. In general, firms can give away too much of their control to outside bodies, and this may affect the entrepreneurial spirit that has made the venture successful in the first place.

- *Timing*: As already mentioned, the timing of the financial inputs should be linked to the critical development stages of the firm.

A key analysis technique for analysing the financial health of a firm in accordance with the FRICT model is ratio analysis. There is a multitude of ratio analysis techniques that firms can employ at various stages of financial management activity. These ratios analyse the liquidity and profitability of the firm *vis-à-vis* industry and competitor averages. The key ratios used by firms include the following:

- Return on Investment

- Debt/Equity Ratio

- Current Ratio

- Quick Ratio

- Return on Sales

- Credit Ratio

- Collection Ratio.

## 11.3 LEVEL TWO — TACTICS: ACQUISITION AND DEPLOYMENT

The total amount of funds required by a firm depends on a complex of factors, some of which can be influenced by the firm itself. Major factors include the firm's life-cycle position (as already discussed the cost structure of the production process, the volume output, and the own or lease policies of the firm.

## 11.3.1 Cost Structure — Capital *v.* Labour Intensity

A major factor influencing capital-funding requirements, over which the firm has some choice, concerns the degree of capital versus labour intensity. This is a complicated decision area, and not all manufacturing processes allow latitude in the selection of the degree of capital or labour that may be used. Caraplas Ireland, based in Dublin and purchased in 1995 by Hoechst, is a manufacturer of recyclable plastic. The nature of its industry and its process is such that it is a capital-intensive industry. Contrast this with Dubarry Shoe Company, which has an amount of capital but where labour costs are also of paramount importance. An important factor is that until recently industrial policy in Ireland not only favoured capital intensity, but only new capital equipment was grant-aided. Second-hand equipment, with a shorter pay-back period and less risk, was not grant-aided. Consider the Japanese philosophy in relation to World Class Manufacturing, where the maintenance of existing capital equipment is extremely important, so avoiding funding requirement for new capital equipment. Sometimes more labour can be used instead of more equipment to increase output, and this will change the cost structure and the capital requirements. (To be effective, it may also require a change in personnel philosophy.) In the absence of adequate equity funding, however, labour-intensive operations may allow a firm to commence operations which can later be mechanised or automated as funds from operations accrue, as the market is established, and as a track record is built up with bankers and other funds sources.

## 11.3.2 Output Volumes

The expected output volumes and the production economies of scale applicable to any specific business, together constitute a third major determinant of capital-funding requirements: capital intensity versus large volume outputs. In general, the more capital-intensive the production process, the more likely that there will be a requirement for large volume outputs. If labour is the major ingredient of the cost structure, output volumes can be increased — up to a point — without further capital equipment, e.g. hand-made crystal at Waterford Glass. Similarly, if raw material inputs or marketing costs are very high, the cost of permanent working capital will be critical, e.g. the energy costs at Irish Glass Bottle Company and Ardagh plc, or the marketing costs at Lyons Irish Tea. If there are important economies of scale in any of these areas, the firm must aim for production volumes which will capture these economies, or else it must have developed appreciable competitive advantages in other areas to offset the cost disadvantages. Industry sectors that require start-up scales larger than that needed to supply the Irish market (for example, an Irish-made, designed and marketed PC computer) have little chance, in the absence of proven export markets.

### 11.3.3 Owning *v.* Leasing Fixed Assets

The policy adopted by or forced upon a firm in relation to whether it owns or rents its fixed assets is a further important factor influencing the level of total capital required. For a number of reasons, Irish firms, both large and small, have a high proportion — two thirds — of their fixed assets tied up on land and buildings. For start-up situations in particular, financing these kinds of unproductive fixed assets can be very onerous, and leasing can, in a sense, become an important source of finance by freeing up working capital for other development requirements.

In looking at the need of indigenous Irish firms for capital, we see, on the one hand, a majority of traditional-industry firms, either struggling to survive in the face of import competition (such as the clothing and footwear industries), or surviving because of logistic competitive advantages. On the other hand, a few young or revitalised companies are geared to export markets or to import substitute markets as a preliminary to exporting (for example, Lake Electronics in import substitution and Bailey's/ Emmets Cream Liqueur in exporting). Development capital required to take an existing firm into a growth phase does appear to be available, but only under conditions that are too stringent for many traditional firms to avail of. In practice, many management teams cannot find a strategy to overcome either the severity of import competition or the natural limits on non-traded products. For new ventures or for export projects, development capital may be readily available, notwithstanding a patchy track record, once export or domestic growth can be demonstrated. Even so, the risk factor must be greater for Ireland, especially where there is such a small domestic market as a fallback.

For incipient new ventures in the feasibility and early commercialisation stages, the necessary equity capital would appear to be scarce. How much this is caused by the capital impoverishment of would-be entrepreneurs, and how much is the result of a lack of truly plausible projects which could attract initial equity investors, must remain an open point. The state currently resolves this situation through the Business Expansion Scheme and the 0.08 per cent of pension funds going to venture capital.

### 11.3.4 Sources of Finance

There are two basic sources of finance available to business firms, equity and debt, and there are several types of each. Each type of capital source has different implications for cost, control and flexibility, and the total composition of capital funding is a major background factor in the company's strategic position.

### *Equity Capital*

Michael Smurfit once said "Equity is to our firm like blood is to the human body". In theory, shareholders subscribing to a company's equity control the company. In practice, the amount of influence that ordinary members have over business strategy may be very limited, and there may be considerable separation of management from ownership, so that management can effectively control the equity shares. The firm's profit is entirely attributable to the equity owners, and thus the lower the proportion of equity to total funding, the higher the returns to equity. However, other sources of capital become more expensive and less available as equity diminishes as a proportion of total funds, and so there is a limit to how little equity is possible. The cost of equity can be estimated by several approaches if there is a market for the shares of the company. For companies where shares are untraded, the cost of capital is approximated by the opportunity cost to shareholders of retaining earnings in the company for future investment rather than receiving dividends and investing them elsewhere.

The Irish Stock Exchange has become a major source of equity to Irish companies. There are now several ways to achieve a Stock Exchange quote, without going through the rigour of a full Stock Exchange examination, via the Unlisted Securities Market (USM), the Smaller Companies Market (SCM) and the Exploration Companies Market (ECM). In 1996, the Irish Stock Exchange plans to merge these three markets and add them to the official listing, in addition to creating a Developing Companies Market (DCM) to cater for medium-sized companies in the development phase of growth.

### Retained Earnings

A second type of equity source lies in the firm's operations, through the generation of profits, asset disposals, and capital appreciation of the equity shares. Surplus funds not distributed as dividends are retained by the firm and reinvested in the business, and they are generally consolidated into the capital base by the issuing of new equity shares.

### Grant-Aid

For manufacturing firms in Ireland, Government grant-aid is an important source of capital funds. If the contract conditions are adhered to, the grant-aid is gradually amortised and becomes part of shareholders' funds. This equity is free, but it also imposes conditions that may impact on strategic or operational freedom. It may, for instance, lead to the investment intensity trap or to high-bridging finance costs while awaiting transfer of funds, or to higher operational costs than a lower-capital-funding alternative, or to unrealistic but acceptable formal strategic plans, designed to "capture" the grant-money.

### Debt

Debt, like equity, also comes in different forms. At one end of the spectrum are formal loans, mainly from banks and other financial institutions. Banks put a high premium on risk, preferring fully secured and shorter-term loans. Another type of formal borrowings make up what is called "off-balance-sheet" financing — provision of medium-term assets through leasing and hire purchase agreements. These assets are used but not owned by the company, and their cost is expressed as annual expenses to be deducted from profit, rather than as an addition to total capital. A third form of debt is that provided by the cash-flows from operations. These arise where revenues are obtained before payments must be made for the component costs. Companies have some latitude in stretching payments to creditors and the Revenue Commissioners, and this is commonly used to balance short-term cash-flow. It is a common cause of business failure in Ireland to allow this "inadvertent" debt — especially to the Revenue, whose collection mechanisms have in the past been much slower than commercial firms — to become exorbitant, and in the end unpayable.

## 11.4 LEVEL THREE — MONEY-FLOW MANAGEMENT AND FINANCIAL ACTIVITIES

This section looks at how strategic and tactical financial decisions are converted into action on a day-to-day basis in Irish firms. It begins by looking at the financial controls employed by firms, and goes on to analyse the main reporting and information procedures that firms use. The section continues by looking at the use of budgets and responsibility centres and the whole area of working-capital management, and ends with a discussion on the financing of intangible assets and other activities within the firm.

### 11.4.1 Financial Controls

There is no single comprehensive method of controlling every aspect of a firm's activities. In practice, several different kinds of control mechanism are used in combination. Financial controls are used to evaluate a firm's overall performance in financial terms. Budgetary controls are the most common method of allocating resources and authority to implement strategy. The development of budgets is a major component of the planning process, and the budgets which finally emerge constitute the single most important tool for co-ordinating and controlling all organisation activities. Computers have greatly improved the speed and accuracy with which quantitative data can be gathered, communicated, analysed, and presented for decision-making. When used properly, even small systems can provide extremely good control. Computerisation can allow financial statements and budgets to be monitored and updated daily, or even on a real-time basis.

Four of the most common and useful kinds of financial control methods are financial statements, ratio analysis, break-even analysis and, more recently, value-added analysis.

### Financial Statements

These describe in monetary terms the flow of goods and services into, around, and out of the firm. They are summaries of the firm's accounting records and are concerned with three key areas of financial performance: liquidity, general financial health, and profitability. These statements are always prepared with past information, and so their usefulness as a short-term control mechanism is limited. However, they do provide managers with useful information about trends and major disruptions, and quarterly or monthly statements can often allow managers to take corrective action in time. Financial statements are also the primary source of data used by outsiders to assess performance.

Balance sheets describe how an organisation has performed up to a particular point in time, in terms of assets, liabilities, and the net worth of the owners. Assets are given in the form of current, fixed and intangible components; liabilities are classified in terms of current and long-term elements. Net worth is the residual value after total liabilities have been deducted from total assets.

The income statement shows a company's financial performance over an interval of time. All costs, including taxes, are deducted from gross income, and profit (or loss) is shown as the residual. This amount is then available for paying dividends to stockholders, or for reinvesting in the business.

Cash-flow statements, also known as sources-and-uses-of-funds statements, show where cash or funds came from (operations, loans, reduction in debtors etc.), and where they went (capital investment, dividends, reduction of creditors, etc.)

### Ratio Analysis

As already mentioned, ratio analysis statements are useful to managers and outsiders (such as investors and bankers) in evaluating a firm's past performance, but alone they do not provide all of the information that is necessary for good decision-making. The picture can be filled out further by means of ratio analysis, which measures financial performance relative to something else — the firm's past achievements, or the performance of competing firms in the industry.

Financial ratios are calculated from information contained in the financial statements, and they express relationships between items in the form of percentages or fractions. There are many kinds of ratio used to measure relative profitability, liquidity, activities, and leverage. The single most commonly used measure, and the broadest in scope, is Return on Investment (ROI). This is usually given as an annual percentage return on assets employed, and it is used to measure the productivity of assets. Other ratios in common use are the current ratio (current assets to current liabilities) to measure short-term solvency; the debt ratio (total debt to total assets) to show leverage, or the relative amounts of internal and external funding; and activity measures (such as stock turnover), which are of particular importance to the firm or industry being analysed.

### Break-even Analysis

Break-even analysis tries to set out the relationship between cost, sales volumes, and profits. It is possible to determine how changes in volumes and/or costs will affect the bottom line (sensitivity analysis), which can be used to calculate the volume necessary to break even, or to make a given level of profit.

The limitations of break-even analysis are that it is sometimes difficult to decide whether costs are variable, fixed, semi-variable or semi-fixed; whether variable costs per unit are constant; whether fixed costs are constant; and whether prices will remain constant. On the other hand, break-even analysis is fairly easy to understand and use, and it provides information accurate enough to be useful in many actual decision-making and control situations.

### Value-added Analysis

Value-added analysis is more sophisticated than break-even analysis, and correspondingly more valuable and more difficult to perform. It attempts to analyse the entire cost structure of the firm, with the dual purpose of understanding the factors which drive each cost element, and also of understanding precisely how each of the firm's activities contributes to the total value-added that the firm generates.

### 11.4.2 Reporting and Information

Closely related to the overall control activities of the firm is the process of creating financial information for internal and external purposes. On one level, the firm has a statutory requirement to report the financial health of the organisation for taxation and shareholders where applicable. On a second level, the firm needs to provide financial and managerial accounting information for internal "customers". This information plays a key role in the marketing information system as mentioned in Chapter Nine, and fuels such activities as new-product and market development. Figure 11.3 graphically describes the flow of financial information through the firm, from the financial plan through the operations, cash and capital budgets and on to financial control, which in turn influences the financial plan for the proceeding year.

*Figure 11.3: The Financial-Information Flow*

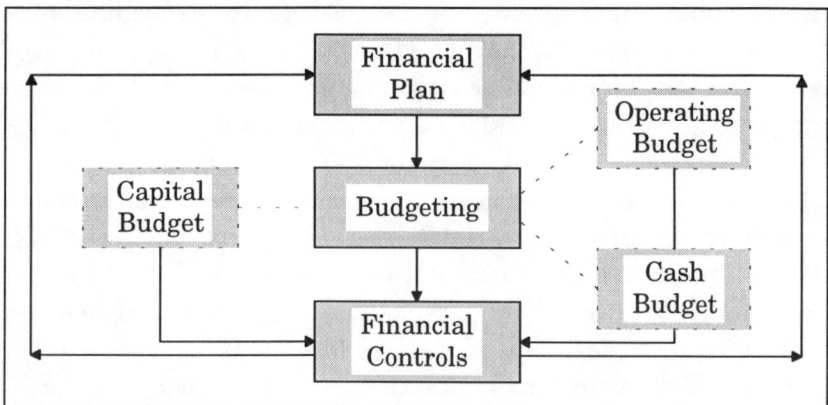

### 11.4.3 Budgets and Responsibility Centres

Budgets are quantified statements, either resources committed to a defined task or of some level of desired performance, which are to be achieved within a given time period. They contain within them, by implication, the authority to access and employ resources, and the corresponding responsibility for their performance. They are the most widely employed formal means of planning and controlling activities at every level of a firm. Three types of budget exist:

- The Operating Budget
- The Cash Budget
- The Capital Budget.

They are widely used because, being quantitative, they provide clear and unambiguous standards of performance within a specified time-frame. At regular intervals during the time period of the budget, actual results are compared with budget figures, and this allows deviations to be detected and corrected. As well as being a control device, budgets are perhaps the major mechanism for integrating and co-ordinating the firm's different activities. Part of the co-ordination and integration task is carried out by using the information contained within the budgets, and part is accomplished by the process of drawing up and agreeing the budgets in the first place.

There are extreme cases where budgets are completely imposed from above, or are originated entirely at lower levels in the organisation; but generally speaking, budgets are drawn up by lower-level managers in response to guidelines set by higher levels. The detailed budgets are amalgamated as they go upwards, the general guidelines are teased out in detail as they pass downwards. Final decisions are made by top management, but most good intermediate managers know how to retain some discretion over their own allocations.

### *Operating and Financial Budgets*
There are two broad types of budgets: operating budgets which deal with the physical quantities of inputs and outputs as well as their associated costs and revenues; and financial budgets, which spell out intended revenues, total expenditures, and sources and uses of funds. Operating budgets can be further classified in terms of the activities they are intended to control, either ongoing

organisational functions or time-bound projects. Operating budgets can also be divided according to the major organisational functions of marketing, operations and human resources, depending on the scope of responsibility of the manager concerned.

### Revenue Centres

Revenue centres are units in the organisation for which the manager is mainly responsible for outputs, which are not directly compared with the units input costs. The marketing department would be an example of this, where sales targets would be the main budgetary measurement, and although there would probably be a cost budget associated with the department, this would not be related to achievements of sales targets. Revenue budgets — the forecast volume of sales multiplied by the expected price per unit — are the most uncertain, dealing as they do with future demand. (On the other hand, the marketing mix is the tool by which future demand is influenced).

### Cost Centres

Cost centres — or expense centres — are built around organisational units for which demand is fixed (such as a production unit), and the focus is to measure and control the monetary cost of inputs. It is the inverse case to the above. Cost or expense budgets may be said to be "engineered", when costs can be estimated with a great degree of reliability. The actual-to-budget variances then measure production efficiency. Expense budgets may also be "discretionary", when costs cannot be estimated in advance with any reliability, and managers spend largely at their discretion to obtain the necessary results.

### Profit Centres

Profit centres come into existence when a manager has a large degree of control over both input and output activities. It is then possible to compare inputs with outputs directly, with monetary measures. Each firm as a whole is necessarily a profit centre. It is possible to make cost and revenue centres at any level into profit centres, if suitable internal "transfer" prices can be agreed. In this event, each of the firm's activities makes a notional profit (or loss) which together add up to the realised profit or loss. This is the type of accounting needed to perform a value-added analysis, mentioned above.

### Investment Centres

Investment centres are responsible, not just for profit, but also for the acquisition and disposal of funding. They develop and control the financial budgets, which deal with cash management, funding flows, capital expenditures and balance-sheet requirements. The investment budgets show whether operations are, or will become, viable. They point out gaps in the financing that must be filled, and they trigger action plans to fill the gaps. They also show how the effects of operating strategy will be reflected in financial position.

### 11.4.4 Working-Capital Management

The shocks to the Irish business system since the beginning of free trade in the mid-1960s have forced Irish managers to focus most of their efforts on survival rather than managing growth, on liquidity rather than on profitability. With inadequate equity structures and limited availability of long-term debt, survival becomes increasingly linked to successful working-capital management.

Working capital is essentially the funds required to enable the company to continue its operations, to pay for production and stock, and to provide credit to its customers. The total funds required to operate the business are balanced by the firm's creditors and short-term debt, usually a bank overdraft. Working capital is the difference between current assets and current liabilities on the balance sheet, and is also called "Net Current Assets" or "Net Current Liabilities". The main components of current assets are cash, trade debtors and stock; current liabilities are trade creditors, short-term loans and current taxation and accruals.

There is no set composition to working capital, but the nature of the business is perhaps the most important factor: the amount of raw material, work-in-progress, and finished goods inventory; the relative amounts of debtors and creditors, and the terms of trade with them; seasonal patterns in purchasing or selling, and so on. The objective in working-capital management is to minimise the net amount requiring bank funding, while ensuring that the short-term claims on the company can be met by its short-term revenue sources. Where working capital is negative — where current liabilities exceed current assets — short-term demands on assets cannot be met, and some kind of financial restructuring is necessary, such as the sale of capital assets, additional equity injections, additional long-term financing or bankruptcy.

As mentioned earlier, working capital in Ireland is almost always financed by bank overdrafts or "private sources". But since a certain level of working capital is always required (even though the amount fluctuates), it is in reality a permanent capital need, and should therefore not be financed solely from short-term funds, especially because the ability to borrow short-term funds for genuine short-term purposes — the fluctuations in working-capital requirements — is hampered when such funds are seen by bankers to be in permanent use.

### Strategy and Working Capital

Although the nature of the business plays a large part in deter-mining the level of working capital, management policy decisions also play a part. In particular, current assets are used to support sales, and the ratio of current assets to sales depends on policy with regard to the credit terms granted to customers (the more liberal, the higher the debtors total), and the acceptable level of stock-out risk (the lower the inventories, the greater the risk). Whether liberal or tight policies are followed, the level of perma-nent working capital increases with sales growth.

The working-capital requirement is of strategic importance be-cause any sales growth is accompanied by increases in stocks, debtors and cash flow. Thus, one strategic problem is how to finance the increase in working capital (beyond increasing the liability components of creditors, expenses, tax due and so on). Another strategic aspect of working capital is its relationship to other elements of the strategic plan, such as the marketing of production strategies. The marketing strategy might, for instance, envisage increasing credit to customers or increasing stock levels as a part of the marketing campaign. On the production side, a strategy of greater product differentiation will normally lead to greater inventory costs. The impact of strategies in these areas must be traced back to the net effect on working-capital needs. On the other hand, a thorough knowledge of the mechanics of working-capital management can pinpoint areas where latitude is possible or where constriction is necessary — information which can then be incorporated into the formulation of functional plans.

Since most working capital is permanent in nature (major exceptions are the highly seasonal, resource-based industries where the concern is to balance cash flows), it should ideally be financed by long-term capital. However, most Irish companies probably fund their working capital through an overdraft facility. (There are some well-established working-capital finance schemes for seasonal businesses.) Overdrafts have the advantage of being cheaper than other forms of finance, and are more flexible. They have the disadvantage of using up creditworthiness, so that it may be difficult to obtain bank financing either for capital expenditure or for genuine short-term financing requirements.

### Problems of Inadequate Working Capital

Inadequate working-capital financing leads to a common cause of business failure: overtrading. This situation arises when a firm, though profitable, cannot realise the profits in time to pay current liabilities as they become due. Often what happens is that payments due to creditors are delayed. The temptation to withhold tax payments, in particular, is very great in these circumstances, and can be very damaging. Employment taxes amount to about two-thirds of wages and salaries paid, and VAT payments often fall in the range of 10 to 20 per cent of turnover. Current taxes due to the Revenue Commissioners are usually the single biggest component of current liabilities, and they are also the easiest component to withhold unilaterally (in the short-term), since the collection mechanisms are much slower than in commercial practice. However, the tax mills grind exceedingly fine, and there are punitive, compounded interest rates once the system catches up. Withheld current taxes are the most expensive form of working-capital funding, and the burden can ultimately lead to collapse.

## 11.4.5 Financing Intangible Assets and Other Activities

Success in today's environment of increasing competitive pressure and continuous technological progress hinges on possession of certain "intangible" assets, which, although they cost money, are not associated with physical goods or fixed assets, and which often cannot be measurably related to performance. Brand names and R & D capability are two important types of intangible asset, though there are others, such as workforce flexibility and management capability, which can be enhanced by investment in, for example, training, motivation and improvement of the work environment.

Funding marketing and R & D is a major problem, rarely given the importance it deserves, which seems strange in a country carrying out so much export trade. Instruments to finance these kinds of expenditure have not yet been developed. This is reflected in the very limited number of internationally-known Irish brand names, the exceptions including Waterford, Bailey's and Kerrygold. The importance of brand names has been shown by the very high prices that international companies are prepared to pay for companies with well-established brand names; Irish examples are Nestlé's purchase of Rowntree Mackintosh, CPC's purchase of Goodalls, Kerry's purchase of Ballyfree and, most spectacularly, Pernod's acquisition of Irish Distillers.

In conclusion, although some changes have been made in recent years (for example, the BES and DIRT), the tax régime in Ireland still strongly favours investment in Government stocks and property over investment in industrial equity. Ireland has some distance to go, in comparison with other countries, to ensure that manufacturing industry receives an adequate return on investment:

- Fixed assets are relatively easy to finance with bank debt, but it is almost impossible to obtain bank finance for intangible capital expenditure on, for instance, marketing or research and development.

- Companies with prospects for rapid growth — almost invariably export-oriented modern industry — have very good equity financing prospects via venture-capital firms, the Unlisted

Securities Market (USM), the Smaller Companies Market (SCM), and, after 1996, via the Developing Companies Market (DCM). However, capital for the development of firms with slower growth prospects is hard to come by.

• The level of grant-aid for fixed assets is being reduced, and state agencies are shifting focus somewhat towards intangibles financing.

## SUMMARY

Competence in financial management is becoming a key competitive advantage in business as it enters the twenty-first century. This chapter examines the crucial role that financial management plays in the implementation of the overall business strategy of the firm. The main points which should be considered in review are as follows:

• There are two major aspects of financial management. The first concerns the acquisition and eventual deployment of funds which fuel the functional activities of the firm. The second concerns the measurement and management of money as it flows into, around, and out of the firm in the course of its operations.

• As with marketing and manufacturing, business strategy permeates financial management on three levels: the strategic finance level, the tactics used in acquisition and deployment, and the money-flow level.

• On the first level, the firm must match financial with strategic requirements. The most important factor which determines funding needs is the life-cycle stage in which the firm finds itself.

  – Seed Capital is finance provided to research, develop and assess an initial concept before a business idea has reached the start-up stage

  – The Venture-Capital phase proper moves the project from the feasibility stage into commercial production and past the knot-hole stage. Capital funds are needed to set up the production system, to fund market development, and to provide for initial working capital.

- Development Capital is the finance required to exploit the growth potential of a firm or business idea with a good record and prospects.

- Decision-making on this level of strategy should account for the five FRICT factors of Flexibility, Risk, Income, Control and Timing.

• The second level deals with the acquisition and deployment tactics employed by the firm in financial management activities. At this level, the cost structure and output volumes should be considered to assess the cash flow and day-to-day funding requirements of the firm.

• The third level relates to flow of money through the firm and the management of this process. This includes reporting and control, budgets and responsibility centres and working capital management. In addition, the firm should consider the intangible aspects of business — such as market development, brand building, new product development and human resource development — as crucial strategic elements, and fund them as such.

• Venture capitalists are tending to focus on a small number of potential investments, usually in the fast-growth traded sector. There is an almost complete absence of seed capital (pre-start-up and start-up capital) in Ireland. Small firms have difficulty accessing loans of £30,000–£50,000 and for time periods in excess of five years. Much of the problems mentioned above can be explained by the fact that lenders and other analysts believe that many of the management skills and, in particular, strategic management skills, are underdeveloped among small firms. State-aid concentrates on the traded sector and, therefore, precludes most small firms from accessing funds, although this is changing through the County Enterprise Boards.

## FURTHER READING

Butters, Fruhan, Mullins and Piper, *Case Problems in Finance*, ninth edition, Richard Irwin Inc, Homewood, IL, 1987.

The Chambers of Commerce of Ireland (CCI), "Finance for Small Firms, an Examination of the Main issues", April 1994.

Department of Enterprise and Employment, "Equity Capital Survey of Irish Indigenous Industry", December 1992.

Kinsella, Ray, *Fast Growth Small Firms: An Irish Perspective*, Irish Management Institute, Dublin, 1994.

McIver, Colin and Geoffrey Naylor, "Marketing Financial Services", The Institute of Bankers, London, 1984.

Walsh, Michael and John Murray, "Pension Fund Investment, for the Steering Committee on Pension Funds", November 1993.

# CHAPTER TWELVE

# HUMAN RESOURCE MANAGEMENT

*I*n the preceding chapters we looked at strategy and how it impinges on the essential management functions of marketing, production and finance. We now focus on a fundamental component of organisations — the people who work in them. The managerial functions are sometimes seen as the tasks the organisation must perform in order to compete; but it also describes the work that people do. The fact that people have to carry out the tasks that strategy calls for is often forgotten in analysis. People bring their full personalities to work with them, complete with motivations, will and desires. Management at all levels has to cope with the problems this may cause. Management has to go further: the energy, creativity, experience, productivity and determination of employees must be mobilised and directed to achieving the strategic task of the organisation. In essence, people are the "ultimate resource".

The way people work, and the way that firms are approaching the organisation of work, is changing in line with the concepts of Total Quality Management, re-engineering the company and World Class Business activities. Ireland possesses an educated workforce which, as will be seen later in this chapter, is of tremendous strategic importance when competing internationally. This chapter addresses these issues and looks at how the Irish firm can harness the Human Resource Management (HRM) function to create competitive advantage. Human resource management is first defined, before analysing the trends in Human Resource (HR) strategy. The three levels at which overall strategy interfaces with the HR strategy are then examined, namely at an overall strategic level, a tactical level and an operational level. This chapter is not meant to be an exhaustive review of HR theory, rather a synopsis of the links between business strategy and the human resource strategy of the organisation.

## 12.1 OVERVIEW OF HUMAN RESOURCE MANAGEMENT

### 12.1.1 Definition and Description

The original idea of the personnel function as being concerned essentially with the administration of employees has been replaced by a much broader concept, often referred to as Human Resource Management (HRM). The HRM viewpoint takes in a much wider range of human behaviour in organisations, and it embraces ideas of organisation structure and culture, of conflict and power within organisations, of the mutuality of interest between workers, managers and owners, and of how strategy, organisation characteristics and performance are related.

Difficult as the subject of HRM may be, firms and managers have good reasons for trying to come to grips with it. The general business environment of firms is undergoing continuous and accelerating rates of change, and one aspect of this is intensifying competition. Under these circumstances, a broad strategy question emerges: how can the firm adapt to the changing business environment? As environmental complexity increases and change rates become even faster, the issue becomes how the firm can maintain continuous adaptability. Business strategy alone is not enough, since it is people within the firm who must develop and implement the strategy. It is people, both as individuals and in their group behaviour, who must adapt. The result of their changed behaviour is manifest in the firm's performance. Consider the performance of Wal-Mart in the USA, a people-intensive retail chain with 2,000 outlets in a very competitive environment, which has had 96 consecutive quarters of record sales and profits and where its people are seen as associates and not employees. An Irish equivalent would be Superquinn.

It is now accepted that a firm should involve its people in order to harness human potential better, which allows it to respond better to its business environment. Another factor for consideration is that the firm is obliged to take people into account because of the demands of the people themselves. These demands and the ensuing relationship between managers/owners and productive workers has changed greatly over the course of industrial history. In early times, the relationship was extremely coercive. Gradually, the relationship became a contractual one, an agreement to supply "work" in return for pay and other conditions. Cultural, social and political changes continue to influence expectations about how people should be treated at work. Although the viewpoint that the relationship is merely contractual still prevails in many working situations, there are many others where "work" is coming to be seen as the mutually acceptable alignment of employees' needs with the business needs of the firm.

At the same time, businesses exist for economic reasons and must maintain a correct balance between social obligations and financial goals. A human relations strategy does not have a stand-alone *raison d'être*; this must flow from the business strategy. However, it should always be understood that bad industrial relations can ruin a "good" business strategy and, on the other hand, high employee commitment may be a key success factor.

### 12.1.2 The Human Resources Environment in Ireland

Before analysing in detail the various levels at which human resource strategy affects overall business strategy and implementation in the firm, the HR environment at a national or macro level is reviewed. The HR environment in general relates to three key activities: the funding and provision of training and education in the skills required for competitive business, industrial relations, and law reform relating to the legal rights of workers and equality within the workplace. Human resources policy at this level is developed and administered by a group of institutions and agencies, the main players being:

- The Department of Enterprise and Employment and the EU
- FÁS — The Training and Employment Authority
- The Irish Business and Employers' Confederation (IBEC)
- The Labour Court
- The Labour Relations Commission
- Rights Commissioners
- Employment Appeals Tribunal
- The Employment Equality Agency (EEA).

## Training and Education

As mentioned in Chapter Three, the state plays a major role in ensuring that Irish firms have the right mix of skills to be competitive in the global marketplace, by offering a range of training and education services. Much of the training and education for business undertaken in recent years has been funded by the European Union via the European Social Fund (ESF).

The **Department of Enterprise and Employment** is the National Authority in Ireland for the European Social Fund (ESF). In the period 1989–1993, over £1 billion or almost 40 per cent of Irish structural funds transfers were sourced from the ESF. This made a major contribution towards financing education, vocational training and employment programmes delivered by a range of Government departments, public and private agencies, as well as community and voluntary groups across the country. The Human Resources Operational Programme in Ireland is set to spend nearly £2.4 billion in Ireland up until 1999. The main beneficiaries of EU funding from the ESF are the Department of Education, FÁS — the Training and Employment Authority, and Rehab — the National Rehabilitation Board.

Three EU initiatives on human resources funded under the ESF are NOW, Horizon and LEONARDO. New Opportunities for Women (NOW) is focused on equality of opportunity and access for women in the workplace. Horizon addresses the training and employment needs of the disabled and the disadvantaged. LEONARDO helps to develop new and innovative systems of training, with an emphasis on transnational co-operation to transfer best practice from one part of the EU to another. Another scheme, Euroform, pilots innovative approaches and training methodologies, qualification systems and the identification of new employment opportunities.

**FÁS — the Training and Employment Authority** was established in January 1988 under the Labour Services Act, 1987. Its functions include the operation of training and employment programmes, the provision of a placement service and support for co-operative and community-based enterprises. Following on the recommendation in the Culliton report, a new industry division was established in FÁS with a view to improving the quality and quantity of training of employees from all areas of Irish business. FÁS continues to assist industry through the Training Support Scheme (TSS), which gives grants to assist employers in providing training for their employees. During 1993, 27,996 people completed training programmes under FÁS. In addition, FÁS administers training aimed at the unemployed through a variety of schemes. In 1993, 28,402 people completed FÁS employment schemes and 6,400 people were placed in employment through the FÁS employment service. The Social Employment Scheme (SES) was the main scheme, and 15,987 participated in it in 1993. In addition, 5,210 people participated in the Community Employment Development Programme (CEDP) run by the Department of the Taoiseach. The SES and the CEDP were replaced by the Community Employment Programme (CEP) in 1994, providing voluntary training for nearly 40,000.

### Industrial Relations and Institutions
Industrial relations is a key element in the overall HR environment in Ireland. The level of industrial relations unrest in Ireland reached very high levels in the 1970s and the first half of the 1980s, fuelled by high inflation rates which put considerable strain on the decentralised wage-bargaining process which prevailed at the time. Since 1988, centrally-negotiated pay agreements have reduced industrial unrest considerably. Figure 12.1 shows the number of strikes and days lost between 1982 and 1993. It is clear that both the number of days lost and the number of strikes has decreased considerably since the 1980s, and that the average amount of days lost per strike has decreased at a faster rate. In 1993, an estimated 48 strikes occurred, resulting in a loss of 65,027 working days. Fifty-one per cent of these days were lost through two public service strikes and one semi-state strike. As already mentioned, the decline is to a large extent caused by the existence of centrally negotiated pay agreements under the Programme for National Recovery (PNR) and the Programme for Economic and Social Progress (PESP) of 1988 to 1993.

The **Irish Business and Employers' Confederation (IBEC)** represents the needs of businesses and employers in Ireland. IBEC was formed in the early 1990s with the merging of the Confederation of Irish Industries (CII) and the Federation of Irish

Employers (FIE). It represents 3,700 firms employing 300,000
people. IBEC influences the formation of economic and human resource policy at national, European and international levels. It
also provides assistance, advice and information for members on
industrial relations, pay bargaining, occupational health and
safety, and economic and legal issues.

**Figure 12.1: Number of Strikes and Days Lost in Ireland,
1982–93**

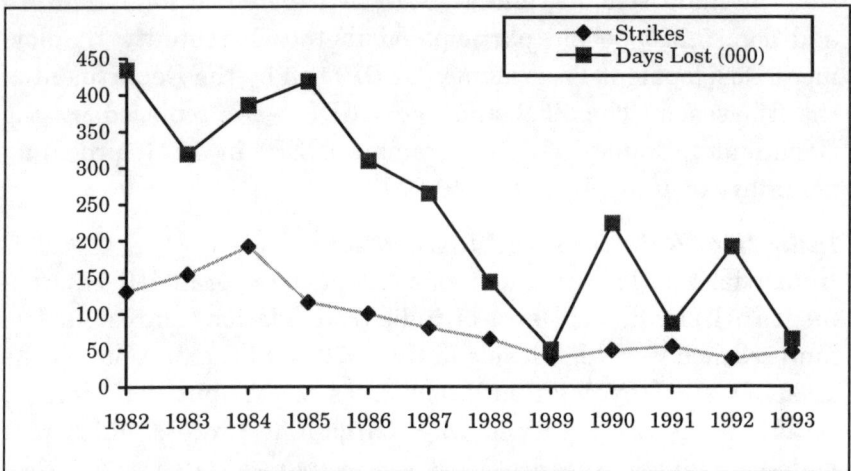

*Source*: Department of Enterprise and Employment, Annual Report, 1994.

### Law Reform, Employment Rights and Equality

As already mentioned, employment rights are a key issue in
terms of human resource management, and law reform in the
area is being influenced and directed by European employment
law and reform, which focuses on employment equality, unfair
dismissal and safety and conditions in the workplace. The legal
framework for dealing with employment-related issues comprises
the Labour Court, the Labour Relations Commission, Rights
Commissioners, the Employment Appeals Tribunal and the Employment Equality Agency.

The **Labour Court** was established under the Industrial
Relations Act of 1946, and provides the machinery for the resolution of industrial disputes. The court also makes Employment

Regulation Orders prescribing legally enforceable minimum rates of pay and conditions of employment in those sectors covered by the Joint Labour Committees.

The **Labour Relations Commission** was established on 21 January 1991, and has overall responsibility for the promotion of good industrial relations in the state

**Rights Commissioners** are appointed by the Minister of Enterprise and Employment under the Industrial Relations Act, 1969, to investigate trade disputes other than disputes relating to pay, hours or times of work or annual holidays. They also investigate cases under the Unfair Dismissals Act, 1977, the Maternity Protection of Employees Act, 1981, and the Payment of Wages Act, 1991. Rights Commissioners' recommendations are not legally binding and may be appealed to the Labour Court, the Employment Appeals Tribunal.

The **Employment Appeals Tribunal** was established under the Redundancy Payments Act, 1967. The purpose of the Tribunal is to determine matters in disputes arising from legislation on redundancy and insolvency payments, minimum notice and terms of employment, and unfair dismissals

The **Employment Equality Agency** (EEA) promotes equal opportunity in employment between men and women and works to eliminate discrimination in employment which is based on sex and marital status. The EEA advises on the operation of the Anti-Discrimination (Pay) Act, 1974, and the Employment Equality Act, 1977, and can advise, represent individuals or take a case itself under these acts. It also has certain functions relating to enforcement in the public interest. The EEA may seek a High Court injunction in respect of persistent discrimination.

### 12.1.3 The Three Levels of HRM Strategy

As with the other management functions, the overall strategy is filtered into the activities of the firm at different levels of business management:

- The **Strategic** level is where competitive advantage and HR are matched (specifying what has to done).

- The **Tactical** level of HRM explains how strategic-level decisions are to be matched with the firm's structure and needs (specifying how it is to be done).

- The **Operational** level describes decisions and their conversion into specific activities on a day-to-day basis (where decisions are converted into action).

Figure 12.2 below graphically describes the three levels of HR strategy, and the sections that follow describe in more detail the concepts, tactics and activities involved.

## 12.2 LEVEL ONE — HUMAN RESOURCES AND STRATEGY

This section looks at the first level at which strategy permeates the HR function, that is, at the strategic level. It examines how competitive advantage is being created via the HR function, the human factors involved and the importance of organisation and culture.

### 12.2.1 Competitive Advantage and the HR Factor

As mentioned before, a central thread of strategic management is to define the "business mission" appropriately. Definition of the product/market niche, the industry, or "the business we are in" depends heavily on human choice — the wishes of the people who are determined to make the enterprise work. The criteria of choice — for example, the level of acceptable risk and the assumptions about the future — are highly subjective decisions, determined not by analysis but by individual experience, and help in defining the organisational purpose. Somehow, this definition must go beyond merely defining the product/market niche and extend to a definition of what the firm does uniquely well in relation to its competitors (its core competence), and how it will translate this into a competitive advantage.

In starting up entrepreneurial firms, the initial impetus usually comes from one person or a small group of people with complementary skills. As time passes, and the original owners cease their involvement — as is the case with many older traditional industry firms in Ireland (e.g. Odlums Flour Mills,

*Figure 12.2: The Three Levels of Human Resource Strategy*

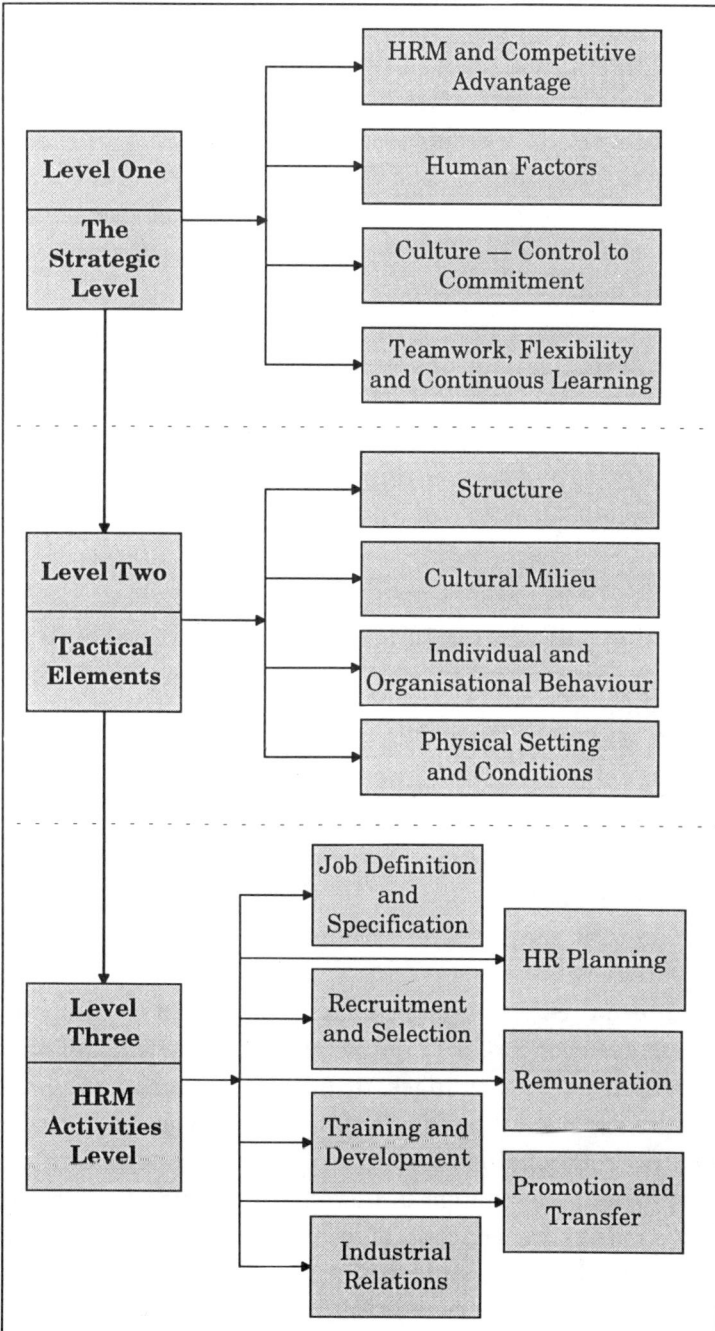

Level One — The Strategic Level
- HRM and Competitive Advantage
- Human Factors
- Culture — Control to Commitment
- Teamwork, Flexibility and Continuous Learning

Level Two — Tactical Elements
- Structure
- Cultural Milieu
- Individual and Organisational Behaviour
- Physical Setting and Conditions

Level Three — HRM Activities Level
- Job Definition and Specification
- HR Planning
- Recruitment and Selection
- Remuneration
- Training and Development
- Promotion and Transfer
- Industrial Relations

Jameson Whiskey), there is a danger that the firm will lose its clarity of vision and fixity of purpose. In a relatively unchanging competitive environment, such a firm can persist for some time, until environmental change eventually causes either collapse or successful adaptation. In well-established and larger firms, which have reached the stages of professional functional management or divisionalisation, the group of people with inputs into decision-making may be enlarged, but the resulting strategic choices are still very much the product of individuals' wishes, constrained, of course, by the power they can bring to bear in getting others to go along with them.

Strategic management, therefore, needs to take into account the human ramifications of any business strategy and build these into the overall scheme. A good strategy must have not only the consent of those who will implement it, but also their commitment, loyalty, active co-operation and dynamism. Sometimes this fact can become lost in the quantitative analysis leading to a strategy.

### 12.2.2 Industrial Change, Flexibility and Team-Working

A second major strategic thread is the organisation of work within the firm. Internal structures and processes must be designed to enable the firm to deliver its goods and services to its customers. These deliveries have to be in the right place and at the right time, possess the right quality/price mix, and be within a cost structure that allows an acceptable level of profitability. The strategic manager needs to be able to analyse the elements of organisation so that they can be arranged, or re-arranged, to implement strategy.

The internal characteristics that allow a firm to compete well in one business context may not be as suitable when the business context changes. The changes to process technologies, products and administrative systems can produce changes in work habits, hierarchical relationships and in many other aspects of the organisation. Where the change is incremental, firms may be able to adapt by using the concept of continuous improvement to its fullest effect. However, sudden, large changes can be very traumatic, and sometimes very painful. It is possible to prepare a firm for change, both in the case of a planned purposeful change in response to or in anticipation of outside circumstances, and also for a change that will allow the organisation to become more resilient and internally efficient.

Given the nature of industrial change in the 1990s, it has become extremely important for both management and the workforce alike to be flexible, to facilitate team-working and to be continuously improving and/or learning. Table 12.1 outlines the emerging organisation characteristics that are coming about as a result of industrial and societal change. It summarises the main implications of industrial change for internal company organisation according to the Industrial Research and Development Advisory Committee of the Commission of the European Union (IRCDAC). The main trends have their origin in one or more of the following changes:

- A demand for quality and flexibility in company outputs (products and services)

- A competitive response through innovation and continuous improvements

- Company adaptation through flatter and less rigid structures, involving decentralisation and optimal use of human resources.

The emerging organisations are utilising the concepts of Total Quality Management (TQM) and World Class Business (WCB) as outlined in Chapter Ten, which noted the importance of effective human resource management in the TQM and WCB.

Another recent development is the trend towards part-time employment. Work forces increasingly consist of permanent and part-time staff. There is also a growing proportion of non-traditional employment relationships, such as subcontracting, secondment, and temporary employment. This blurring of the traditional concept of employment is a response by firms to increasing competitiveness in the market, but it is also caused by individuals' personal desires, and changing values and attitudes in society.

## Table 12.1: Industrial Change and Internal Organisation

| Traditional Organisations | Emerging Organisations |
|---|---|
| • Vertical organisation with divisional structures. Compartmentalisation and separation of functions (management/design/production/marketing) | • Predominance of organic models. Professional division of labour with emphasis on flexibility, adaptability and mutual adjustment. Integration of R & D, design, production and consumer needs |
| • Many hierarchical lines, with line management focus on leadership and control. Centralised management | • Flatter structures with less management levels. More functional, project-based management. More decision power at the lowest level |
| • Full employment. Fixed working hours and schedules. Task and Job stability | • New and flexible employment patterns. Job rotation and mobility |
| • Product- and process-oriented structures with predominance of tangible assets (hardware). Management of production flows by allocation of production resources | • Knowledge-based structures, with predominance of intangible assets (people, research, patents, licenses. Management of information flows and skilled human resources |
| • Low-cost strategy. Acceptance of defects. Retrospective quality control | • Quality comes first. Full internal quality strategy with on-line control |
| • Rationalisation by mechanisation or automation of tasks. Division and specialisation of production for productivity gains | • Total optimisation of processes and production flow, Integration of production, maintenance and management |
| • Workplace with specialist, single-purpose equipment, many identical machines | • Multi-purpose and adaptable equipment. Flexible workplaces containing full range of different equipment |
| • Mass production for stable demand and batch for other. Importance of stocks and transport | • Flexible fast response for all demands. Few stocks. Transport is part of the production process |
| • Productivity gains are achieved and implemented in big steps | • Continuous and incremental technological improvements. New forms of technology transfer |

*Source:* IRCDAC 1994.

Finally, there are several pragmatic reasons why strategy-makers should try to understand organisational issues. A knowledge of the human processes at work can be used as a tool to manage strategic and organisational change. For example:

- Existing patterns of belief and behaviour can blind managers to strategic possibilities. Clarification and discussion of these patterns and central values may suggest strategic options or remove unnecessary taboos.

- Understanding the organisation's internal workings can help managers in analysing and predicting how other agencies might behave or might be influenced — competitors, customers, suppliers and others.

- Understanding organisational forces and dynamics opens up the possibility of deliberately managing the elements (the structure, people, physical setting and culture) to be continuously flexible and adaptive to its environment and to maintain its drive.

- The ideas of organisation can be used to help assess the fit between the firm and other companies with which it is contemplating a long-term relationship — mergers, venture-partners, licensers, distributors and so on.

In strategy implementation, when large-scale changes are required — for example, introducing new administrative systems, installing a formal strategic-planning system, setting up an export presence, or indeed when a company is set up for the first time — an understanding of the organisational factors involved should be incorporated in order to design the new organisation.

### 12.2.3 Human Factors

As stated earlier, people bring their entire personality and all their personal attributes to the workplace, and bring with them too a wide range of behaviour. However, only a limited range of behaviour is required at work, and not all personal characteristics are relevant to the work situation. Work stations differ greatly in the degree to which individual personality and individual differences matter to the completion of the task. Highly structured tasks, which can be specified completely in terms of behaviour, require mainly that specific skill combinations be assembled and controlled. No initiative is required or allowed, and to employees, the purpose of the organisation may be reduced to the control and reward system. Another situation is where highly unstructured tasks involving uncertainty and judgment cannot be carried out on the same basis, as they may require and usually permit a wider expression of individual personality. However, irrespective of the situation, it is essential to pay attention to individual personalities. It should be understood that attitudes, values and beliefs are the shapers of the individual's style of decision-making, of conflict resolution and of problem-solving.

Therefore, the individual brings to the workplace the skills, knowledge and experience needed to perform the work and, in theory, the collection of individual technical skills should be adequate to carry out the overall strategic task. It ignores people's need for a level of interpersonal skills in order to be able to relate functionally to others. Interpersonal skills increase as one goes up the management hierarchy. For the strategist, training and development programmes to increase technical or behavioural skills should always be considered as an element in strategy implementation.

In considering human factors and strategy, it should be understood that interaction and communication between members of a firm can make a considerable difference to strategy implementation. Individual members of the organisation, embedded in cultural, physical and structural backgrounds, interact with each other to carry out the organisation's task. These interpersonal interaction processes tend to form patterns which can be analysed on several different levels, and changing the forms of these patterns of interaction is the usual purpose of an organisation development intervention. Interaction also takes place between individuals, among individuals in groups, and between groups. Individual and group behaviour can be conducive or detrimental to the implementation of strategy. Therefore, the way in which conflict is resolved, the way in which influence and power are exercised, the way information is obtained for decision-making, and the consideration with which people are treated are important factors in strategy implementation. It should be emphasised that the appropriateness of given behavioural patterns depends very much on the unique circumstances of the firm, its external environment, and the other elements of internal organisation.

A full analysis of the behaviour taking place in a firm is neither possible nor necessary here, but the manager and the strategist must be aware that behaviour is the first outcome and manifestation of strategy; that economic performance of the firm is dependent on appropriate behaviour of individuals; that behaviour cannot be dictated by work design and control systems alone; and that there are possibilities for management to elicit higher productivity and effectiveness by understanding and improving the fit between the individual and the organisation.

### 12.2.4 Organisation and Culture — Control to Commitment

Work is carried out not just in a particular physical setting but also in a particular social context. This social matrix can be thought of as a set of patterns, not of behaviour itself but of beliefs and assumptions about behaviour. The sets of patterns are unique to each firm, are shared by all its members, and provide a general background for decisions and behaviour. These assumptions are held because they have worked at some stage in the past to enable the firm to cope with the twin problems of adopting to its external environment and maintaining effective organisation internally.

These patterns of thought are not absolutely fixed, and are blurred by individual interpretations, but in the absence of major change they do display enough stability to be analysed and taught to new members as norms of behaviour. Examples of such norms might be "I'm not/he's not paid to do that", "The customer is a nuisance/king", "You can't beat the system/you can change the system if you can show it will work", and so on.

There is more to the idea of culture than just internal states — beliefs, values, expectations, attitudes and so on. The central idea is that these are shared among members of the culture. In fact, culture is the collection of tangibles, which can be shared by members and observers. Examples of these cultural artefacts in business firms would include such things as dress codes, in-house jargon, the typical manner in which managers and their subordinates interact (management style), in-house success stories, and many other subtle but detectable shared behaviours. They serve to mould individual interpretations of behavioural norms into a working consensus. When looked at in these terms, it is clear that every organisation has a culture. Cultures can be strong if there is widespread agreement about the central tenets, if there is a strong reinforcement of these, and if there is a strong relationship between the beliefs and people's behaviour. Weak cultures do not express clear values, or there is no widespread acceptance of them, or they are not felt deeply enough to exert positive influence on behaviour.

Culture is important to the strategist in that it is a powerful shaper of individual and group behaviour. It is a conservative influence, because it has worked in the past, and because people have invested a lot in its creation and maintenance. Especially in large and bureaucratic organisations, such as in the civil service, cultural momentum is considerable, and changing it is a major, time-consuming, and expensive exercise. Smaller and newer firms deliberately manipulate the culture in order to elicit behaviour more favourable to achieving strategy. The development of the culture of McDonald's and its corporate culture and behaviour can be cited as one of its competitive advantages.

Culture is particularly significant in the development of a distinctive competence. The prime shared values behind work activity should support and enforce the things that the firm is particularly good at doing. A supermarket competing on the basis of personal service to customers has to get its staff to be of service at all times, and only a widespread cultural value can do this, e.g. Superquinn in Ireland. A firm dedicating itself to constant new product development must create and maintain a central value of innovation — Microsoft being a good example. A firm competing on the basis of cost must extend cost-consciousness into every aspect of operations and obtain employee commitment and initiative to search continually for ways of reducing cost, as in the case of airlines throughout the world. The initiative-based behaviour that employees must perform in order to develop a distinctive competence cannot be obtained by purely coercive means, though control systems and the organisational structure do play a part. If the cultural values shared by employees are aligned with the strategic intentions of the firm, the costs related to control and organisation are reduced.

It should be pointed out that there is room for more than one cultural theme, but if they do not compliment each other, there can be detrimental results. Significant conflict between sub-cultures may lead to a breakdown in effective organisation. There is another kind of breakdown possible, stemming from what might be called cultural "weakness". This reflects a lack of deeply felt and shared values, a particular risk to firms that, having been successful in the past, have reached a growth plateau. A firm whose members do not have a strong, clear, and widely shared set of values in relation to the work they carry out in common is an unlikely candidate for the development of a unique distinctive competence. This relationship between culture and strategic effectiveness applies mainly to situations where initiative is required of the workforce to maintain a distinctive competence and competitive advantage. Where work can be specified completely, and supervised adequately, it is enough to require the specific behaviours formally and to monitor the control systems. However, in nearly every work situation there is some scope for productivity improvements through working more effectively, and enhancement and exploitation of cultural values is one line of approach.

The setting and maintenance of strategically important cultural values is clearly the task of the Chief Executive or the owner/manager. The solution to problems related to culture is to have a strong and unified strategic vision, whose implementation includes the development of a culture. The culture should strongly express and reinforce values which shape the behaviour expected of employees in the work context. However, making a change in organisational culture is not easy. Small groups — and the top management team in a firm is such a group — tend to choose leaders who embody their norms. A successful change in leadership usually involves changing norms, beginning with that of the top management group.

Although company culture is not lightly or easily changed
(weak cultures are easier to change than strong ones), a rounded
strategy demands that it be taken into account. The formulation
of strategy should include a brief description of important cultural values and an assessment of the risk they contain for implementation. If the risks are very high compared to the difficulty of
changing the cultural elements, the strategy may have to be re-
formulated. If, on the other hand, cultural change is necessary,
the management literature provides a few tentative guidelines:

- Know what you are doing, that is, know how the organisation
  elements interact to affect strategy and what the desired end
  result is.

- Gradual change is best, beginning with a clear statement of
  new values, seen to be shared at the top.

- The new values should be communicated and reinforced by
  top-management example and by the reward system.

- Cultural change should be co-ordinated with other strategic
  changes being carried out.

- Initiate specific development and training courses that can be
  directly related to the change, perhaps interpersonal-skills
  training.

- Try limited pilot programmes first, aiming for a few early successes as a signal to others.

- Start with weak cultural elements that don't involve much
  disruption.

- Prioritise areas of change, starting with the most important
  incompatible element. Sequential attention to different areas,
  and evaluation procedures to monitor progress are important.

Finally, cultural influences, together with the organisation structure, the physical setting, and the control mechanisms in operation, combine to exert a great deal of pressure to shape human
behaviour in the work context. The final element in the mixture,
which determines the actual behaviour of organisation members
is the set of properties attaching to the individual human beings
involved.

## 12.3 LEVEL TWO — HUMAN RESOURCES AND ORGANISATIONAL ELEMENTS

Human resource, which is the ultimate resource, must operate within an organisational frame. This is irrespective of whether the organisation is rigid, flexible, hierarchical or flat. Therefore, organisational theory has a considerable impact on Human Resource Management. Although organisation theory is "softer" than theory in other management disciplines — it is not as easily quantifiable — it has so far yielded a body of general ideas, which help us to look at what goes on in behavioural terms inside organisations. Much of the research is concerned with business firms and other large organisations. Very large and complex firms have been at the forefront of this research, since they often have enormous problems co-ordinating and organising their operations.

Theory has confirmed that there is no universally correct way of organising, and that successful firms achieve a unique combination of internal arrangements in response to the specified circumstances of their unique external environment. Nevertheless, patterns are observable, and many of the insights derived from research in larger firms are applicable to smaller ones also and small-firm studies are increasing. To simplify the mass of detail that makes up even a small organisation, it is useful to look at four elements, which, though they affect each other intimately and profoundly, can be considered separately for analytical purposes. These elements are:

- The physical setting and conditions of work

- The organisation structure

- The cultural milieu of the firm

- The human behaviour that occurs in relation to work.

These elements are knitted together by an organisation's purpose and strategy. Perfect integration is rarely advanced in practice, although there are examples available of organisations that were outstandingly successful, at least for a time, in business and in other spheres of activity — IBM being a good example. The environment, internal decision-making and spontaneous processes occurring within the organisation are all sources of change which conspire to make a given fit inappropriate. The strategist is helped, therefore, by an understanding of how organisational elements interact to support or undermine the business strategy, and how they influence the evolution of strategy itself.

### 12.3.1 Physical Factors and Conditions of Work

In assessing the effect on strategic implementation of the human factors at work in a firm, management should pay close attention to its physical factors. It is important to understand that physical work that has to be carried out by organisation members, and the setting in which it takes place, have a major effect on people's behaviour at work and their attitudes to it.

There is firstly the setting where work takes place. This is largely determined by the technical task: the buildings, plant and equipment needed to carry out the work; the kinds of technical expertise required; the detailed job and work-flow design; and the technical control procedures and systems in force. These factors play a large part in deciding who will interact with whom, as well as the content, frequency and channels of communications between organisation members. Some firms have leeway in how these factors can be assembled, especially when the tasks are more intellectual in nature; but the core technology is usually critical in deciding the way that physical facilities are arranged.

A second set of physical factors relating to the work environment is less dependent on the nature of the work being done, and is more under the control of management. This includes the architectural setting, the way space is configured and decorated, and the quality of light, heat, noise and cleanliness. Ergonomics — the study of how man-made objects can be optimally designed for human use — can offer many suggestions about how the physical work environment can be improved.

As stated earlier, human factors at work in the firm have an impact on strategic implementation. As a result, close management attention is warranted in relation to physical factors. Many small but important aspects of the physical environment can be changed quite easily to yield practical results. For instance, improvements in communications can often be obtained by moving offices or workstations so that people who must communicate frequently or intensively with each other are close together. A concern to keep the workplace clean and well-maintained expresses a norm of the firm's culture. It has been found that involvement of employees in making the physical arrangements is a practical way of expressing their participation.

Spatial arrangements, décor, and particularly maintenance, all convey information that helps form workforce attitudes to work and to their superiors, subordinates and peers. They are the props and the stage on which behaviour at work is exhibited. For the organisation to succeed in carrying out its various tasks and in implementing its strategy, the stage, props and cast should compliment and enhance each other. (To continue the metaphor, there must also be a good script and a good director, with a clear vision of what is to be accomplished.)

A final set of factors — not quite "physical" in one sense, but worth considering in the context of the work environment — is the detailed mechanics of how control of work is carried out. Physical supervision, mechanical supervision, rules and regulations, supervision by means of reports, by budgets, by periodic reviews and by many other means of control, all contain varying degrees of coercion and autonomy and are used in many combinations. Control systems and procedures must exist, of course, and it is routine in strategy formulation and implementation to consider the adequacy and appropriateness of these. However, the control systems themselves do not operate neutrally in terms of the effects on human behaviour. A time-clock not punched by everyone makes a clear statement about two groups of people who, at least in terms of the control of time spent at the workplace, are not equal. People are not equal, in the sense that they have different skills and status, but their perception of equality of treatment and fairness is a major factor in obtaining commitment to the firm's strategic plan in building distinctive competence and solid competitive advantage. Thus, the control mechanisms need to be looked at, not just in terms of the adequacy with which the work is integrated, but also in terms of the ways in which they influence the perceptions of those subject to them.

### 12.3.2 The Organisation Structure

A major issue of organisational theory is how strategy and organisation are related. Organisation structure is really a formal model of how people are supposed to relate to each other in terms of authority, responsibility and information flows. It is intended to control and co-ordinate work. However, real-life human behaviour causes an "informal" organisation to come into being, and this may sometimes work against the formal structure and what it is trying to accomplish. The organisation structure formalises many — but not all — of the rewards that employees derive from working: status, non-monetary privileges and, usually, pay. The structure is designed to segregate and control work, but it is not neutral in terms of the human values which it embodies and promotes. Organisations and top managers have to work hard to control them.

Formal organisation structures — the hierarchy of responsibility and authority which can be expressed as an organisation chart — tend to reflect the complexity of the overall task. In general, if the type of work to be done — the technology — is routine and predictable, the organisation can be highly structured, resulting in some form of bureaucracy, like in the public service. If the work is non-routine, like writing software, or if there is uncertainty about how to do it, then the best approach seems to be to increase autonomy, to use temporary project groups and to have multiple lines of authority and communications. The primary determining factor seems to be rooted in the information-processing requirements of the task, which is determined in turn by the technology used. Different parts of an organisation may face different degrees of routine and novelty, and thus sub-units may have different structures.

As production and administrative technologies evolve, the nature of work changes, and different kinds of relationships of authority, responsibility and reward may be more appropriate. The introduction of computers into business may serve to illustrate this process. In the early 1970s only a few very large Irish firms had computers — mainframes that had to be maintained in air-conditioned rooms and operated centrally by a staff of specialists. Now, even small firms have computers, and in large firms, workers who need to do so can directly access the system without requiring specialist help. A great deal of service, maintenance and system-development work is now subcontracted, leading to specialist companies that cover all aspects, like Cara Computers Ltd. There are, of course, other profound changes caused by the introduction of computer technology, but it must be understood that the change in technology, causing changes in work done both by computer professionals and by non-specialists, has radically altered the way in which computer departments are structured. Some jobs have disappeared, some functions are performed by non-computer staff, new specialists have arisen and other functions are carried out by outsiders.

The traditional and emerging job patterns as a result of industrial change, according to IRCDAC, are summarised in Table 12.2 below. As task definitions become broader and occupation becomes a function of flexibility and adaptability, traditional human resource policies may not be able to deal adequately with the change. Human resource policies in preparation for the twenty-first century will have to be flexible and malleable in line with industrial and business change. The policies will have to spur competence and commitment; they will reward innovation, risk-taking and/or goal achievement.

Earlier the question was posed as to how business strategy and organisation structure are related. Strategy, by defining what the firm will do in terms of specific products, markets, technologies and scale of operations, determines structure in one sense. By deciding on the total tasks to be carried out, a certain type of organisation structure is implied, rooted in the information processing needs required by the task. However, the determination is not complete, because the optimum way of organising may not be known, and because there is usually (except in the case of new ventures) an existing structure, with existing vested interests.

Another organisational structure problem to consider is that there may be great divergence between how the firm is actually structured and the way it should be structured for efficiency and effectiveness. Competitive forces will tend to check this, and indeed the discovery and successful application of an improved structure may itself be a source of competitive advantage. In

*Table 12.2: Emerging Job Patterns*

| Traditional Job Patterns | Emerging Job Patterns |
|---|---|
| • Narrowly defined jobs. Single and fragmented tasks. Compartmentalisation of knowledge. Task-oriented job specification | • Broader task definitions with a longer time horizon. Multiple and multi-disciplinary tasks and knowledge needs. Result- and project-based job requirements |
| • Rigid employment framework. Occupational classification based on skill and seniority. Individual tasks and accountability | • Flexible and changing employment. Occupation as a function of adaptability. Team-work, interacting with colleagues, customers or suppliers. Evaluation of group performance |
| • Straightforward paper, control or assembly work. Prescribed work. Much routine work of low level. Separation of thought and action. Low personal advancement | • More abstract and intellectual work. Less supervision. Routine work disappears and need for anticipation, creativity, decision-making and problem-solving. Combination of thought and action. Importance of self-advancement |
| • Jobs require skill, dexterity and speed of manual execution | • Emphasis on speed of perception, reaction and intelligent co-ordination |
| • Predominance of heavy work, sometimes dangerous and unhealthy. Tangible relationships with product and material. Technology is a physical concept | • Move to communication and computer-based work. Stress intensive. Less use of physical energy and strength. Safety of workers. Interface with product or material. Technology penetrates all aspects of a job |
| • Adversarial industrial relations. Collective bargaining and agreements to solve conflicts. Power-based relationships | • Explicit long-term compromises between management and workers/employees (via job tenure and/or sharing dividends). Participative attitude |
| • Higher wages to get consent to poor job content. Pay based on results, output and productivity. Status separation between job categories | • Human resource policies to spur the competence and commitment of workers. Alternative payment systems, more based on risks and goals achieved Blurring of status |

*Source*: IRCDAC, 1994.

relation to the generic business strategies of low cost or differentiation, the types of strategies themselves are of less importance in determining organisation structure than the technology used. (It must be stated here that industry and firm history has played a large part in determining the structures obtaining in older industries and firms, which are influenced by generations of collective bargaining and government actions).

In conclusion, it should be noted that while organisation structure is a tool for carrying out strategy, it has some influence on how strategy is shaped. One such influence is the conservative one: the existing structure has rewarded those in powerful positions, and a change that threatens these positions will be resisted. The established structure also influences strategy formulation in the way in which it facilitates or hinders information and communications flows between the formulators.

## 12.4 LEVEL THREE — MANAGEMENT OF HUMAN RESOURCE ACTIVITIES

As mentioned earlier, there has been a widening of the concept of people management from earlier ideas to a present position that takes account of the full range of relationships between employees and the firm, the work environment, and also outside bodies such as trade unions and professional and trade groups. Analysis of the wider organisation context and how its elements fit together to match strategy is the domain of strategic management. However, people still have to be considered as part of a routine management function.

In addition, the routine tasks that the personnel function carries out are mechanisms that can be used to considerable effect in implementing strategy. Since these mechanisms have an effect in any case, it is worthwhile to consider them specifically in terms of how the business strategy can be promoted. Figure 12.3 graphically depicts the key tasks and activities that are undertaken by the firm in implementing its human resource strategy.

### 12.4.1 Work Specification and Job Definition
Work Specification and Job Definition are derived directly from the strategic tasks and goals. Of course, it may be that strategy is

set in terms of existing task capability; nevertheless, accomplishing the strategic task demands a necessary and sufficient combination of people with the right skills.

*Figure 12.3: **Human Resource Activities***

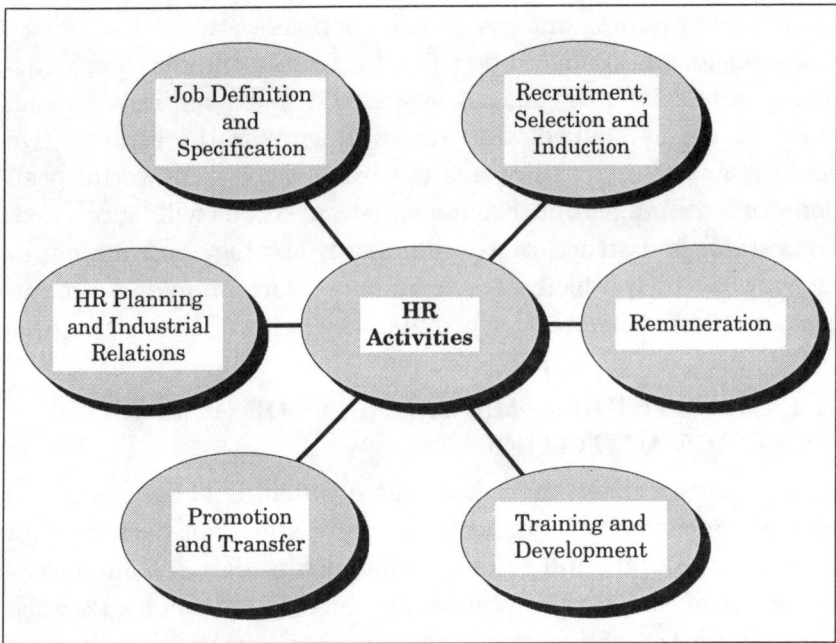

## 12.4.2 Human Resource Planning

Human Resource Planning is also derived in the same way from strategy, where the work and job specifications for the overall task are translated into the number of people required, a list of skills to be acquired or developed, and a timetable for having the right people in the right place at the right time.

## 12.4.3 Recruitment, Selection and Induction

Some employees, while remaining within the letter of regulations, do not contribute what they could or should. When these kinds of problems occur after induction, the firm has to expend resources on correcting them. The recruitment and selection procedures should be used to avoid this problem by consciously assessing the potential recruit's fit with culture and their behavioural skills, in addition to job-related skills and experience. The induction period should be meticulously designed to communicate the firm's cultural values so that the new recruit willingly adopts them.

### 12.4.4 Remuneration

Monetary compensation is a set of rewards and signals with a very direct effect on employee behaviour. The amount that people are paid, the form it takes and the criteria on which it is based should be carefully aligned with strategy. Incentives need to be precisely — and publicly — linked to specific results, which in turn require careful choosing. Profit-based bonuses, for example, may be increased in the short term by cutting strategic capital expenditure. Incentives and specifically profit-based bonuses have in recent times been the subject of controversy. Was the push for profit bonuses responsible for the demise of Baring's Bank, in that controls were relaxed on their employee in Singapore who at one stage was responsible for 20 per cent of profits?

### 12.4.5 Training and Development

All training and development programmes run by, paid for, or subsidised by the firm should be specifically tied in to long-term strategy. Conversely, the strategy-formulation process results in a manpower plan which sets out the skills that have to be acquired to implement strategy. As well as specific task-related skills that need to be developed, the strategic firm will give consideration to how employees and managers generally can be developed to become more productive. Training and development can sometimes be linked informally with the reward structures, further reinforcing desirable behaviour. It is also a major tool in carrying out strategic organisation change.

### 12.4.6 Promotion and Transfer

It is very difficult to articulate a company policy in relation to promotions. They tend to be the unique products of circumstances — the person, the job, the times, political forces at work, tradition and many other factors. However, it is feasible to try to develop such a policy, linked to long-term strategy. People with potential can be actively sought within the firm, given opportunities to obtain varied experience and skills, and be developed as a pool of candidates for promotion. Smaller firms have fewer management posts, but they can sustain much higher growth rates than large firms, opening up new positions as they grow. The long-term success of firms depends on the ability to formulate and implement good strategy continuously. Good strategies must pay attention to their own succession, and promotions and transfers, being the path to top management, should be strategically controlled.

### 12.4.7 Administration

There is a great deal of paperwork attached to the administration of personnel. Work controls (e.g. time-cards), pay administration, tax returns, holiday and sickness calculations — there is a long list. Very large companies tend to have one personnel administrator for about every 200 employees. IBM (turnover nearly twice Ireland's GNP) has an unusually high ratio of 1:100. It should be understood that personnel administration is very time-consuming even for small to medium-sized firms. It may even be worthwhile computerising the process with only about five employees. It is important to understand that the manner in which the system is operated may carry overtones of repressive control, and in general these administrative systems form part of the cultural and physical background of the work situation.

### 12.4.8 Industrial Relations

The existence of the sub-function of industrial relations points up the adversarial nature of relations between employees and management, which stems from both social history and the history of the company. Strategies aimed at coping with the business environment can be rendered ineffective by internal strife. Successful strategy implementation should therefore include a proactive stance towards employee relations, moulding the climate for diminished divisiveness and enhanced co-operation.

### SUMMARY

This chapter examines the key role that human resource management plays in implementing strategy. Utilised properly, the HR function in management can act as a key tool in facilitating competitive advantage in today's business environment. The key points covered in this chapter are as follows:

- The HRM function has become a necessary strategic tool in dealing with change in the modern business world. The changes making this happen include a change in demand for quality and flexibility in company outputs, and a change in competitive response through innovation and continuous improvements. Companies are adapting through the use of flatter and less rigid structures, involving decentralisation and optimal use of resources.

- The key to adapting to change is combining overall strategy with HRM policy. As with the other functions, strategy affects HR policy on three levels: the strategic level, the tactical level and the operational level.

- On a strategic level, HR policy in the 1990s is closely linked to World Class Business (WCB) as described in Chapter Ten. The key related concepts are flexibility, team-working and continuous learning and improvement. HR policy in the twenty-first century will reward and motivate non-traditional job behaviour such as risk and initiative. Strategy will also have to continue to account for the human factor with individuals and their responsibilities. This is critical in moving the culture of the firm away from being control-based to a base of commitment and shared values.

- On a tactical level, the firm must decide on the appropriate structure in order to ensure flexibility and competitiveness. In addition, physical setting and conditions of work are becoming increasingly important.

- On an operational level, there are certain daily activities which are undertaken in the HR function. They include HR planning, industrial relations, job specification, recruitment and selection, training and development, remuneration, and finally, promotion and transfer.

- As discussed in Chapter Ten, a key aspect of World Class Business is cost minimisation, which in many cases causes tension and insecurity and, inevitably, lay-offs in many instances. HRM is the mediator in this situation and should play a key role in making change less painful, while minimising the mismatch between strategic and operational requirements.

---

## FURTHER READING

Department of Enterprise and Employment, Annual Report, Government Publications, 1994.

Directorate-General for Employment, Industrial Relations and Social Affairs (DG V) COM(94)381, *Employment in Europe*, European Commission, 1994.

Drucker, Peter F, *The New Realities*, Mandarin Paperbacks, London, 1989.

Hamel, Gary, and C.K. Prahalad, "Strategy as Stretch and Leverage", *Harvard Business Review*, March/April, 1993.

Hamel, Gary, and C.K. Prahalad, "Competing for the Future", *Harvard Business Review*, July/August, 1994.

Handy, Charles, *The Age of Unreason*, Arrow Books Ltd., London, 1989.

Industrial Research and Development Advisory Committee of the Commission of the European Union (IRCDAC), "Quality and Relevance — The Challenge for Education", European Commission, 1994.

Waterman, Robert H., Judith A. Waterman, and Betsy A Collard, "Toward a Career-Resilient Workforce", *Harvard Business Review*, July/August, 1994.

Wood, Stephen, *The Transformation of Work? Skill Flexibility and the Labour Process*, Routledge, London, 1989.

# INDEX